Growing a Feast

Also by Kurt Timmermeister

Growing a Farmer:
How I Learned to Live Off the Land

Growing a Feast

The Chronicle of a Farm-to-Table Meal

Kurt Timmermeister

W. W. Norton & Company

New York · London

For information about permission to reproduce selections from this book,
write to Permissions, W. W. Norton & Company, Inc.,
500 Fifth Avenue, New York, NY 10110

For information about special discounts for bulk purchases, please
contact W. W. Norton Special Sales at specialsales@wwnorton.com or
800-233-4830

Manufacturing by Courier Westford
Book design by Kristen Bearse
Production manager: Louise Mattarelliano

Library of Congress Cataloging-in-Publication Data

Timmermeister, Kurt.
  Growing a feast : the chronicle of a farm-to-table meal / Kurt
Timmermeister — First edition.
    pages cm
  Includes index.
  ISBN 978-0-393-08889-2 (hardcover)
  1. Timmermeister, Kurt. 2. Dinners and dining—Washington
(State)—Vashon Island. 3. Cooking—Washington (State)—Vashon
Island. 4. Dairy products—Washington (State)—Vashon Island.
5. Timmermeister, Kurt—Homes and haunts—Washington (State)—
Vashon Island. 6. Timmermeister, Kurt—Friends and associates.
7. Cooks—Washington (State)—Vashon Island—Biography.
8. Dairy farmers—Washington (State)—Vashon Island—Biography.
9. Agriculture—Washington (State)—Vashon Island. 10. Vashon Island
(Wash.)—Social life and customs. I. Title.
  TX649.T45A3 2014
  641.59797—dc23
                                                        2013031570

W. W. Norton & Company, Inc.
500 Fifth Avenue, New York, N.Y. 10110
www.wwnorton.com

W. W. Norton & Company Ltd.
Castle House, 75/76 Wells Street, London W1T 3QT

1 2 3 4 5 6 7 8 9 0

To Byron and Bill Palmer,
two fine souls whose legacies live on here at the farm

Contents

Introduction: The Feast Is Established 3

ONE Two Years Before the Meal; the Birth of a Calf 10

TWO Eighteen Months Before; the Hard Cheese
Is Made 19

THREE The Cheese Cave and the Aging of the Cheese 39

FOUR Early Planting in the Garden 49

FIVE Nine Months Before; Alice Is Bred 57

SIX Springtime on the Farm 75

SEVEN Summer Arrives 105

EIGHT Preparation for Dinner Begins 124

NINE Two Weeks Before; Alice Calves 147

TEN Four Days Before; Foraging and Harvesting 153

ELEVEN Milk, Cream and Butter 171

TWELVE Saturday Morning; Tyler Arrives 185

THIRTEEN Saturday Afternoon; Dinner Preparation
Is Finished 217

FOURTEEN The Guests Arrive; the Feast Begins 227

FIFTEEN The Second Half of Dinner 266

Appendix: Recipes 285

Acknowledgments 295

Index 297

Growing a Feast

The Feast Is Established

Although I went to bed later than usual last night, I am up at six, easily an hour earlier than expected. I am hungover. Not in the sense of a headache and nausea and all that, but rather I am still enjoying the previous evening. I quickly walk the short distance from the Log House to the Cookhouse. I have mistakenly left the lights on over the dining table and as I approach I can see the room illuminated. It is the second week in October, still a bit dark at six, but not as dim as it will be in a couple weeks' time. The halogen spotlights beaming down on the table shine brightly—it appears as if the sun is shining in the Cookhouse. Both Daisy and Byron lag behind me, staying in their dog beds in the Log House; my enthusiasm for last night's dinner does not extend to their dog lives. In an hour's time they will awake and join me, checking out the rugs under the long wooden table for food scraps.

When I open the clumsy French doors held closed with the tedious brass cremone bolts, I see the remnants of last night's large feast. I should have stayed up later to clear the table and wash the last of the dishes and glassware and silver, but I did not. I was exhausted and wanted to climb into bed and rest. I have spent all of my adult life working in restaurants and I was taught early on to completely clean up the kitchens and dining rooms at the end of a shift. As I work for myself, it is easy to fudge the rules.

The table is sixteen feet long, made of Doug fir and can seat eighteen people easily. Twenty were here last night. It is deep, more than four feet across, giving ample room for plates and wine glasses and large platters of food, but also propelling the diners to be quite loud in an effort to be heard by those across the fir divide.

Scattered among the dirty plates and forks and napkins are the cards that I printed up with the menu from the night before. I quickly printed them on my computer in a furtive effort to make the dinner appear a bit more formal. Odd that twenty minutes of work on a not terribly advanced home computer can produce a menu that still has the cultural weight of a century ago when having cards printed would have taken days. The menu cards read:

Thin, crispy pizza from the wood-fired oven with tomato sauce, chilies, fresh herbs

Winter squash soup of Brodé Galeux d'Eysines squash, pureed, finished with cream, garnished with brown butter, fried sage

Hard rolls, sweet cream Jersey butter

Antipasti: hard, aged eighteen-month cows' milk cheese, membrillo/quince paste, black pepper crackers, pickled Long Island Cheese pumpkin, chanterelle mushrooms, fresh whey ricotta

Fresh slaw of shaved cabbage, with apple cider vinegar, pickled red currants

Poached farm eggs, sauce béarnaise, sautéed Lacinato kale

Tagliatelle, butter, chicken gizzards, hearts and livers, bread crumbs, cippolini onions, grated hard cheese

Beef bottom round roast, braised in milk, sliced, with gravy and boiled bay leaf potatoes

Tomato upside-down cake, butter cookies

Coffee

I worked on the menu over the last few days and finalized it just before dinner yesterday. That is not to say that dinner preparation started last week. Rather, it started months ago.

Just a bit of the menu came from my supermarket, most came from my farm; I grew this feast.

The menu is neither arbitrary nor capricious, but still it is casual. It reflects what is available for this time of year—the second week of October; the beginning of autumn—and what I had preserved from the past months of growing at the farm. I looked for ways to best use the cabbages in the garden, the pumpkin on the vines and the beef in the freezer. Beautiful cheeses were ready to be eaten that had aged for months in the cheese cave, and the cows have been producing excellent cream that I could churn into the best butter of the year. The melons that I had hoped would be ripe and sweet and juicy were overripe, moldy and disappointing by the time of the dinner. They certainly were not included on the menu. Thankfully the quinces had reached their full potential in the days leading up to last night. And I found the time to pick a few of the fragrant firm fruits and cook them down into a gritty membrillo for the antipasti course. I was worried the quinces would not be ready in time; occasionally I get a bit lucky. Last night was such a time.

There were a few ingredients that were not picked or harvested or grown on this smallish thirteen-acre homestead. Primarily the flour, sugar, salt, pepper and a pound of green coffee beans to roast and brew into coffee for after the meal; and I bought a case or so of wine to make the meal that much more pleasurable, to keep the conversation going, to loosen up friends who were a bit too quiet for the others. But in essence, dinner last night reflected Kurtwood Farms in October after a long, but not terribly hot, summer.

I walk around the table picking up the linen napkins. Some were left casually on the table, a few dropped under the table and one was folded a bit too preciously. I find the remnants of the cookie plates that I passed around last night at the end of the meal. A few cookies remain and I happily munch them for breakfast. The large French-press coffeepots have a bit remaining. I pour the cool coffee from the two press pots into a small copper saucepan, light a burner on the large gas stove and warm the coffee for myself. It seems wasteful to grind a bit of coffee and brew it this morning. I can't toss a couple cups of coffee down the drain. I hate waste.

When the coffee is hot but not quite boiling I pour it into a nice china cup, sit down at the long table, find the last remaining cookies and go over the evening. Twenty friends came out to the farm to enjoy this dinner. It wasn't a commercial venture, just good friends coming together and sharing an evening. All knew it would be one of the last warm evenings before the cool breezes and the endless rains of the Pacific Northwest winters arrived. It wasn't a dirge of a night, however, but rather a celebration of what summer had been; what the growing season had produced.

I have lived on this farm for more than twenty years, every year growing a bit more food than the past year. Presently the farm is primarily in grass pasture to feed the twelve Jersey cows that live on these acres with me. Twice a day I milk them and throughout the day transform that milk into farmstead cheeses. Although most of the acreage is in pasture, I still keep an orchard and a vegetable garden, a few pigs, a couple dozen chickens and three beehives. Not to sell, but simply to keep myself in food, to make sure there is always enough food to feed those who work with me on the farm and anyone who may stop by for lunch. I also grow an abundance of food so that there is a reason to host dinners such as last night's feast.

For five years I had served a dinner such as this every Sunday as a commercial venture. Each weekend twenty guests would pay one hundred dollars for a seat at this table, for a chance to experience a farm and to eat a meal composed entirely of local ingredients. I loved serving this meal and took great pride in it. By the end of the half decade, however, my cheese business was taking more and more time, leaving little time for me to work on growing enough food for the Sunday dinners. I would often be making cheese on Sundays while preparing the meal in the kitchen, a combination that made for poorly executed cheese and less than stellar attention to the dinners. I chose to devote my time to making cheese and let the Cookhouse dinners fall.

After the last Cookhouse dinner in December I expected a great bit of relief. That respite lasted a few days, but then I missed the excitement of serving a dinner each week on schedule. The Cookhouse dinners gave me something to look forward to. I knew that new people would be walking through those clumsy French doors at four-thirty on the next Sunday without fail. I needed to be ready for that entrance and the farm needed to be ready as well. Knowing that guests were scheduled kept Jorge and me on task to keep the lawns mowed, the vegetable garden weeded, the kitchen floors mopped. Without those Sunday dinner guests expected, the lawns got a bit scraggly, the gardens a bit disheveled and the floors a bit ignored. The production of milk, however, increased, and likewise did the production of cheese. What Kurtwood Farms has become is a small farm producing a respectable volume of very tasty farmstead cheese. What I lost in the deal was the vitality of people eating and drinking and enjoying themselves every Sunday.

I like to control things. It has always been my goal to make my world tight and tidy. I want the vegetable plants in the garden lined up on a grid, spaced equidistant and parallel. I long for the cows to be the same shade of tan, with the same conformation and temperament. And without question the goal of my cheese making is to produce identical, consistent cheese all of the same weight, size and flavor.

These are all goals of some value, but they ignore the breadth and variety of people. When the dinners ended and the people stopped arriving each weekend at precisely four-thirty the vitality left. What I had formerly looked at as frustrating— the guests who missed the ferryboat and came thirty minutes late, those who drank too much and so were too loud, the sullen eater who could not be charmed—now I missed.

During the months after the final Cookhouse dinners I flirted with the idea of moving my cheese business to the city, dropping the "farmstead" descriptor and changing it to "artisan" cheese. As it turned out, I didn't leave the farm and the island, but rather kept at it. I stay because I like the food. Actually I love the food. I grow the vegetables, tend to the fruit trees, raise the animals and keep the bees. I don't do it always particularly well or always with glee, but I get through it. It is the center of my being. I want to be connected to the food I eat. I must admit that I don't know if it is my distrust of the large national food companies or if it is my belief that homegrown food is better tasting and of a superior quality. It may be that I am just too damn stubborn to give up my farm before I have mastered it. Perhaps it is a combination of all three.

What I did change was to invite folks over to the farm again for big dinners—to capture a bit of the excitement and nervousness and the loss of control that the dinners represented.

I can easily muster together twenty friends willing to leave the city, take a state ferryboat and head over to Vashon Island to have a dinner. I am confident the food here is good. Actually that it is quite good. Although the ingredients are superior, I do have some assistance in transforming those raw ingredients into the final prepared meal. Yesterday morning, not as early as I am awake now, but still early, Tyler came out to the farm to help cook the meal. Tyler has been a chef around Seattle and Portland for years and relishes the chance to work with great ingredients in a relaxed kitchen. We have worked together from time to time for the past four years and work well together. He knows that I can light a fire in the pizza oven far better than he, but I would never think of rolling out the pasta dough; he can make tagliatelle with greater skill than I ever could.

Together the two of us spent the day working in the kitchen preparing the meal. Yesterday was without question an important day in the creation of last night's meal, but it does not speak to the entire preparation. This multi-coursed meal began many months prior with the birth of a young female calf in my barn. That simple act—seemingly unrelated to the feast enjoyed by twenty friends—contributed immensely to the meal. Most of the items on the menu contained butter: rich sweet cream butter that I churned a couple of days ago. I needed six quarts of rich Jersey cream to make that butter. When that young calf came into milk two years after her birth she would produce the finest cream on my farm. The story of this meal begins with the birth of that calf in my barn two years before the guests sat down at the long fir table. The story of all meals begins days, weeks, months before we sit down. It begins when those first seeds are planted, the animals are born, the cucumbers are picked and pickled. This is the story of that glorious fall feast.

ONE

Two Years Before the Meal; the Birth of a Calf

It is late in the evening on a cold, dark October night, and a bit of rain is coming down when I decide to return to the barn. I have already left the warmth and light of the house an hour earlier. I am worried about Dinah and put my mud boots on for a second time this evening to make the walk back through the mud to Dinah's stall. This beautiful cow, Dinah, was born here on Kurtwood Farms six years before. The only time Dinah is in this stall is when she calves, generally once per year. Now she is very soon to have her next calf.

There is little reason for me to be nervous. Many cows have given birth over the past ten years since I started this dairy. They have never had a problem, at least never a problem that I couldn't solve with the vet's help. Boo was the cow that gave me the most worry. An older cow, she calved early, before I could get enough calcium into her. She was hit with milk fever soon after the birth of her calf, falling to the ground with little chance of ever getting back up. The veterinarian was called and over the course of a week of IV injections of calcium she was saved, but since that time I have been on edge whenever a cow—one of my much-loved cows—is about to give birth. Tonight is no different.

I spend just a few minutes in the stall of the barn to look in on Dinah. She is lying down, looking a bit uncomfortable, with her large, oversized udders awkwardly trying to find a place to rest. The stall is the one room in the barn where I can confine a cow. Just large enough to hold an adult and her eventual calf, it measures twelve feet by eighteen. On one side are the large cedar sliding barn doors that lead out to the paddock in front of the milking parlor. Above the doors the gable is open to the outside. Thankfully the cedar-shake roof has a large overhang and little rain ever falls into the stall. The floor is covered in fresh rye straw. It is golden in color, bright, brittle and folksy. No large dairies would ever still use straw as a bedding material. Their preferred material would be sawdust. I use straw for a couple of reasons. Primarily because it composts well with the manure, but also simply because I like the aesthetic qualities of it. When I walk over it, it crunches under my boots with a bit of a give and with a bit of noise. It looks like my romantic vision of a farm. The cows seem to enjoy it as much as I do; it rustles under them as they awkwardly drop their large, hulking bodies onto it.

On the other flank of the room is a large, low manger. From the concrete alley where I am standing the manger is the only thing between myself and Dinah. If I want to get closer to Dinah I would either need to climb over the feeding trough or walk out of the barn and open the sliding doors to enter. Outside the barn, the paddock is full of manure and mud and the rain is still coming down, so I choose to awkwardly climb over the manger and into the stall to check on Dinah one last time tonight. There is little medical reason for me to be here, and I have no active part in the process of her having a calf, but I simply want to make contact with her. Certainly more for me than for her, but I can still convince myself I have a role in the calving process here at the farm.

Having checked in with Dinah, I flip off the overhead lights in the barn, walk down the long aisle toward the north side, open the half door and head back down the path to my warm, light-filled house on the other side of the dairy buildings. I can sleep with just a bit of worry about Dinah. My hope is that she is still hours away from birthing, but I am fully aware that in fact she may calve in the minutes after I leave the barn.

When the sun comes up the next morning, it is much colder

than I had expected. Autumn has certainly ended and the cool winter weather has arrived early. I can see that there is ice on the windshield of my truck as I walk past it and head over to the barn. I am fully dressed, but with such a haphazard manner that I surprise even my usually messy self. My blue jeans are bunched up in my muddy boots, socks still left on the dresser in the house, shirttails hanging out and multiple layers of down vest, hoodie and coat in disarray. The thought comes to me that I should have spent the entire night in the barn, just in case Dinah had had a problem.

The barn is on the small knoll near the entrance to the farm and there the sun hits it well before other parts of the rambling farm. There is no need to turn on the overhead lights as I quickly walk down the alley of the barn and head toward the stall. As the full stall comes into view I quickly scan the space and see Dinah has just started to give birth.

Dinah is lying down, all of her weight on one vast side, her legs extended out awkwardly in a pose I only see when a cow is about to calve. Her head, usually calm and downward-facing, is arched back and fully extended. Although Dinah has had three calves previously, she still appears to be surprised and confused by the labor.

As I stand across the manger from her I see two small, ivory-colored hooves appear slowly—the pristine little nuggets of the calf contrast with the tan, fawn-colored adult cow. Even though I have no role other than to worry and to attempt to be empathetic, I am nervous. I want the birth to be quick and painless for my cherished cow. My ability to control the farm does not extend to the bovine birthing and I am forced to wait patiently, completely out of my character.

The two small hooves soon become two small ankles, their light brown hide darkened by moisture, both legs tight together, almost as one. Once a bit of the torso appears, Dinah brings her extended legs under her and with great power and absence of style stands up. She paces and twirls in the small stall, obviously hoping to move the birth along. Her exhaustion and frustration is palpable and unchangeable. But she returns to the ground quickly, a pose that appears to me to be more productive than her imitation of a whirling dervish. Once Dinah regains her grounded position, the calf continues to slide out in its slow birth. Its head appears, and then the final two hooves gently slide to the hay beneath Dinah. The minutes-old calf is still encased in a gossamer sack that envelopes its entire young body. It is moist and, I know from past experience, slippery. In the past I have become too impatient and attempted to help the birth along by pulling on the first sign of the hooves to no avail. I learned my lesson then and now let the cow perform the birth unaided.

Dinah quickly stands up once again, turns around and begins to break the sack, removing it by licking with her coarse, powerful tongue. Once the head is freed of the thin veil, she continues to lick the calf's hide and mouth and nose, causing her offspring to begin to breathe in the new, crisp air for the first time. Dinah continues methodically working around the calf, licking it, drying it, cleaning it. At times her tongue is forceful, nearly flipping the lightweight body over with its dedicated power.

Gently I climb over the manger, slowly, so as not to scare Dinah. I walk over to the young calf, and can see that it is dry, breathing and apparently healthy. As I reach down toward it, the long-term implications of my next task flash through my head. If this calf is a male—a bull calf—he will be a loss for the farm, castrated in two weeks and sold off in eight. I will realize little in profit from him—at best $200. If this calf is a female—a heifer—she will live out her years here at the farm as a productive and profitable member of my growing herd of Jersey cows.

I lift up a back leg and lean over to peer down upon the minutes-old, smooth, suede-like body. In fact, I see four small teats lined up on a grid, the sure sign of milk-producing udders in the not too distant future. A new calf is born, and a female at that. My mind immediately leaps to the future. This calf will be part of my milkers in two years. I quickly name her in order to confirm that this newest member of the farm is in fact a female and here to stay: Alice.

I will only leave Alice in with her mother for a single day. The next morning I pull open the large sliding doors and let Dinah out to the surrounding paddock. Tomorrow Dinah will retake her place as one of the milking cows. Today, however, Alice will have a chance to drink as much colostrum as she can. Dinah's udders are filled with thick, sweet, dark yellow milk rich in antibodies that the young Alice needs for her growth and to build her immune system. It is essential that she consumes amply and throughout this first day. I will assist her, holding her eager mouth to one of Dinah's teats and keeping Dinah from pushing her away. This is not Dinah's first calf, but she still has some hesitation when Alice attempts to suckle. Most likely it is simply that her teats are sensitive and sore and the actions of her overeager calf are too much.

Once Dinah is moved out of the barn stall, Boo will be moved in. Boo is the oldest cow in the herd, most likely over twelve years old. Although her milk is of a quality too low to be used for cheese making, it is still of high enough quality for feeding the young calves. Boo has become the de facto wet nurse of the farm. With her many years of life has come a tremendous calm. She cares little that calves other than her own nurse off of her. She is ideally suited to her task. She will spend a couple of days in the stall with Alice until I see that they have bonded adequately and then I will move them to their own paddock. Alice will have weeks to drink a mother's milk, even if Boo isn't her own mother.

Learning to be a dairyman was a slow process, with errors made on my part. Early on, I fell for the most common mistake. The first calf that was born here was nine years ago. Dinah—the original Dinah, that is—had a calf very soon after

I bought her and brought her to the farm. She had a beautiful bull calf, and in an effort to be thoughtful and kind I left the two of them together. I left them together for days. It all looked very natural and appropriate and full of common sense. I felt that I knew more than experienced dairymen. And then at the end of three or four weeks I decided I should separate them so that I could have some milk to sell, as the weeks-old calf was rapidly consuming all that Dinah could produce. At the time the farm had far less in the way of infrastructure and the only way I could separate mother and calf was to keep them in adjacent pens. The calf that first night began to cry out for his mother. My guess was that the mother found it to be a great relief to not have the now-strong bull calf suckling throughout her day. Dinah would wander the pastures eating grass at will, but the impudent young charge cried incessantly for his mother. I fed him by bottle an adequate volume of his mother's milk, but he found it inadequate and let me, and my neighbors, know it.

It was a mistake for me to keep them together for an extended period of time, but then I made it worse. I gave in and returned him to her pasture so that he could nurse and so that my neighbors and I could get some sleep. This only compounded the problem. Eventually I sacrificed my sleep and my neighbors' good graces and kept them apart until the bull calf ceased to wail all through the night. I vowed to do better with future calves.

The calves of this farm now spend a short day with their mothers.

Up until the new year Alice will spend her days in a large fenced paddock with Boo. Every morning and evening I will bring a few flakes of alfalfa to feed Boo. For the first couple of weeks Alice will be nourished entirely by nursing on Boo, and then little by little she will begin to nibble at the hay that is brought to them. By the end of two months, she will have begun to get half of her nutrition from the dried alfalfa, and by the time that I let her out of the paddock to join the other cows, all of her nutrition will come from the hay. Although she would prefer to continue nursing off of Boo for as long as possible, once she has the ability to consume grasses, I will take her off of the teats. Boo will need relief from the constant suckling to regain her strength and fatten up a bit in anticipation of the next calf born on the farm and needing her milk.

Dinah spends the first day with her young calf Alice and in those hours Alice has a chance to drink as much as she can of the colostrum that Dinah produces. After Dinah has rejoined the herd and begun her daily milking her first few milkings will contain that same thick yellow milk. I will not pour that milk into the bulk tank with its eventual use for cheese, but rather will pour it into the large heavy concrete trough for the pigs to consume.

On the third day after the birth of Alice, Dinah's milk will be ideal and will be mixed with the milk of the other cows. The milk is poured from the tall, shiny milk cans into the bulk tank located in the milk room. Neither myself nor Jorge milk the cows by hand per se. We use a small system run by an electric vacuum pump, where the milk is collected in sealed stainless-steel cans. When they are full, or too heavy to lift easily, we unhook the milk tubes and haul the cans from the milking parlor into the milk room a few feet away. The bulk tank is a large refrigerated kettle that holds forty gallons of the freshest milk, until I can use it for cheese production.

A week after that chilly winter evening, Dinah will settle down into her new routine. She'll line up with the other cows every morning and evening. As one of the oldest members of the milking herd, she usually will be near the front of the line to be milked. The cows are tremendously hierarchical. The oldest cows, the largest cows, the strongest cows are always at the head of the line. The youngest settle in at the rear. I am surprised that the ranking is fluid, however. For weeks Baby may be the first in line and push away any usurpers, and then the next morning, oddly, Andi will be the lead cow, with little if any challenging by the former head cow Baby.

Alice too after that first week will settle into her role on the farm. She will be content to suckle from Boo and will rapidly gain weight. In the first few weeks I'll spot her running around in ever larger circles faster and faster, apparently aware of her body's abilities. Within minutes of birth she can stand, and within hours she can most certainly walk, but during that first month all Alice will be fully conscious of is her great strength and agility.

On this winter day it is hard to believe that the eventual milk of this young calf Alice will be used in the dinner. She is but a small calf—barely larger than my yellow lab Byron. She might weigh thirty pounds this week. Her teats are barely visible. She has limited ability to eat grass and hay and would prefer to suckle from her mother, or from Boo, for the rest of her life. The idea that this calf, this young Alice, will produce rich, fatty cream that I can churn into a golden, grassy butter seems unfathomable today. I trust in the process. I have had calves born before on this farm and have watched them grow into fine cows. I have been present from their birth until they reach maturity and come into milk. Yet even saying that, it is still hard to picture young Alice walking into the milking parlor, transfixed by a bucket of grain in front of the steel stanchion and hooked up to the milking equipment. I know that it will happen, but on this cool, crisp winter morning I am skeptical.

Dinah, Alice's mother, soon will be back as a member of the milking cadre at the farm. I will take the milk from her and the other mature cows and will transform it into large wheels of hard grating cheese. As the sun sets early this afternoon and the temperature begins to drop to freezing, I am not thinking of a meal on a sunny warm evening of a future October. I am only concerned with finishing up my chores, getting the cows milked, fed and watered; making sure the pigs, the chickens and the cows are ready for another dark, chilly evening in October. I am looking forward to kicking off my muddy muck boots, pouring a glass of wine and holing up in the Log House with my dogs. The thought of a boisterous dinner with many people around the long Doug fir table in the kitchen seems like years away. In fact it is nearly two years away.

TWO

Eighteen Months Before;
the Hard Cheese Is Made

Winter held on for far too long this year, in my opinion. In years past this has been a glorious time of year as the temperature rises and the rains cease; this year there has been no glory. The rains continued through March and April; low nighttime temperatures kept the soil from heating up and the plants from growing. It is only now, in early May, that any sign of the approaching summer has appeared. The pastures are finally beginning to awaken, the grass growing ever so slightly. I did stop feeding the cows much of any hay a couple of weeks ago however. Mostly because I had run out of hay stored in the barn. I simply could not call up the hay hauler and order another six tons of alfalfa so late in the year. It made no sense to have the large gooseneck truck and trailer pull down the long road to the farm and back up the knoll and into the barn when the lilacs are blooming and the sunset lingers until eight. I also couldn't find the cash to pay for any more hay. One of the great joys of the warm summer months is not having to write large checks to the hauler. The entire summer is easier in a financial sense because the hay expense doesn't arrive until the deep heat of the end of summer burns up the pastures and makes grazing impossible. It is then that a truckload of expensive alfalfa is needed.

The pastures here are now ten acres by my somewhat educated guess. Every year I clear a bit more land, push the amount of land in pastures a bit more and reduce the amount of land in scrub and brambles. I have trouble doing the math, but if the grass grows just an inch over these ten acres from the higher temperature, it amounts to a tremendous volume of nourishment for my dozen cows. It is enough to increase the milk production of the six cows presently in milk and raise the quality of the milk immediately. That is not to say that milk from cows eating hay for most of their diet is substandard. It is quite tasty and healthy. I would just say that milk from cows eating 100 percent of their diet on fresh, green grass is superior.

The volume of milk from the cows has increased in the last two weeks. It is time to begin making hard cheese. I do make a wheel of it here and there through the winter when I have too much of Dinah's Cheese. Today, after the morning milking, I will begin a batch of Francesca's Cheese, the hard cheese. Dinah's Cheese, the fresh, Camembert-style cheese, is the primary cheese that is made at Kurtwood Farms and is responsible for the farm's fiscal success. Without Dinah's Cheese, I long since would have had to give up this farm, return to a job, or find another way to make this business profitable.

Francesca's is a cheese similar in style to Parmesan or Grana. Or at least that is what I like to believe. Each wheel weighs around eight pounds, is made of whole milk and is aged for a minimum of sixteen months. I have spent the past three years making this cheese and it is slowly getting better, but by its very nature it is a challenge to improve the quality. Any change in the recipe will not show up for more than a year. Perhaps if I were far more experienced I could anticipate the outcome of a change in method, but at this point in my cheese making career I have to wait for the full sixteen months to see how the cheese will perform. I'm thankful the milk is of very high quality.

The bulk tank in the milk room is a third full this morning; the milk from last night's milking was poured into the tank and it quickly chilled in the early evening. Jorge has already started working when I walk into the creamery to begin the day's cheese.

By seven, when I crawl out of bed and walk over to the creamery, Jorge has been up for at least an hour and a half. With the
staggered way the farm buildings line up, I can look out my
bedroom window in the Log House, past the Cookhouse gable,
past the gutters of the milking parlor and the creamery, and
see just a bit of the space next to the barn where Jorge parks
his truck. It is a bright cherry-red pickup truck with a Lady of
Guadalupe pendant hanging from the rearview mirror. I can
see that vibrant red clearly against the dark greens of the veg-
etation and the dull concrete of the creamery and brown siding
of the barns.

Jorge is just so damn cheery as I blearily open the door of
the milk room to say hello to him. There he is, getting ready to
milk the first cow, singing along to the Mexican banda songs
piped into his ear buds, his short muscular body bouncing up
and down to the beat. I have to tap him on the shoulder to alert
him to my presence. And still he is good-natured and excited
to see me. I worry that one of these days he will ask me how
it is that I can't get out of bed before seven. I doubt that day
will ever arrive, but I worry about losing his respect. Amazing,
that he has respect for me. Luckily for me, the culture of the
patrón gives me some leeway to sleep in and be a bit sloppy in
this and that.

I spend the next few minutes transferring the milk from last
evening's milking into the cheese vat in the next room. It is
a simple task of opening up a stainless-steel gate valve and
filling a large four-gallon heavy plastic container, walking it
over to the vat and pouring it in and then returning to the milk
room for another bucketful until the bulk tank is empty. By the
time I've finished, difficult for me at this early morning hour,
Jorge has milked two cows and filled one of the squat stainless-
steel milking buckets with the morning's milk. Instead of pouring this very fresh milk into the bulk tank to cool, it will be
poured directly into the cheese vat.

After eight trips from the milk room to the make room with four gallons of milk in each trip, the vat is full. I switch on the heating element that gently warms the milk from the water bath that surrounds the vat. Slowly the temperature will be brought up to the requisite ninety degrees. I switch on the temperature probe and place it in the milk. The probe is accurate, responds quickly to the change in temperature and is regularly calibrated by the state Department of Agriculture. Although the hard cheese is not pasteurized, it is handy to use the equipment used in the pasteurization process. I will stir the milk by hand using a long stainless-steel wand that can reach to the bottom of the vat so I can guarantee the even heating of the milk.

I stand by the side of the vat gently stirring the milk, keeping my eye on the digital electronic temperature display on top of the probe. I will wait for it to hit just below ninety degrees, as the inertia of heating thirty-two gallons of milk continues once I shut off the heating element.

Ninety is the ideal temperature to introduce the cultures into the milk. It is often referred to as "blood" temperature, as it is close to the temperature of one's blood. Sure, our internal temperature is ninety-eight-plus, but the idea is there. Ninety is the temperature of life; it is the place where life happens and things grow. It is the temperature at which the cultures will grow and reproduce and thrive. Two cultures will be added to flavor the eventual cheese and also to bring down the acid level of the milk. Both are thermophilic cultures, meaning they are able to withstand a high temperature when the curds are cooked in the process of making the hard cheese. Only a gram each of the fine, single-strain dehydrated cultures is added to the milk. The cultures are weighed on a small digital scale accurate to one hundredth of a gram. This is the point in the process where I realize that cheese making more closely resembles lab work than my early vision of cheese making as cooking.

The cultures are distributed over the surface of the rich,

warm milk, allowed to hydrate for a moment and then I gently stir them into the milk with the stainless steel wand. Once I am confident that the cultures are evenly distributed among the thirty-plus gallons, I walk away and allow them to regenerate throughout the sugar-rich milk. The bacteria will eat those sugars—the lactose—and transform them into lactic acid, raising the acid level dramatically.

I have a bit of time before I need to tend to the milk. I leave the warmth of the make room for a few minutes to catch up on other activities on the farm. Three days ago Jorge moved Andi into the small stall at the end of the barn in anticipation of her having her next calf. A few times a day I shuffle off to the barn, walk down the alley and peer into the stall in anticipation of a new calf. Each time I am disappointed, but eagerly return a couple hours later. This morning, getting the milk into the vat, I have had less time to check in on Andi, one of my favorite cows. So with this break in the cheese making I head over to the barn, expecting little more than a lovely cow soon to calve.

In fact, Andi has dropped her calf earlier this morning. My thought is that she tired of my unwanted attention and waited for a chunk of time without my constant intrusions.

When I come down the alley and the stall comes into view, what I see is a very contented cow, happily sitting on the bed of straw and with a small, yet fully dry and clean calf to her side.

I climb over the low manger and proceed to check the gender of this beautiful young beast. A quick examination, and where Alice showed a small grid of four pubescent teats, this calf has no such indicators of its future milk production. This is a bull calf.

The disappointment is tremendous but with little recourse or appeal. Nothing is possible except to accept the lack of value to the farm of this small, sweet bovine. I have no names ready for a bull calf and the only thing I can think of on the fly is Boy.

I lose no time in sending a text to Jorge and return to the

make room. This afternoon we will find a use for this unwelcome addition to the farm.

When the milk is sufficiently cultured I can then add the rennet. The rennet will coagulate the milk—in essence creating cheese from the liquid milk. Rennet is made from the stomach of a days-old, unweaned calf. The rennet is a group of enzymes present in the abomasums of the young calf. As the calf is still exclusively feeding off of its mother, it needs enzymes in its stomach to break down the milk into a form that it can digest. This same characteristic of the rennet can also break down milk in cheese production into the two components—the curds and the whey.

These very young stomachs are harvested when young bull calves are slaughtered as veal. Although the raising of veal has a long and unpopular history in this country, it is a necessary part of commercial dairies. The female cows are bred annually to keep them in milk production. Each of those annual pregnancies results in a calf, predictably producing half bull calves and half heifers. Generally the bull calves are immediately removed from the farm and sold, to be quickly raised for a few days or weeks and then slaughtered for veal and for their stomachs for rennet production.

In a cow dairy, this is a relatively small issue, as cows generally only produce one offspring per pregnancy. Goat dairies, however, have a tremendous challenge, as goats can regularly produce three or four young kids per year, and statistically half of those would be males. The ugly secret of the goat dairies, and by extension of the production of goat cheese, is that routinely a vast number of male goats are destroyed every spring when the goats kid. Because goats produce a much smaller volume of milk per animal than a cow, a goat dairy could have hundreds of goats in the herd and each could produce one to three males that need to be destroyed. There is a market for veal, but less so for baby goat meat.

Thankfully I have a cow dairy of just twelve cows and have

at the very most five or six bull calves born per year. There is also a market on the island for calves my neighbors can raise on their small hobby farms for meat.

The rennet that is produced from the stomachs of these calves is in a concentrated form. Just one tablespoon is added to the vat to coagulate the more than thirty gallons of milk. Its power astounds me every time I use it. Today I add the rennet, diluted in a small volume of water, and gently but completely stir it into the warm, cultured milk. When it is equally distributed throughout the vat, I remove the stirring wand and the thermometer and allow the milk to come to rest. The enzymes in the rennet are creating long chains of casein proteins, in effect curdling the milk. The time it takes the milk to be transformed from liquid milk to jellylike curds is tightly monitored. In my case, I use the stopwatch function on my iPhone. Not the way the Old World shepherds made cheese, but it works in my life and in these times.

The degree of coagulation is determined by a clever trick. A small plastic bowl, like a to-go container for a bit of egg salad or such, is used to indicate adequate coagulation. The bowl is left to float on the milk after the rennet is introduced. It will freely spin as long as the milk is not yet coagulated. Once the rennet has adequately firmed up the milk, the thickness of the curds will cause enough resistance to keep the lightweight plastic bowl from spinning.

The amount of time it takes to reach this level of thickness is termed the flocculation time. This monitors the progress of the coagulation of the milk, which varies depending on the temperature of the milk, the acid level achieved by the cultures and the quality and age of the milk. That little throwaway plastic deli bowl is the best way to gauge that progress. With that information I can calculate the entire time needed to create a firm curd.

Once the curd is fully developed the more active part of cheese making begins. The vat is filled with rich, golden milk that now resembles a large, slightly rigid bowl of Jell-O. In just a few minutes, with just a tablespoon of rennet, the milk has changed form, from liquid to a gel. And now it needs to be cut.

The tools used to cut the curds evenly and consistently are beautifully crafted lyres made of stainless steel. One is constructed of eight long, thin, sharp blades, arranged in parallel three-quarters of an inch apart. The blades are long enough to reach the very bottom of the three-foot-deep vat. The second lyre is also made of similar thin, sharp stainless steel blades three-quarters of an inch apart, but these run horizontally, just six inches across, thirty-six blades in all. The first slices the curds vertically, the second horizontally. For hard cheese both blades will be used to cut the curds as small as possible. Francesca's Cheese is a hard cheese.

The hardness of cheese comes from the extraction of the whey from the curds. The relative amount of whey removed produces the relative hardness. A soft, fresh cheese retains a higher percentage of its whey than does a hard, aged cheese like Francesca's Cheese.

The first step in removing the whey is to cut the curds as finely as possible so that there is the highest amount of surface area for the whey to exit. In this case I will cut the curds with the thin blades until they are one-quarter of an inch square, if possible. Once the cutting is done, the blades are washed and put away and the curds are allowed to rest for a few minutes. When I return to the vat, the curds have begun to expel the whey and have fallen to the bottom of the tank. Now as I look at the vat all I can see is the yellow, slightly opaque whey. It is thin, still with some body and color, but certainly not the slightly golden milk of just a few minutes earlier.

Cooking the curds also contributes to reducing the whey. I flip on the heating element in the vat's surrounding water jacket and slowly begin to heat up the curds and whey. The heat will cook the curds, drying them out and making them firmer.

With the long stainless steel wand I slowly stir the curds,

watching the temperature slowly increase. The goal is to reduce all of the curds to the size of a grain of rice, equally cooked and equal in size. The constant motion of the stirring helps to guarantee this. I must admit that it is tedious, standing at this kettle stirring incessantly for the hour that it takes to raise the temperature from the high eighties to the eventual goal of 124 degrees. It is not my nature to be patient. At all.

I dutifully stand there, methodically stirring, one eye on the temperature indicator and one eye on my iPhone and Facebook or the like. Over the course of the hour, the curds shrink and the texture becomes more rubbery and chewy. Steam will begin to rise as the whey approaches the temperature goal.

I reach down into the vat of steaming whey with the rice-sized kernels swirling. I grab a handful of the hot curds, pull my hand from the vat and squeeze my fist around the ivory-colored cheese. A moment later I open my now-bright-red hand, not burned at all, but certainly warmed from the heat. The small, individual curds have come together with the pressure of my fist and hold together. This tells me that the curds have been cooked adequately. I flip the switch on the control panel of the vat, cutting the heat to the water jacket, and allow the curds to slowly settle to the bottom.

Even with the tedium of watching the slowly heating curds, I still revel in the excitement of the quick transformation of the liquid milk to the solid cheese. I witness this change, and feel it in my hands as I squeeze the warm curds.

While the freshly cooked curds settle to the base of the kettle, I turn to the cheese molds. I pull five of the cylindrical molds down from the high shelf in the make room. They are made of high-impact plastic, six inches tall and eight inches across and perforated. On the shelf next to the molds are five followers. These round disks slide into the cylindrical molds and are also made of high-impact plastic. The followers have rigid concentric circles that strengthen the disks and make it easier to press.

Also from the stainless steel shelf I muster a stack of cheesecloths that will be used to line the molds. Each is twenty-four inches square, made of a tight muslin fabric and sanitized after the last use. The all-cotton fabric wrinkles and shrinks after the high-temperature washing, and consequently the squares appear to be just a dozen inches across.

The long draining table in the make room is stainless steel, six feet long and three feet wide. Surrounding the table is a two-inch curb, giving the table the look of a very short and very expansive sink. At one end is a single drain. The draining table is mobile; at the base of each of its four legs is a large caster, to give me the ability to roll the table to where it is needed in the make room.

The draining table is used just as its name implies. On it I line up the five plastic molds, with the five corresponding followers behind each mold. One by one I grab a square of cheesecloth and dunk it into the vat behind me filled with the steaming whey and curds. Once the cloth is completely soaked in the hot whey, I remove it and wring it out, making sure it is fully saturated. I can now stretch it into its true shape and size and lay each into one of the awaiting molds. The edges of the square cloth drape over the round mold and I move on to the next one until all five molds have a damp cloth liner.

Then I gather every large plastic container I have in the make room. Nine tall Cambros, named after their manufacturer, litter the floor of the room around the vat. Each will hold three gallons. At the base of the vat is the gate valve that will drain the contents into the empty Cambros.

At this point the small individual curds are settled to the bottom of the vat, with gallons of whey above. The drain is located on the very lowest point on the front of the vat. It is through this hole that all of the whey will drain. Hanging on the wall of the make room is a four-foot-long sheet of flexible stainless steel perforated with small holes. It is eight inches wide and will slide in perfectly down the inside of the vat onto the drain to hold back the curds.

I take the stirring wand and bring the small bits of curds back into suspension, then bend the flexible steel band into a half circle and slide it down the side of the vat as close to the edge as possible. I push it all the way down to the bottom of the vat, all the while hugging the vat's side. The whey is very warm and my hands are burning, but I like the feel of the hot whey. It feels like I am accomplishing something; that I am paying a physical price for the creation of a great cheese.

As I pull the first Cambro into place and open the gate valve, immediately hot whey pours out and fills the tall plastic container. Quickly all nine Cambros are filled to the brim with the opaque, steaming liquid.

As the level of the whey in the vat descends, the volume of curds on the bottom of the vat is revealed. It is both more than expected and less than expected. At first glance it is a large pile of golden yellow curds and it seems miraculous that all of these beautiful nuggets came from milk that was a simple liquid just a couple hours earlier. And then on closer inspection it is remarkable that surrounding the vat are nine large containers filled with the by-product of this process. Even with a beautiful pile of curds in the vat, soon to be formed into cheese, the vast majority of the volume of the milk is to be discarded.

I load up a small bowl full of the curds and transfer them to each mold in succession. I pack the curds down with my fist, pressing the curds into the sides of the cloth-lined mold. The goal is to make the cheese solid and without air pockets within the curds.

The entire time that the cheese curds have been pushed into the molds, the whey has been slowly draining out the small holes in the rigid plastic molds. It slowly runs down the slight incline of the draining table and into a plastic bucket. When the molds are full I continue to push down on the still-warm curds, trying to push out more of the whey. Hanging from the sides of each mold are the edges of the cheesecloth. The four corners of the large square extend beyond the confines of the cylindrical mold. Once the curds have been pressed enough that the curd is level with the top of the mold, I fold those four edges onto the top of the cheese curds. The cheesecloth will help give the cheese a final smooth face and also assist in wicking the whey from the curds. The followers are then pressed into the molds, fitting tightly. These tasks are physical; the bowls full of curds are weighty and the punching down and compressing of the curds takes some strength. All around the floor are the large buckets filled with the still-steaming whey. The room is filled with steam and my hands have been deep in the whey for the past hour. I lean onto the table to get my full weight onto the molds. My shirt is soaked with whey and my hands are red from the heat.

While the five cheeses are settling, I turn to remove the buckets of whey that remain on the floor of the make room. They will be sent to the barn to be fed to the pigs once they have cooled. It might take a few days for the pigs to drink the entirety of the twenty-plus gallons but they will drink it greedily each time it is poured into their concrete trough. It is filled with nutrients—proteins, amino acids and riboflavin.

I turn to the slowly cooling vat and clean it out, scrubbing down the interior of any residual bits of curds and the whey that has cooked onto the sides of the heated interior. I don't relish the cleaning part of cheese making, but there is a bit of pleasure in seeing the burnished smooth surface of the shiny stainless-steel vat return. The vat is a beautiful thing. It was made in the Netherlands by the C. van 't Riet Company and it has a presence that demands respect. It is not a flimsy, temporary tool that will be replaced every few years, but rather a well-designed and well-built machine. The welds are apparent and methodical and precise. The controls are large and bulky and have a firmness to them that indicates their quality.

There are few exciting moments in cheese making, but the next step is one of them. Each of the cheeses must be rewrapped and flipped. The followers are each in turn removed and the cheesecloth unfolded to reveal the cheese. The mold is flipped upside down onto the draining table. I remove the mold, leaving the cloth-lined cheese on the table. The mold is filled with many small holes and the sound of the air leaking out from them to release the cheese is audible. What was a mass of small rice-sized curds thirty minutes earlier now resembles a cheese; it has the final form—cylindrical with straight sides and, with a bit of luck, a level top and bottom.

As the cheesecloth is removed, what is revealed is a cheese— a bright, golden yellow, still-moist cheese. Amazing that it can stand up on its own in such a short time, but it can.

The cloth is spread out flat on the table adjacent to the resting cheese. I pick up the fragile accumulation of curds by grasping the sides and lift it onto the center of the cloth. Although it looks like the final cheese in form, it does not yet have either a great deal of the strength or stability.

I pull up the sides of the cloth with the cheese in its center and position it over the mold. With a bit of luck, it can be lowered back in, the air pushing out quickly through those holes with a pleasing whooshing sound. The follower is returned to the mold and pressure is added to squeeze out more whey.

In another half hour I will repeat this step, flipping each of the cheeses, rewrapping them and then putting them back in their respective molds, with more pressure each time. After two flippings, I move them to the side counter in the make room to be pressed. Overnight they will sit on the counter with weights on the followers, further knitting the curds together and expelling as much whey as possible.

The press is a beautiful, ingenious contraption, yet is very simple in design. Above the counter is a four-foot-long stainless steel rod mounted a few inches out from the wall like a towel rack. Five brackets slide along the rod, each one with a two-foot-long handle. On each of the handles slides another bracket with just a short six-inch rod attached. Each of the five long handles can be moved left and right along the length of the wall-mounted rod and each of the short rods can slide along the long handles.

I set a cheese-filled mold on the counter, position one of the long rods above it and adjust the short rod until it is directly over the center of the follower. The long rod acts as a lever with a small amount of weight on its end, giving a larger corresponding pressure onto the cheese.

Once the cheeses are set up in the press with the weights hanging from the handles, the whey slowly dripping from the molds, I flip off the lights and leave the make room. It is late in the afternoon and time to milk the cows. The vat is empty, the floors have been hosed down and sanitized and the temperature has dropped from the warm steamy room of a couple of hours earlier. It is a pleasure to leave the make room and return to the bright sunlight of May. It is not warm out, but it is quite pleasant; the pastures are bright green from the winter and spring rains, and the cows have begun to lose their hairy winter coats for the sleeker, flat coats of summer.

———

The next morning starts like any other at the farm. The cows are waiting to be milked, lined up outside the milking parlor by order of dominance.

It has warmed up in the past few days and I slept with the window open, airing out the Log House after a winter sealed against the cold. From my perch in the north bedroom I can see down the line over the Cookhouse to the milking parlor and the barn. With the casement window open I can also hear the activities in the milking parlor. The cows are milked with bucket milkers—vacuum-driven milking machines that funnel milk into large stainless steel buckets. Each of these buckets holds the milk of two cows at the beginning of their lactation, and three later in their season when their volume has dropped. Each bucket is three feet tall and a just over a foot across. The buckets aren't particularly heavy, but they are almost pear-shaped and not terribly graceful to move about, particularly when they are filled with fifty or sixty pounds of fresh milk.

The noise that resonates from these buckets as they hit the concrete floor of the milking parlor is distinctive. The bell-shaped steel buckets bellow as they hit the hard concrete when they are set down next to a cow. The sound is greater when they are empty and ever more quiet as they are filled with milk from the first and then the next cow.

That distinctive sound tells me, from the luxury of my bed, that the cows are being milked. It isn't too great a physical distance, perhaps 150 feet, but it is a great distance from lying under my thick down comforter to being the one down in the milking parlor cajoling a stubborn cow into the stanchion in the early morning.

When I peek from under the comforter and look out of the window I can see that, instead of Jorge's bright cherry-red truck with the Guadalupe sticker, the other herdsman's truck is parked in front of the creamery. It is also a Ford truck, but one that represents a different end of the cultural range of farmworkers. It is a F-250, a larger model than Jorge's F-150, dark black, with six-inch lifts, locking hubs, a toolbox in the bed, diamond plating on the gunwales and a distinctive diesel roar that indicates a vehicle owned by a white boy farmer. In this case, a very well educated white boy farmer named Ben.

Ben started here at Kurtwood Farms during the dark months of winter, moving over from another farm on the island when I needed more help milking the cows and managing the pastures. Half my age, yet with a comparable maturity, Ben stepped in to bring the pastures into shape. I managed them with more emotion than science, letting cows graze longer than was beneficial, damaging the pastures yet making the cows happy in the short term. Ben came from Cornell, the foremost bookish ag school in the country, and could tick off all the reasons to implement a serious rotational grazing program on my nice but not well managed fields.

Ben studied "Science of Natural & Environmental Systems and Agroecosystem Science." At least I think that is what he studied. I have spent the past two decades on this farm reading about agriculture and animals and food, and I haven't a clue what that means. When he got here he certainly knew a great deal about the science of farming and the politics of small farms, but I will contend that I am better with the cows than he is. He does represent a large percentage of the folks working on small farms today. He is just out of school, educated, twenty-five years old, terribly bright, idealistic, intent on having a job that has meaning for him. And he is opinionated. Perhaps he is even stubborn in his beliefs.

Although he worked at other small farms before arriving here, I have watched him slowly realize that most of this work is tedious. Each and every morning the cows walk down the hill from the pastures and line up at the milking parlor where he is waiting. He spends an hour letting in one cow and then the next, milking them out and then herding them back to the pastures, or to the barn during inclement weather, only to repeat this process a few hours later during the evening milking. Even though I never attended a large Ivy League university, I would guess that they never really taught this idea: that farmwork is primarily tedious, monotonous and manual. I do not mean to imply that it is unpleasant, but rather that it is repetitious. Whether it is milking cows, plowing a field or weeding carrots, it is all rather monotonous. I enjoy the nature of it: getting to know the actions and personalities of the cows from day to day. The making of a cheese every day with the goal of an entirely consistent product is a challenge compounded by different seasons and fluctuating milk quality.

I worry, however, about the construct of a nation of small farmers who are well educated, bright and creative. Should those young men and women be doing farmwork—jobs that were at one time deemed "stoop labor"? I would say that it is these new, imaginative, inventive minds that will solve the challenges of our present agricultural system; these students of Joel Salatin and Michael Pollan and Rudolph Steiner who will bring a new way of growing high-quality food that is good for us and for the environment.

I enjoy having Ben here at the farm milking my cows, managing my pastures and guiding this farm into a new phase of its development. From my bedroom window I can hear every time he brings that milking can from the milk room into the milking parlor and sets it down on the concrete, knowing how far along he is in the morning chores. In a couple of minutes I will head down to the Cookhouse and brew myself a cup of coffee, then heat up the gas oven and begin to make the corn muffins that are our customary farm breakfast. When he has finished with the last cow, he will return to the Cookhouse with a handful of dirty towels that he used to clean and sanitize the teats of the cows, headed for the washing machine. After he drops them off, he will return to the long counter of the main room of the Cookhouse as I am pulling out the turn-of-the-last-century cast-iron pan filled with the warm, just-baked muffins. They are still steaming, crispy from the deep black iron of the pan and golden from the pasture eggs and rich milk in the mix.

For a few minutes we will methodically work our way through the pan of eight muffins, four each. Myself with a cup of black coffee on the side, he with a tall mug of raw milk straight from the bulk tank. The conversation will range from politics, to music, to island gossip, to my apparent lack of appreciation of everything new and current in the world.

Ben represents a new class of young farmers in America certainly, but he also plays a more personal role for me.

Ben is half my age with a few months to spare. He is fit and active and energized by all that is new and exciting about this farm. He has a great sense of wonder about it all. He doesn't know what the future will hold for him, even if I have a pretty good idea. He is at that great tipping point of our lives—when the uncertainty and immaturity of childhood and college is replaced with finding the first steps of a great path toward adulthood. He doesn't have a family yet, nor his own farm, but he will. He has finished his education and now is striking out on his own, and he relishes it, even if he doesn't always show it.

I myself, however, have long since passed through that phase. I am in no way elderly or frail, but I can no longer pick up a seventy-five-pound bale of alfalfa hay with anywhere near the grace that I could when I started here. I rarely if ever drive the John Deere tractor around the farm any longer, my eyesight so damaged by an accident with a cow a couple years ago that I cannot gauge the distance of the front bucket and have crashed into the odd fence post and barn door too many times. And bending down under the low udders of a mature cow to attach the inflations onto the teats makes my knees ache like I never thought possible when I was just twenty-four.

Thankfully the business of this small farm has improved greatly in the past couple years and the selling of cheese has allowed me the financial wherewithal to hire Ben to do a lot of the physical work of running a dairy. I have moved from milking the cows each of the fourteen shifts every week, to ten when Jorge came on board, to now just two, with Ben taking the majority of shifts. Jorge still keeps three shifts every week as well. Officially I still hold two shifts—Thursday evening and Sunday evening—but it is common knowledge that I give them away at any chance, passing them off to Ben or Jorge when a weekend party invitation comes in or any such diversion.

I don't always relish this position of management. It feels dilettantish and silly. My mud boots sit by the door for too long unused; I don't always head to the upper pastures daily to check on the cows as I did every day for years. My days are spent in the office, or wrapping cheeses in the make room, or at a cheese festival offering samples of our cheeses. What it means to be a farmer crosses my mind far too much; I'm often convinced that I have lost the right to the title I spent so many years earning.

Ben represents so much of this. He comes into the Cook-house with his Carhartt jeans caked with manure on the leg, his cuffs stuffed into his mud boots, his hoodie up around his ears to keep out the morning cold and he has just come down from the far pastures, checking on the dry cows, filling the stock tanks and throwing hay into their paddock. He is the embodiment of the youth that has escaped me.

When the last muffin has been consumed, the pan returned to its place above the range and the mixing dishes in the wash, he will return to the milk room to wash out the milking equip-ment, and then to the barn for hay for the cows and grain for the chickens, and I will head to the make room to check on yesterday's hard cheese.

Through the night the bulky lead weights that were hung on the end of the long stainless steel handles pressed the fol-lowers down onto the cheese in their molds. Through the night the whey slowly dropped out from the many small holes in the rigid plastic molds. The trays beneath the molds are now filled with enough whey to coat the bottom of the broad aluminum trays. Not gallons by any means, but a cup from each indi-vidual cheese.

I lift up each of the long handles, propping them against the wall, where they will rest until the next batch of cheese is made. It is good feeling, like shutting down the power with large electrical toggle switches. The handles are clunky and loud and bang around a bit, making the task seem much more dramatic than it is.

The molds are moved back to the draining table, the fol-lowers removed, the cheeses inverted onto the table and the cheesecloth carefully peeled away. What remains are five beau-tiful, still slightly moist golden cheeses, and with some luck and skill they are level and straight and true and even in size with one another.

Hard cheeses such as these are salted by brining. I make up a supersaturated solution by adding boxes of kosher salt to hot water in the same Cambros that held the whey from the vat yesterday. The test for supersalination is to keep adding salt until the water can hold no more, and then to add more until the salt falls out of suspension. Into this salty bath the cheeses will be floated for more than forty hours—nearly two days. Every few hours I will flip them and make sure that they remain submerged. If any part remains above the surface, I will dredge it with dry salt as well. I always want to believe that I will without question remember when I began brining the cheeses and when they are due to be removed; instead I write it down explicitly, as I have never actually remembered on my own.

Starting the brining is a quick task and I am in the make room just a few minutes. It is satisfying and hopeful. Nothing has gone wrong at this point. It doesn't occur to me that anything other than a lovely cheese will come from these five simple forms bobbing in the buckets of salt water. After this quick task, I turn off the lights, leave the make room and move on to other tasks, only returning to flip and check on the cheeses throughout the day and early evening. It is a pleasant task, a comfortable break from other chores around the farm.

THREE

The Cheese Cave and the Aging of the Cheese

After forty hours in the brine, the cheeses are ready to begin their aging. I reach into the Cambros and pull out the wet, somewhat slippery cheeses. A quick drying off of the salt water is helpful and then I load them up for their trip to the aging room. I head out of the make room with the cheeses, down the driveway and up to the barn. Then, with a bit of balancing, I unlock the main gate, lock it behind me and continue up the north road, past the curious pigs, and to the base of the hill. Here, to the left, is the entrance to the cheese cave. From the road it is startling to visitors. Generally they remark that it looks like the entrance to a hobbit house. It does in fact bear that resemblance.

At the base of the hill is a long gravel path that starts at the north road and goes straight into the hillside. Twenty feet from the road the hill begins to rise, and on both sides of the gravel path are large boulders that act as a retaining wall leading to the door of the cave. The gravel path begins to decline where the boulders begin and it drops a few feet by the time it reaches the door of the cave ten feet along. The boulders that line the pathway down are large, some very large. I've heard rocks termed one-man rocks and two-man rocks. I used to think that one-man rocks were those that were as large as one man—presumably in a fetal position. I was later corrected that a one-man rock is one that a single man can move. A two-man rock would take two men to push and shove into place. I watched these rocks being put into position—some were difficult to move with a large hydraulic track hoe. Perhaps these boulders are ten-man rocks.

At the end of the ten-foot path is a door. I call it the first door because, unbeknownst to the first-time visitor, there is an identical door four feet behind this first door. I must state categorically both of these doors are the most beautiful I have ever seen.

The first door is set into a concrete wall that rises up fourteen feet from the path. It is six feet wide, and all that is seen is this simple vertical wall with a beautiful door set into it, a light above and a light switch to the right. It is rather disorienting. Behind and nearly above you are the many large boulders, ferns growing between them, and beyond that is the sod of the pasture that surrounds the boulders and goes up the hill to the upper pastures.

The doors are works of art. They were made by Frédéric, the island Frenchman who also built the cow barn here and the roof of the Cookhouse. They are made entirely of Douglas fir and contain no nails, only pegs of black locust wood, known for its strength. The frames of the doors are four and a half inches thick—meaty—and the doors themselves are three and a half inches thick—also quite meaty. And those are straight measurements, not the confusing modern lumber measurements we now accept.

The hinges are bullet hinges that Frédéric buys in France periodically, stows in his luggage and brings back for his projects. They look and feel nothing like the poor imitations for a hinge that can now be found at a Home Depot or local hardware stores.

The basic design of the doors is traditional: each has a top and bottom rail, with a hinge stile and a lock stile. Dividing the top and bottom of each door midway up is a cross-rail as well. There are two additional, smaller stiles that divide the top half of the door and two more that divide the bottom half. This creates a framework of six areas. Each of these is filled with a floating panel. These are the nonstructural parts of the doors and are decorative. In this case they are very decorative. Each was hand-carved by Frédéric in a classic French motif. The design is of a long, vertical ribbon that flows from the center out. The panels appear to be tall, skinny, open books where the pages flow out from the central spine.

The carving is superb. I often run my fingers up and down these Douglas fir ribbons to feel the subtle flow of the wood and pick up on the subtle handwork that is apparent. What is surprising is that the backs of the doors also have carved panels. One of Frédéric's qualities that I have always admired is that he adorns that which is in sight and tends to ignore that is which is hidden. It is his economy of work. There is no need to beautify the hidden. In this situation a case could be made that I can see the reverse of the doors when I exit the cheese cave, but it is a thin argument. More likely is the fact that the winter when I hired him Frédéric had little or no work and needed the cash. If he made them more intricate he could bill me additionally. I'm happy with either reason—they are beautiful and I appreciate them every time I go in and out of the cave.

The two doors are each locked with a dead bolt. My house is not locked, my truck never, but I keep the cheeses under lock and key all of the time. The sound and the feel of locking these two doors is tremendous. They both have identical dead bolts that are of very high quality and which are very well engineered. The heavy, dull clunk that is audible when they are turned is reassuring. The doors are equally well designed and engineered. They fit precisely within their frames. Add to the effect the resonant quality of the cheese cave. The sounds of the dead bolts and the door handles and the opening of the doors are greatly amplified by the reverb chamber that is the cave. This is further enhanced by the experience of coming to the doors. On this spring day it is quite warm, not hot but certainly pleasant. Walking the ten feet down to the entrance of the cave is dramatic. The temperature drops precipitously during this quick walk. On both sides are the cool stones of the retaining wall, shaded by the ferns growing from their crevices. The entrance faces north and the sun rarely glares down this approach to the entrance. It is a physical change I experience, approaching the first door to the cheese cave. Turning the key and hearing the resonant sound of the dead bolt further tells me that I am somewhere different. This is not the front porch of a simple house in the suburbs.

When I open the first door of the cave, I am confronted with a small vestibule—just four feet square with a ten-foot-high ceiling. The two walls and the ceiling are all cast-in-place concrete, the floor as well. There is only an industrial light in the center of the ceiling in this small room. Directly opposite this first door is the second beautifully adorned hand-carved door. It resembles the exterior door—the ribbons, the pegged frame, the bullet hinges.

The vestibule is simply an air lock. It is to guard against bringing in too much warm air in the heat of summer or too much cool air in the depths of winter. I close the first door behind me and enter the small chamber. The caged light overhead is lit. I unlock the second door, the dead bolt giving an even more ominous thud, and I push open the second door.

The cheese cave is 330 square feet, all of cast concrete. From the doorway I can see to the end of the rectangular room. Above me are three more of the industrial lights. On the left and the right of the center nave that divides the room are the floor-to-ceiling wooden shelves that hold the cheeses. Frédéric built these as well—the frame that holds the individual shelves is made of Douglas fir with black locust pegs.

Each of the shelves is made of spruce, the wood of preference for aging cheeses due to its absence of deep odors. The shelves are loose; they are not attached but rather simply rest on steel pegs that come out from the fir posts of the framework.

The ceiling is barrel-vaulted, curving down from its apex of eleven feet to the six-foot-high side walls. The gentle curve is designed to encourage the air to roll down the sides as it heats and cools; in a flat-roofed room the air would stagnate in the corners. The vaulted ceiling also keeps moisture from dripping down onto the cheeses. If moisture rises up in the room, it will hit the cool ceiling and roll down the vault to the sides rather than collect and drip straight down.

This tidy bunker was built three years earlier on a whim. I had made a hard, aged cheese five years ago. I made a lot of different cheeses then: Tomme, mozzarella, Camembert, Gouda. Some were good, some ended up as pig food, but the Grana-style cheese after a year of aging was magnificent. I had one wheel of perhaps six pounds and I ate most of it myself. I shared what little remained with folk who had a good palate and some experience with cheese. I am not sure what all the comments were, but the ones that got through to my overly confident ears were all positive. I was convinced to begin making this cheese at my creamery.

I knew I needed a cave to produce it consistently and in a professional manner. I must correct that. I wanted a cave because they are beautiful structures; I could have made great cheese in an industrial building with a refrigeration unit. The final product is important to me, but equally important is the process. I like food to have a story, a pedigree, a tale to tell.

I drew what I wanted on a cocktail napkin or a scrap of paper and began asking around for advice. An architect friend of mine set me up with an out-of-work architect who had worked in his office before the building boom ended. She gladly took up this unique project.

There are few true cheese caves in this country and little information on their design. With great gusto she investigated all that she could find, emailing other creameries and calling around for tips on the design. Thankfully they are rather simple contraptions.

The basic element needed for success is depth. The entire goal is to keep the interior of the room at a consistent temperature year-round, despite a highly fluctuating outside temperature. Although mechanical refrigeration can accomplish this, I wanted a much lower-tech solution: burying the room underground can satisfy the temperature concerns.

The temperature of the earth below the frost line is consistent. In this part of the country, that line is at four feet. If you were to dig down four feet in your garden today—or any day, for that matter—the earth will be a bit above fifty degrees. It is never thirty, nor eighty, but rather an ideal fifty. Perhaps in the desert of Arizona that depth is ten feet, but here in the moderate Pacific Northwest four feet is adequate.

When Dawn calculated the thickness of the concrete and the height of the room, together with the needed barrel-vaulted room design and then the thickness of the bottom slab, the depth of the hole needed for this room was impressive.

What was needed, therefore, was a hill. Only then could the entrance to the cave easily come out to daylight without a long staircase down to reach it. Being able to easily access the entrance was a design necessity. Dawn and I walked around the thirteen acres of Kurtwood Farms repeatedly before deciding on the only possible site.

This site had everything we needed, the hill first and foremost, but also access to a road for construction work and also for its eventual use, proximity to the main water line, and with room for the construction equipment and vehicles. It was a long distance from the cheese production area, but I was confident that would not be a deterrent.

Once the location was set, she drew up the plans with the assistance of a soils engineer, a structural engineer and a wetlands scientist. My seemingly simple project became dramatically more complicated once reality entered into the project. We were building a room underground where I would work for an hour or two at a time. I really didn't want to die inside of a crushed subterranean concrete bunker. Doing the extra work to guarantee that the cheese cave was structurally sound was paramount.

Once the plans were drawn and approved by the local building authority, the contractor began his work. The first step was to remove the existing hill. I like writing that and thinking about that task. We removed an entire hill from the farm. What was remarkable was that it was not a time-consuming project. Two small track hoes went to work continually moving dirt for three days. The difficult part was not the digging but rather moving the soil as it came from the hole. One track hoe dug the hole and passed the dirt to the next piece of heavy equipment. The second would then pile the dirt around the excavation.

They did this in studied unison. Both Stuart and his young daughter are well experienced in earth moving and could make it appear effortless, and steadily the hill disappeared and in its place two large piles of dirt appeared.

What made it more interesting was that there were cows watching at all times; a herd of terribly inquisitive cows. I learned that they are more agile on their feet than it appears and they would climb to the top of each of the two tall, profound dirt piles and stare down with curiosity into the hole deep below. They never slipped, they never fell, but they appeared to precariously balance on the edge of the shifting soil.

After three long days the hole was complete. Twenty feet below grade was the base where the cave would be built. It was leveled and squared and then Stuart and his daughter began to build the wooden forms that would contain the cast-in-place concrete. The structural engineer had specced out—at least to my uneducated eyes—a massive volume of steel rebar to reinforce the concrete.

The engineer explained to me that the hydrostatic pressures—which I assumed just meant water pressure—applied to the sides and top of the concrete structure could be substantial. There was to be a large quantity of soil—and in winter, wet soil—pressing down onto this bunker. In addition, there needed to be the ability to withstand the possibility of trucks driving across the upper pasture and, unbeknownst to the driver, traveling over the largely hidden cave beneath. Although I had little understanding of the structural forces at play, I was convinced that the wet soil would indeed be weighty and the water pushing against the sides of the concrete was not a small force. Again, I remembered my initial request that I would prefer not to die in a collapsed pile of concrete rubble.

Stuart and his small crew followed the plans diligently and began to fill the forms with concrete. Once the base was poured, they moved on to the side walls and then the barrel-vaulted ceiling and the entrance. For days the same procedure would repeat—building the wooden forms, adding the steel reinforcing bars, pouring the concrete, stripping the forms and then building the forms for the next section. By the end of three weeks, in place of the empty hole deep below the pastures stood a small concrete bunker—solid, massive and heavy.

And then began the backfilling of the soil. What came out quickly in three days took longer to return to its original location despite the great advantage of gravity. The soil was pushed back into place, compacted and settled, then more would be added to raise the level higher and higher. Slowly the concrete bunker disappeared, covered by the ever-greater mound of relocated soil. Once the concrete was no longer visible, the soil was mounded on top of the subterranean structure. More than four feet of soil was needed to fully insulate the interior room from the changing heat and coolness of the weather outside the cave.

Once the bulk of the soil was mounded over and around the concrete, the retaining walls holding up the earth on either side of the path down into the doorway were set. Two dozen large boulders were collected from the surrounding pastures and woods and dragged to the site and set into position.

By the end of eight weeks the hill had been removed and replaced with a sturdy concrete box hidden within it. In the coming weeks the doors would be set, the shelves installed and the pastures reseeded on the surrounding hillsides. All so that today I could walk down the short gravel path, unlock the pair of carved wooden doors and bring in five freshly made cheeses to be aged.

I have been making just a few of these hard cheeses each week for the past few months. There are four sets of shelves on either side of the windowless room. When it is fully utilized, it will hold nearly a thousand of the eight-pound wheels of cheese. Today there are at best seventy youthful cheeses in residence. Today five more cheeses will be added to the ranks of the aging, here four feet below the pastures and the cows. I find the next empty shelves in the rack and place the cheeses on a spruce wood shelf. A tag with the number of the make goes on the end of the shelf and the cheeses now will live out their time in the dark, cool space. Once the cheeses are all lined up on the loose shelf, I turn and go back through the pair of doors and out to the farm. The doors are locked in succession as I leave, the heavy thud loud and apparent as I close each door and lock the dead bolts.

It is a bit jarring to come out of the cave and walk back up the short gravel path to the north road of the farm. The cave is confined and small, with deep echoes and a limited range of sensations. It smells deeply like the cheeses that inhabit it, but you can hear nothing of the outside world and feel no vibrations or movement from outside. It is a room of stability and calm. The temperature is stable, the humidity as well. Outside of the cave, the surroundings are immediately vibrant and full; high overhead planes pass by on their way to the airport, the cows are methodically grazing on the grass above the cave door, the trees are filled with small, quick wrens and the faint sounds of the highway a few thousand feet through the adjoining woods can be heard when a large commercial truck drives by. The sun filters through the tall Doug firs on the north road and a canopy is created by the adjoining madrone tree, blocking the light until the wind begins to blow, disturbing the leaves. I wasn't in the cave for more than a few short minutes, putting the new cheeses on their shelf and then checking on the older cheeses. I spent a couple of minutes perusing the crates of wine that are also stored on the floor in the back of the cave. It was enough time to get used to the quiet, the faintly dull existence in the monochromatic gray box, and enough time to be alarmed, and frankly also relieved, to walk out into the vibrant, bright, chatty surroundings on the other side of the thick wooden door.

FOUR

Early Planting in the Garden

Fall has arrived at the farm; the heat of summer has settled down but the heavy rains have yet to arrive. The garden is at its tipping point. The lush tomato plants are still filled with fruit, some deep red and ready to be picked, others green with little chance of ever ripening on the vine. The pumpkins are full-sized, deep orange and ripe, yet their large green leaves are browned on the edges and beginning to fade. The onions and garlic were harvested a couple of weeks earlier and are in the kitchen drying, soon to be used in cooking through the winter months.

Although it appears to be the end of the growing season, it is also the beginning for one plant: the garlic. To achieve full, large, bulbous heads next fall, I will plant the garlic this week. October has arrived but there is still warm weather for at least four more weeks, ample to get the garlic sprouted and established in the ground. In the kitchen I sort through the heads of garlic I picked a couple of weeks ago. Some are small, some grew better and are larger and then a few grew too much. When the individual cloves are too large—most likely from harvesting too late—they burst from their paper coverings and are more vulnerable to rot than those completely tight and covered in their dry outer skins.

I select a dozen of these robust heads, all with large, full cloves. I break them apart with the heel of my hand, fully separating the individual cloves. The table is now covered with at least a hundred cloves of garlic. Thankfully Jorge has prepared a bed in the garden for me, improving it with a couple wheelbarrows of compost and turning under the weeds from the summer months.

I plant four long rows of garlic, filling the bed. Each clove is planted with the root down, just below the surface, a few inches apart from one another. The soil is already moist from a couple of light rains last week and the temperature is an easy fifty degrees today. I am confident that by the end of October each ivory-colored nub will have sent down an inch of roots into the soil beneath and a small green shoot will have emerged. Although little growth will occur through the cold winter months, this initial start will guarantee success next year. The weather in this region can be mild during the depths of winter, even if a few odd weeks drop well below freezing. Those days in the forties and fifties will certainly help the garlic crop along.

The task is simple, quick and easy. Getting my hands dirty, if only for three-quarters of an hour, is enough to reconnect with the soil. The frequency of working in the garden seems more valuable than the duration.

After scrubbing up in the Cookhouse, I head up to the cave to check on the cheeses. Once per week I enter the subterranean bunker to look in on my charges. They change little in the span of seven days, but it is a schedule easy to maintain.

Walking down the gravel path and through the double doors into the cave has little of the drama that it did in the heat of the spring and summer. Today is dull and cool. The sun is barely out and the skies are gray and flat. Consequently, the atmosphere of the interior of the cave resembles that of the exterior.

There is a lintel above the door, partially hidden by smaller boulders and soil and ferns and the pasture, but it is certainly a lintel, the horizontal element above every door that both physically and visually supports the opening. I look up at it as I approach the cave and am always reminded of the phrase that I should have had inscribed on it but did not. I wanted it to read ET IN ARCADIO EGO. I forgot to ask Stuart to find a way to cast it into the concrete as he made the forms. I also thought it would appear to be pretentious and forced. It may be better that I know what should be above the door, and that I am reminded every time I enter, and that it is just for myself.

Et in arcadio ego is a Latin phrase that I first came across years ago while reading *Brideshead Revisited* by Evelyn Waugh. In the 1980s a miniseries had been made of this book about the wealthy of England before the First World War, and I was drawn into the rich interiors and decadent lives that Waugh had so beautiful described and which the television series presented. I found a copy of the book and pored over it, enjoying the petty lives as they began to crumble in the early part of the twentieth century.

The Latin phrase is the title of one of the first chapters in the book and has various translations. I never took Latin in school and have little understanding of the intricacies of this diminutive phrase, but it speaks of arcadia and death. I prefer the translation "the one that lies in this tomb lived in Arcadia." Obviously a lot of additional meaning is attached to these four short words, but I like that interpretation. This cave is without a doubt a tomb, sure to be in existence far longer than anything else on the farm. And I consider this farm to be my Arcadia: my rural, idyllic, pastoral site.

When Stuart finished the building of this cave I asked him rhetorically what it would take to remove it if there was ever the need or desire. He paused for a few moments, and then described the effort that would be needed to dismantle and destroy this room deep in the earth. The concrete is thick and of high strength. It is reinforced by a virtual cage of weighty steel. And it would be quite a Herculean task to destroy. He thought that he could go inch by inch with a jackhammer and break up the concrete, but he appeared to find the question odd and obtuse.

I walked away from our short conversation and thought about what he had said. My Log House is 130-plus years old, constructed entirely of wood, and has little chance if any of not continually degrading back into the earth. I spent ten years bringing it back to a livable state, replacing a sizable percentage of the fragile wooden logs. Many other structures on the property are constructed of masonry, yet all have wooden rafters and purlins that hold up their roofs, and are sure to rot and degrade over the decades. The barn is entirely made of wood, with barely a tiny percentage of steel nails in its structure. Even the roof is made of cedar shingles. At least the other roofs are clad in galvanized metal.

This tomb, however, is entirely reinforced concrete with little if any chance of degradation. It will survive. I have placed something on this bit of arcadia that presumably could remain for centuries. Few people have that opportunity or the desire to leave something behind with such longevity. Certainly the doors will rot, their thick, strong fir structures in essence simply long strands of organic fiber. Cellulose, if you will, parading as permanence.

This tomb will be found decades or centuries later and confuse those who come across it, perhaps thinking it was a bomb shelter from the middle of the last century, or a gothic mausoleum.

I think too much and these ideas pass through my mind today as I walked beneath the lintel, and read the slogan *et in arcadio ego,* pondering its significance even though it has never been inscribed into that concrete.

The task at hand is clever, necessary and tactile. The cheeses need to be flipped. Those made just a few days ago are moist and likely to stick to the board on which they are stored. They need to be flipped so that the dryer top side can now be on the bottom and the moist bottom side can now have a chance to dry. Those that were made weeks or months ago are not likely to stick to the spruce shelves, but flipping guarantees their even curing during the duration of their time in the cave. The act of picking up each cheese, flipping it and then replacing it on the shelf also gives me the chance to rub the molds down, keeping them short and managed. And finally, the possibility of cheese mites living under the cheeses is diminished if the cheeses are constantly flipped and the boards brushed clean.

What is clever about this simple task is the way it is achieved. If I were to simply flip each cheese and replace it in the same spot, that seven-inch round on the spruce shelf would never dry out. Never exposed to the air, always covered by a wheel of cheese, that circle would potentially harbor bacteria— good or bad—and would arrest the drying process.

The remedy for this dilemma is to flip the shelf boards at the same time as the cheeses. Frédéric installed these spruce boards three years earlier laying them on long steel rods that come out from the vertical supports of the shelving system. Each board is resting on two of these simple rods, anchored only by gravity.

I walk down the center apse of the cave and then turn into one of the small naves of shelving. Each shelf is filled with five cheeses, except for one.

The top shelf contains no cheeses. I go to the next shelf down, pick up each cheese, rub it down completely, flip it and then place it on the empty shelf above. When the last cheese is relocated, the now-empty shelf is flipped over and returned to its steel supports. While I have it out of the frame and in my hands, I quickly brush any errant bits of mold or cheese or cheese mites to the floor.

Now I continue with the next shelf down and replace its cheeses onto what is now the inverted second shelf. The top side has had all week to dry; the bottom side, which held five cheeses just a moment ago, now has the next seven days to dry out as well.

I had hoped that my mind would empty as I passed beneath the phantom Latin motto on the lintel, but it has not. The flipping and brushing of the cheeses is mechanical and tactile and my mind can wander. I am struck by the idea of Arcadia. It is in fact a region of Greece on the Peloponnesian peninsula, still rural, mountainous and partially inhabited by shepherds. What strikes me as remarkable is our continued need since Hellenistic Greece to look to an area outside of the cities to romanticize.

This farm is a few miles outside of Seattle, on an island greatly underinhabited compared to its nearby cities and suburbs. There are without a doubt many small farms and homesteads, most with a goat or two, perhaps a pig, and a few that keep cows, such as my farm.

I would not consider myself a shepherd per se, but I do tend to cows on a daily basis, albeit in a modern dairy practice, rather than goats or sheep raised in a transhumance manner. I love this lifestyle, enjoy the nature that surrounds me daily, revel in the beautiful days when the sun shines through the often thick clouds of winter. Yet I also comprehend the reality of this life—the challenges of a business and a life connected to the cruelties of nature. Most everything of daily life and business in a city is controlled—the heating, the air-conditioning, the artificial lighting, the paving—all in an effort to limit the unpredictable effects of nature.

This is a real life. I am cold. Animals die. The mud and manure of winter is overwhelming in the darkest days. And in the summer, on the best days, it is a remarkable, idyllic existence. Until it gets too hot, the pastures dry up and the flies take over the farm.

And yet, on a weekly and often daily basis, I get emails from those who have heard of this farm, of this life, and who express their envy; a desire to experience a place of Arcadia. They want to believe there is such a place of fantasy. A place where shepherding the animals from pasture to pasture in the bright days of summer exists. Where all is calm and verdant and pastoral.

The cruel part of this envy is that this farm and all others like it are not idyllic, nor always pastoral. What most do not realize is that Arcadia is the concept of an idyll that has passed. It is utopia that is the dream of the future. Yet we all crave the hope that just over the water, just a fifteen-minute ferryboat ride away, is a place that we can dream about. And we have been dreaming of such a place for more than two thousand years.

This is where my mind goes as my hands lift the cheeses, rub them and flip the boards and shuffle over to the next row. It is a pleasant thought, neither bleak nor dour. This ancient thought—that of Arcadia—together with this ancient practice of crafting cheeses, connects me to our past.

This flipping of cheeses and flipping of boards takes not even an hour, yet the entire time I have a silly grin on my face. The process of flipping boards is just too clever for me not to smile. I wish I had come up with the idea, but alas it is a method that has most likely been around for generations. It matters little to me; I am pleased each time and revel in the simplicity and great utility of it all.

It is important to me that I age my cheeses here on the farm. There is a trend today in this country to have a separate person and business age cheeses off of the farm. These *affineurs*—the people who perform the *affinage*, or aging of cheeses—are the next darlings of the food world. It is a tradition in France that is slowly gaining acceptance in this country. I see the benefit of it in some cases, but I prefer to keep the control of my young cheeses here in this cave a short walk from the make room, surrounded by the curious cows who are largely responsible for the cheese.

In the new model, the cheese maker produces his cheeses, and as soon as they are out of the molds, they are transported to the *affineur* to be turned and brushed and cared for over the life of their aging, and it is up to the *affineur* to decide when they are ready to be sold.

I am an opinionated and often arrogant bastard, and I feel that I know better when my cheeses need to be flipped or turned or cared for. I am also often incorrect. There are certainly far more knowledgeable folks in the cheese business and I should listen to them more. Trial and error has been my teacher, often with disastrous results. My pigs have fattened well on the missteps of my earlier *affinage*. An added force in this is my wanting to retain full credit for the success of my products in the consumers' eyes and also financially. If I send cheeses off to another facility, I am also sending off part of the profits of my enterprise. At this small scale, attention to retaining every bit of profit is paramount.

Thankfully, this thirteen-acre farm, with now seven cows in milk and another six dry, has managed to become profitable. In the last decade, this small farm has evolved from my initial dream of raising and selling honey and vegetables, to serving farm dinners in the Cookhouse, to selling raw milk, and now to concentrating exclusively on selling the finest farmstead cheeses I can produce.

This refinement has been necessary, if at times a bit exhausting. Goats were attempted, sheep as well. A farm stand was set up and quickly dismantled when it proved impractical. Raising one cow and then a second taught me the necessary skills for being a dairyman. Raw milk was a great beginning, even if it exposed me to far too much liability. By the time I arrived at this point a decade later—as a profitable farmstead cheese maker—I had acquired the skills needed and also the necessary barns, fences, paddocks and vibrant pastures required for the business.

I'm glad I stumbled onto that first Jersey cow—Dinah— early on and quickly realized my great love of Jersey cows. That breed has served me well. The small scale of the cows in comparison to the larger, weightier Holsteins is ideal for the small acreage that I own. The deep golden color of the Jersey milk and the unusually high butterfat content makes for delightful, rich and special cheeses.

FIVE

Nine Months Before;
Alice Is Bred

It is nearly the end of the year. Christmas is just a couple of days away and winter has arrived. The days are the shortest of the year and the weather is characteristic of the Pacific Northwest in December: overcast, wet and dreary. It is not snowing, nor even freezing, but it is difficult to find joy in such damp, dark days. Today I have a project to break up the monotony of these bleak winter days.

Alice is ready to be bred. Although she is still young, and looks rather small in comparison to the mature milking cows, when she calves in nine months she will have gained weight and stature. I check my watch and realize the AI tech will arrive in a few minutes at the farm. The AI (artificial insemination) tech will breed Alice now that she is fifteen months old. To call him a tech seems quite impersonal; his name is Wayne and he has been to the farm many times.

I leave the comfort of the Cookhouse and head out the front paddock, where I can see Alice and also wait for Wayne's mini-van to come down the driveway. He is coming from off-island, so it is very predictable what time he will arrive from the ferry dock, and he does not disappoint. When I noticed that Alice had come into heat early this morning while Jorge was milking the other cows, I called Wayne and he agreed to come out this afternoon to breed her.

While I have had bulls in the past to breed the heifers, I have since switched back to AI. The bulls were simply eating too much expensive hay, the quality of their genes was suspect and, most importantly, I was fearful that they would hurt a visitor to the farm.

Those who have grown up on traditional farms with bulls know of their inherent danger. They are extremely strong, bullheaded and potentially aggressive. Over the years many of the older visitors would tell me harrowing stories of bull encounters with a casualness that always surprised me. Quick comments as, "My uncle was killed by a bull" or "My grandfather was attacked by a bull and only lived by stabbing his bull with a pitchfork" were not uncommon. I grew up in the city and had little such culture in my genes. Over the years I came to respect my bulls, but I was unable to convey that sense to visitors. Many people would put their hands inside the electrified fence to pet the bulky beasts, even with my protestations. When the last one encouraged his young children to do the same and headed for the locked gate of the bullpen, I decided it was time to switch to AI to breed the cows.

Wayne hops out of the deep blue minivan, wearing a polyester cap emblazoned with the name of his national semen company and holding a catalogue in his hand. I meet him by the side of the van and he begins to open the catalogue to the Jersey cow page, showing me the names and stats of the Jersey bulls he represents. My life is full and busy and I have little interest in complicating it further by studying the cryptic tables of heights and weights and potential fat content and ash content of offsprings' milk. He pushes me to pick one and I casually pick a name and a photo that I find appealing. Wayne may judge me as a casual farmer, but he doesn't show it, excited about my choice of bull semen to breed Alice.

He drops the catalogue in the front seat and heads to the rear of the van, opening the doors wide and pulling out a strawful of semen from the nitrogen tank, and a thin plunger together with the needed supplies.

While he is loading up what he needs, I bring Alice into the stanchion of the milking parlor, luring her in with a bucketful of grain. She tenuously approaches and is quickly locked in. Once she begins to eagerly eat the grain, her apprehension falls away and she settles.

Wayne comes into the milking parlor and quickly goes to work. Today he will breed one of my cows, but most of his days are spent at large commercial dairies. He drops numbers that seem incomprehensible—a hundred cows bred this morning, fifty tomorrow, two hundred the next day. Consequently he is rapid and competent in his work.

On his left hand he fits a thin, shoulder-length pale green plastic glove. It is nearly four feet in length and bears little resemblance to the tiny plastic gloves I wear in the cheese make room. With his right hand he squirts a long line of lubricant on the glove starting with the hand and on up to his elbow. He sets the bottle of lubricant down and grabs the syringe filled with the straw of bull semen. While he is putting the glove on and lubricating it, I notice that the plunger and straw are cupped under his armpit, in that way gently warming the frozen semen in the moments before it will be given to Alice.

He then inserts his gloved and lubricated hand into the rear of the cow held in the stanchion. Miraculously, he gently and rapidly inserts his entire hand and arm and elbow up to his shoulder. Alice appears to notice and possibly be confused, but is neither hurt nor particularly concerned. The grain is far more interesting to her than Wayne.

With his free hand, he pulls the plunger and straw from beneath his armpit and precisely guides it into Alice, following the path of his gloved hand. In a moment he is rotating and moving the syringe until it is just where he wants it, then he pushes the handle on the end, releasing the barely frozen bull sperm deep within Alice. The syringe is removed, and then his arm. He offers me the empty straw, which I accept. It is an odd part of the operation. It is marked with the serial number of the bull and the lot, but it feels rather more like he is offering me a cigar, toasting to the future calf. I play the part, and graciously accept the straw.

Wayne inverts the glove as he removes it so that only the clean interior is apparent, and he returns it to his van with his supplies. He has been in the milking parlor for at most two minutes. He quickly writes up the invoice while seated in his van and in a couple minutes he will be headed back down the bumpy driveway off the farm and back to the large commercial dairies that are his usual clients. Alice slowly finishes her bucket of precious grain, I unlock her from the stanchion and she returns to the paddock, seeming unaware of what all has transpired. With luck, she will give birth to a calf nine months later, in the last week of September.

———

Today has very little resemblance to spring. It is still quite cold in the morning, with a bit of frost on the roofs when I stumble out of bed. The days are certainly longer than they were on the solstice six weeks earlier, but not enough to make me think that summer is just around the corner. By the calendar, however, I know that it is time to get ready for spring.

The seed catalogues arrived in the mail more than a month ago and the orders were placed online soon thereafter. Now that the small box has arrived from the seed seller, I can begin in earnest in the greenhouse. I order few seeds for the farm. When I started growing vegetables for the farmers' market and for a CSA eight years ago, Matt was working here and did the seed orders. He is by his nature an optimistic soul and ordered a vast quantity of seeds. At the time I was rather annoyed by his exuberance. Actually, when the Visa bill arrived on my desk I was annoyed. Eight years later I still have a great box filled with vegetable seeds. Granted, the most useful seeds were long since planted and some seeds have short periods of viability. But I still have a few years' worth of arugula seeds, for example. My parsimony keeps me from throwing out the entire legacy of that first year of farming; my sentimentality as well.

I did order fresh onion seeds and a few new varieties of tomatoes and squash, and they are laid out on the kitchen table. The greenhouse is prepared. This small glass house is eight feet wide and fourteen feet long, tiny by commercial standards and large by household standards. It is ample for this farm's needs. From mid-February until June it will hold flats of plant starts, begun in the protection of surrounding glass and planted out into the garden when ready. When the last of the small starts have left the confines of the hothouse, the benches will be removed, the dirt floor augmented with compost and the greenhouse will be directly planted with pepper plants, greedy for the continuing warmth of the greenhouse. By September this confined room will burst with the heady scent of peppers, the capsicum airborne even though the peppers are just ripening on the small, sturdy plants. Halloween will signal the time to pick the final deep red fruits, pull up the exhausted plants and leave the greenhouse empty until it is time to begin again with the flats of onions in February.

Today, the greenhouse is bleak. Completely empty, it appears forlorn and unable to sustain any life whatsoever. As it is an enclosed space, sealed from the elements, no rain reaches the dirt floor of the house. It is completely arid and dusty when I open the stubborn sliding doors even though it has been raining most days this wet winter. A few desiccated leaves and peppers remain on the ground, left from my sloppy cleaning in the fall.

The benches are stored when not in use in the attic above the milking parlor. Wobbly, feeble aluminum tables, they came with the greenhouse when I bought it eight years ago. Every year it is a miracle that they survive, barely able to hold the weighty flats filled with wet soil and plants. And every year I promise to replace them before the next growing season begins. This past winter was no different and today I climb the skinny stairs to the attic and begin to pull the rickety excuses for furniture down for their season of service. In the cramped quarters above the milking parlor are the vacuum pump that runs the milking equipment, the stacks of benches and an assortment of discarded dairy accessories: in-line milk filters, dented milking buckets made unusable by their damage, gallon jugs of dairy detergent, milkstone cleaners, iodine teat washes and antibacterial teat dips, square black plastic flats and hundreds of four-inch plant plots. One by one the six benches are passed down the skinny stairs to Jorge waiting below, followed by a stack of twenty of the flats and a couple hundred of the pots. With a small amount of effort the benches are set up in the greenhouse, lining the walls with a central alley remaining in the middle. In a matter of minutes the greenhouse moves from an ignored, empty space to a greenhouse capable of housing hundreds of small plants in the luxury of climate control.

Onions are the first plants to be seeded in this new year; they need the most time to reach the large, robust size by autumn. Onions are slow-growing and need this early start. They also have a unique characteristic.

Onions have two distinct growing periods in their season. The first is when they are growing their roots and tops. The second is when they bulb up and create the part of the plant that we know as the onion. The plant determines when to stop growing the green top part of the plant and begin to grow the bulb part by the length of the day. In reality, onions are sensitive to the amount of darkness, but for practical reasons, it is easier to think of them as aware of the volume of sunlight.

Because of this fairly unique characteristic, onion varieties are divided into two distinct groups—long-day and short-day. Long-day onions are planted in the northern latitudes of this country, and short-day are planted in the southern latitudes.

What makes this even more interesting is that short-day and long-day onion varieties are not the same in other characteristics. Long-day onions are generally storage onions, with the ability to be held for months after they are harvested. Short-day onions are the opposite, needing to be eaten soon after their harvest. In addition, onions' storage ability is directly related to the quantity of sugars in the onions. The short-day onions are those grown in the southern states such as Georgia, known for its Vidalia onions. The Vidalia onions are character-ized as sweet onions, I would guess as a marketing tool. So it is now assumed that short-day, southern onions are therefore sweeter than their northern long-day neighbors. In fact, long-day onions contain more sugars than the short-day ones. What we are tasting in an onion is its relative pungency. Onions that are sharper, with a great pungent onion flavor, seem to us to be less sweet. It is onions that have less of that sharp onion quality that we perceive to be sweet. It is the relative amount of sulfur in the onion that creates those pungent qualities. As it happens, the counties where Georgia Vidalia onions are grown are low in sulfur in the soil.

This would all be simple, except that Walla Walla sweet onions are in fact, long-day onions grown in the northern lati-tudes, and yet they are less pungent, nonstorage onions. There are always a few anomalies.

I prefer to have the ability to keep onions for weeks after harvest, so the varieties I plant here, at the forty-seventh par-allel, are all long-day storage onions. The two varieties that I ordered last month were Copra, a consistent, sweet stor-age onion and a cipollini onion as well. The Copras are large, robust, yellow globes. The cipollini are white, squat, small onions, nearly flat in shape. When you look at them, they seem like a strange aberration, as if they were stepped on mistak-enly at a time when they were curiously flexible.

I also ordered a small packet of Ambition, a large shallot variety recommended by Leda, a grower on the island. I have always grown shallots from bulbs of the former year's shallot crop, in the same way that I plant garlic. For years, I used this method before asking Leda her opinion on shallots. She assured me that without a doubt I needed to grow them from seeds, and not from saved bulbs. I trust her. The seeds have arrived and will be planted along with the other alliums.

The process is simple and straightforward. One of the square black plastic flats can hold all of the season's onion starts. The trays are sixteen inches square and two inches high. The bottoms are perforated for ample drainage. Under the bottom I lay a single sheet of newspaper, most likely the unneeded and unwanted weekly sales circular from the local supermarket. There is a touch of irony that the publication advertising distantly grown vegetables will form the base for the growing of local, superior produce. I smirk as I pour two inches of potting soil over the brashly colored photographs of onions and lettuce and tomatoes on this chilly February afternoon.

The soil is smoothed over to make the bed a consistent depth, then nine equidistant parallel troughs are created in the soil by pressing in a short wooden stick left in the greenhouse from staking peppers in the last summer months. The troughs are just a half inch deep and V-shaped, the nadir made from the stake, angled forty-five degrees to make the indentation.

Plastic tags are found and the varieties are scribbled with a permanent black marker that will stand up to the months in the shinning sun. One is placed at the head of each small row in the plastic flat filled with potting soil. The seed packets are then opened as needed to seed the rows.

Onion seeds are truly one of my favorite seeds. Seems like an odd item to categorize as good or better or best, but seeds are distinctly different. Brassicas are terribly boring: dark brown or black, tediously spherical and uniform. Squash seeds are large and in fact quite vulgar, almost grotesque in some variet- ies and often still have remnants of the sticky wet mesh of the interior of a pumpkin or Hubbard. Oddly, corn just seem to be not terribly bright. Not sure why, but that is the impression they give. Tobacco is special, but not in a good way; the seeds for a plant that grows to ten feet tall with an incredibly thick, rigid stalk and large, resinous leaves are nearly microscopic. They simply make no sense. They are far too small to produce such a hotly contested agricultural product.

Onion seeds are different. They are black in color, and neither round nor oblong. They remind me of the charcoal pebbles that I would use to filter my fish tank as a child. I doubt if they are tetrahedrons, but they do have flat, chiseled faces. They are certainly very similar in size and shape, but each is unique.

Because onions seeds lose their vitality quickly, I do not want to carry over any remaining seeds to the next year. I have three short rows for each variety and I make sure that all the seeds are used. This may make them very tight side by side, but the roots are quite strong and resilient and the small onion plants can easily and successfully be disentangled when they are to be transplanted into the garden.

When the nine rows are filled with the black nuggets and the paper seed packets are emptied, I will push a thin layer of soil over the rows, covering the seeds, my fingers tamping down the soil at the same time. The potting soil was moistened before I placed it into the flat, so I have no worries about adequate moisture for the seeds to germinate. They do, however, need added heat, as it is still thirty to forty degrees this time of year, even in the greenhouse.

The method of gently warming this weighty, wet flat of soil is to use a heating mat, made of flexible plastic, with an electrical cable running through it carrying just enough current to bring the temperature up enough to help the seeds germinate. A long temperature probe runs from the thermostat mounted on the wall of the greenhouse into the soil in the flat, guaranteeing that it won't overheat on a warm day and burn the tender seedlings once they emerge.

The flat is left sitting on the warm mat, the small red light on the thermostat aglow, on this chilly February afternoon. It is difficult to see ahead eight months to a warm autumn day, picking large, bulbous onions from the warm soil in the garden. At this point the seeds haven't even sprouted, nothing is green, nothing is growing. In the greenhouse is the dusty, dry dirt of the floor with a few dried peppers that fell off the plants last fall and a pile of dried weeds that I pulled up last week when I started cleaning out the greenhouse in anticipation of today's first seeding. I can only rely on my past experience. In a few days the charcoal-colored seeds will sprout, pushing a bright green thread up through the potting soil to the light. In a month each of the nine rows in the flat will be filled with tiny onion seedlings, all growing vigorously. And when the weather turns, and winter turns to spring, they will be ready to be planted out in the large kitchen garden. We will have onions for cooking this fall, I am confident.

———

Whereas the onions are seeded in long rows reminiscent of a field of corn, the tomatoes will be seeded in individual soil blocks. I utilize a clever tool to produce these potless squares of potting soil. The soil blocker is made of tinned metal and is three feet tall. Most of that height is the handle, with a long square tube connecting it to its base.

The base of the soil blocker is a grid of individual cells in four rows of six. Each individual cell is one and a half inches square and two inches deep. This grid is open on the bottom, and the top is made up of individual squares that fit into each cell.

To make the soil blocks, I push the grid of cells into a mound of moist, friable potting soil. The downward pressure pushes the soil up into each individual square chamber. The moisture of the soil together with the pressure keeps the soil inside the squares. I lift the soil blocker out from the mound of potting soil and place it on a short plastic flat. The flat is perforated on the bottom to allow water to pass through, yet rigid enough to hold a hundred of the soil blocks. I press the apparatus filled with wet soil onto the base of the flat and then engage the lever that presses the twenty-four individual plates down into the cells. The movement of the plates presses the compressed soil blocks out of the cells. Once the blocker is removed, the twenty-four soil blocks remain, all lined up on the plastic greenhouse flat. The process is repeated three more times until the flat is full of ninety-six small cubes of potting soil, ready to be seeded.

It is an ideal number for my garden—I will seed ten different tomato varieties. Eight varieties will have eight individual plants, and two will have sixteen plants. Out of the large box of seeds I can easily pick ten different varieties, some from years past and some just ordered this year. I break down the selection into types of tomatoes first—cherries, paste, heirloom and beefsteak. I pick out a couple of different varieties of cherries: Sun Gold and Sweet 100, the former yellow-colored, the latter red, and both sweet and full of flavor. I will plant double of the Sun Golds. For the heirloom varieties I have a few seeds remaining from my favorite tomato packets: Pineapple, Persimmon, Cherokee purple, Constolato Genovese and Marmande. I decide that if I only have two cherry varieties I can have five heirlooms. For beefsteaks I pick two: Early Girl and Taxi. The latter is not really a beefsteak but rather a predictable yellow fruit that is always prolific and holds well. Although the heirlooms have superior flavor and are beautiful to look at, their season is shorter and their output smaller. There are times when I just want a slice of tomato for my lunch sandwich and Taxi will do just fine. Taxi is more reliable than an heirloom even if it isn't the tastiest tomato. I am not really sure why I grow Early Girl, but I think of it more as insurance—against the possibility that the summer is so chilly that no other tomatoes will ripen and I will by default be excited to be eating the Early Girls.

For the paste tomato slots I decide to allocate sixteen plants in the final garden bed. I choose Bill's Tomatoes. You will not find such a variety in any one of the many tomato seed catalogues that overwhelm every gardener's mailbox in the late months of winter. It is as the name implies: Bill's tomatoes.

Bill is a fine older man who has lived on Vashon for more
than forty years. He is skinny and now a bit frail but is still the
chatty, cantankerous man I met twenty years ago when I first
arrived on the island. He shows up at my farm unexpectedly,
but very welcome, on a regular basis. He drives the same white
panel van that he has for years, it sounding a bit less vital
every year. In the van are numerous paint cans and buckets
and brushes and cans of solvents that he uses for his paint-
ing business. On the back bumper of the creaky vehicle is a
faded bumper sticker that states I DIDN'T QUIT—I SURRENDERED!
I have never really understood the sentiment, but I can recognize his van easily in the crowded grocery store parking lot. He
wears the same white painter pants, stiff paper painter's hat
with a company logo on it, a tidy small towel hanging from his
side pocket and dusty brown work boots with few if any drips
of paint on them. I doubt that I have ever seen him in any
other attire. After the front door of the van is closed with a bit
of effort, he goes to the rear of the van, opens wide one of the
doors, from among the sea of paint cans and mixing buckets
picks up a plant that he has grown for me and walks into the
Cookhouse to find me. I can't help but smile every time I see
that thirty-year-old van round the curve in the driveway.

I suppose you could call him an old hippie but that sounds
somewhat facile and uninteresting. It is, however, rather apt.
He moved to Vashon in the late 1960s because it was cheap and
out of the city. He, thankfully, never left. He has often told me
his story of Vashon Island. Prior to the late 1960s, Vashon was
a very blue-collar, conservative place with a small population
of farmers and working-class folk whose families had lived on
the island since it began to be inhabited in the late 1870s. It
was only when he and his kind moved to the island after the
Summer of Love that it began to acquire the deeply liberal,
educated character that it now possesses.

For most of his working years he has worked as a house
painter and, I know from hiring him, an excellent one. He has

painted and maintained all of the many windows and doors on the Log House, the Cookhouse and the creamery. I worry that he is close to retiring and that I will have to find some less experienced kid to paint the thin mullions of the 130-year-old sashes of the Log House.

In addition to his painterly skills, Bill also showed a knack for growing and propagating plants. On his property is a large greenhouse filled with plants. He is too cheap to buy large, expensive trees and shrubs from local nurseries in five-gallon pots ready to drop in the ground thirty minutes after you pick them up at the nursery. Instead he propagates trees and the like by seed or grafts or by root cuttings. Certainly it takes much longer and in many cases years to produce a plant equal in size to that super-grown nursery stock, but Bill's way is much cheaper and the experience much richer.

Bill also is profient at growing tomatoes. Primarily he simply grows starts from seed and then plants them out. The difference is that I order seeds by mail-order from large seed companies with glossy catalogues filled with color pictures of the tomatoes in question. Bill saves seed from the each year's fruit for planting the following spring. It is the much more erudite way of growing tomatoes and one that Bill has inspired me to attempt.

The tomato variety that Bill has brought me I now know simply as Bill's Tomato. I am not even sure how he came across it originally, but he has been growing it for many years. He first gave me one of the fruits five or six years ago and I let it get very ripe, to the point where it was starting to lose its shape, then I cut it in half and began to harvest the seeds that were in the interior. When I cut this beautiful deep red tomato in half, I realized why this tomato was special. The vast majority of it was actually tomato, as opposed to half flesh and half seeds. It was a paste tomato, with thick, dense, ruby-colored pulp ideal for cooking down to sauce. A few neatly arranged seeds ran down a slender valley from the stem end to three-quarters toward the bottom. This also was no usual tomato in its size and shape. Generally paste tomatoes are two and a half inches to perhaps three inches long and an especially long example could run four inches. These Bill's Tomatoes regularly passed the four-inch mark and easily could hit six. Their girth was equally profound. I have had many experienced gardeners pass through my garden and inquire about the bell peppers ripening on the exceptionally tall pepper plants. I take great pride in elucidating to them that, in fact, those lofty plants are tomatoes, and not simply tomatoes, but Bill's Tomatoes.

And now, at the end of each of the past five growing seasons, I hold back a couple of the best-looking, largest, and most flavorful specimens for the next year's seeds. I remove the seeds from the very ripe fruit, pushing the gel-covered seeds out with my thumb down the valley and onto an awaiting paper towel. I separate them in hopes of their quickly drying without molding. In a few days sitting on the counter of the Cookhouse in the warm heat of late September they will fully dry. What remains is a stiff, crusty paper towel with small, flat brown seeds. Difficult to comprehend that they contain the ability to create large, robust, verdant plants the next summer. I must admit that I mistakenly threw out the seed-covered paper towel one year and had to return to Bill, ashamedly asking him for a few more seeds to get me through the coming growing months. I had failed and yet he had no judgment, eagerly giving me a few more precious seeds.

What makes these seeds, these plants so much more precious and special to me is Bill's vision of their place and significance. I mentioned to him one day, when he came by the farm to see how my garden looked, that I was thinking of dropping off some seeds for my friend Leda, a commercial plant grower. I mistakenly expected him to be excited, flattered that I thought he had come across a great new variety, worthy of propagation and distribution to other growers. On the contrary, he explained to me that those seeds he gave me were a personal gift, to me and to me only. I assured him that I respected his wishes and that I would keep the seeds for my own exclusive use.

There are a couple of interesting aspects to his reaction, which I both relish and question at the same time. Bill is fully aware that all someone would have to do is grab even just one single seed from one of his fresh tomatoes, and grow it the next season. That would be fairly easy to do, by simply stealthily sneaking one off the plate while enjoying a beautiful tomato salad on a lovely summer day on the back porch of Cookhouse. That one tiny bit could easily create a six-foot-tall plant filled with ripe ruby fruit the next summer.

The other interesting facet of his conviction is that Bill is not a young man. The chance of him propagating this tomato himself on a grand scale is not likely; he has had a couple of strokes and is slowing down a bit every year. He wants to retain that proprietary nature of Bill's Tomatoes even if it isn't logical. It is, however, passionate, and it is his vision. I can respect his wishes in spite of the purely emotional qualities and lack of logic.

I finish seeding all of the blocks of soil. Ten varieties of tomatoes are represented in the two flats. My priorities and interests are reflected here: what kinds of tomatoes I like—the flavors and shapes—but also the climate here, its lack of hot summers, and also the varied uses these tomatoes will fulfill. I could have planted fifty different varieties, but ten will suffice.

Each variety is tagged with one of the small white plastic markers. The flat is put onto one of the heating mats on the benches in the greenhouse and the leftover seeds are returned to the large box of seeds. The sliding glass doors of the greenhouse are pushed and shoved and cajoled into closing; the runners on the threshold are clogged with dirt from my coming and going over the past couple hours. The latch is closed and I can see the red light of the thermostat is on, indicating that the heating mats are gently warming the trays of onions and tomatoes, helping them to germinate during this late winter day.

Every couple of days during the next two weeks I will stop by the greenhouse and check in on the blocks, to see if the seeds have germinated, if tiny sprouts have broken the surface. On this first day, however, there is little evidence that spring is on its way, that the temperature will warm and the days lengthen and that eventually twenty friends will walk into the Cookhouse and enjoy a slice of pizza with a rich, ruby-colored tomato sauce fresh from the wood oven and then continue on through dinner, eating a large plate of pasta with cippolini onions, chicken livers and grated cheese. It seems improbable on this chilly winter day. It is only blind faith that keeps gardeners going through this ritual, knowing that these tiny seeds will yield great rewards in a matter of months.

————

Just a week after I spent that cool morning in the greenhouse, seeding tomatoes in the flats of moist soil, I received a phone call from a friend on the island. I anticipated a light chat about her recent vacation and catching up on the goings on at her small farm a few minutes up the island from mine. It took me a moment to react when Sara's voice was not her usual happy tone. What she called to tell me was that Bill had died the night before, and that she wanted me to know.

Evidently the man I saw four weeks earlier was not simply a man fatigued from his daily work, but rather one ravaged by lung cancer, unbeknownst to him until the last couple weeks of his life. We ended the conversation quickly, my reaction both shocked and saddened. It was not for a couple more days before I comprehended fully that he had passed and that I would never get another chance to chat with the irascible but giving plant grower.

Once it settled into me, I returned to the greenhouse and checked the small cubes of seeding soil, looking for the bits of green life sprouting from the cubes in front of the white plastic tags with the scrawl of *Bill's Tomatoes* written on them. They were there—wispy bits of leaves poking through the soil, on their way to becoming full-sized, mature tomato plants.

I returned to the box of seeds and dug through the shiny commercial seed packets until I found the simple white envelope with his name written on it. Inside there remained the crusty paper towel with many seeds from last year still stuck to it. I felt relieved that even if I forgot to water the tender seedlings in the greenhouse, I could always start a second batch, or a third, to guarantee the continuance of these now-precious plants.

A walk along the edge of the farm, and I came across three trees that he had given me over the years: a Spanish pine that he was especially fond of and a couple of American larches. Originally I'd had three larches, but they were short and Jorge had mistakenly cut one down with the tractor. Bill admired the European larches I had planted two decades earlier and wanted me to have a couple of American varietals to complement those. Thankfully they have grown nicely and have little chance of being mowed down. The three trees he gave me will grow to maturity and remind me of Bill's contribution to this small landscape. The tomatoes will accomplish even more. Each year I get to plant the tiny dried seeds, watching them germinate and grow leaves. After a few weeks I can plant them into small pots and then, when the weather breaks and the garden is warm and sunny, they will be planted into the raised beds of the kitchen garden. Through the summer months I can prune and water and fertilize them, all for the eventual treat of picking and enjoying the large, robust ruby-colored fruit. It is an active memorial, an active legacy.

Bill fiercely guarded this funny, overweight tomato. I will never know why, but I can now respect it. It is tempting to hand the seeds out to friends and other growers, hoping that many gardens will contain the tomatoes ideal for making rich, thick tomato sauce. But I won't. He wanted them private and special and personal.

My gardens will continue to have a large, long bed filled with the pepperlike plants, however, and come fall, the guests around the table here will enjoy the sauce from those tomatoes, full of the flavors of a warm summer. They may have no idea of the significance of the tomato sauce smeared across the thin pizzas, but I will. Each time someone enjoys a bit of this legacy I can smile and remember my chatty and cantankerous friend in the white painter pants.

SIX

Springtime on the Farm

Vashon Island is, in fact, two islands: Vashon Island, the namesake, and Maury Island, its lesser-known neighbor. The two islands are linked by a small man-made isthmus, perhaps a thousand feet wide and five thousand feet long. From the air it is obvious that there are two landmasses connected by a small band of soil, but when driving from one island to the next it is not obvious in any way.

Those who live on Vashon think of Maury Island as simply an extension of Vashon and rarely if ever make a distinction in any description of their community. It is the Vashon School District, the Vashon Parks District, the bumper stickers common to all here state KEEP VASHON WEIRD and the state of Washington is clear that their ferryboats are headed to Vashon Island only.

For those who live on Maury Island, however, there is an apparent inferiority complex. Occasionally they will push for the inclusion of their community name—the Vashon-Maury Islands Community Council, for example. We, those on the dominant island, find it tedious and unnecessary. Such is the role of the oppressors.

As Maury is more difficult to access—it is necessary to drive through Vashon and then across the isthmus to get to it—it is less populated and more rural. The standard adage is that Maury is the place that Vashonites move to, to get away from all the congestion. Needless to say, even though Maury is less inhabited than Vashon, there are few areas of true density on either island.

Kurtwood Farms is located just outside of town on Vashon Island. It is a quick drive to the town of Vashon where the business district and the road to the ferry dock are located. My attention is drawn to town generally only for shopping and getting a coffee in the local café or to head to the north end of the island to catch a ferry to Seattle.

I do, however, head to Maury Island for one great reason. Located just outside the small shell of a town named Dockton is my friend Leda's farm. She and her family have a very tidy ten-acre farm located on the outskirts of Dockton. Today Dockton has no retail businesses, but in its heyday it was a thriving town. In the Vashon historical museum—incidentally officially named the Vashon-*Maury Island* Heritage Museum—are large photographs of Dockton in 1895. The most striking is one of two large, three-masted schooners at dock. They are so majestic that it is inconceivable that the image represents this small, long-ago-deserted town. At first glance it is a photograph of San Francisco or Boston or even New York.

Leda's farm is just a couple of blocks east of Dockton. The main road across the smaller island comes down the hill into the harbor, and circles around the last remnants of the turn-of-the-last-century town. A few pilings remain visible that once supported the largest dry dock on the West Coast. A row of proud houses line the main street and face out toward the inner harbor. Those five houses have the delightful moniker of Piano Row, the name indicating that the owners of each of those fine homes had the resources to purchase a piano. After a quick, sharp turn at the last stately house, the town continues for a half a block. The building that housed the general store and the post office remains; the local parish church was demolished a few months earlier this year. A quick block later and Leda's greenhouses become visible. The hill slopes down from the road in such a way that you can see the farm below you as you approach it. The farm is not what one would generally imagine a farm to look like—there are no large animals, no barns and very few fields. The largest percentage of the acreage is devoted to greenhouses: expansive, long, plastic-covered greenhouses.

Leda's husband Matt built these greenhouses over the past decade. They are constructed of dimensional lumber from the local lumberyard, nailed together and then covered in plastic sheeting. They suffice admirably even though they are neither graceful, nor grand, nor the industry standard. They extol an attitude of perseverance, industriousness and hard work. The five greenhouses, all approximately two hundred feet long and thirty feet wide, each contain a series of benches lining the long walls.

Those benches, also made of the ubiquitous two-by-four and two-by-six lumber, are covered in small mesh hardware cloth to allow water and air to pass through. The benches hold flats of plant starts—hundreds upon hundreds of flats of starts. Above these long, low benches are propane heaters and fans, the heaters running nonstop in the cold nights of late winter, the fans desperately trying to move the air in the warmer spring days when the heat rises precipitously in the greenhouses.

During the winter and early spring their farm is dedicated to the growing and selling of plant starts. In the summer months when the greenhouses have been emptied of their small plants, Leda and Matt move on to growing vegetables in the fields.

I am thankful Leda greatly enjoys cheese; especially the fresh Dinah's Cheese made at my farm. This makes for a great relationship of barter. I need vegetable starts for my garden, and she enjoys having cheese on her table. This is a solid, mutually beneficial relationship. It is virtually impossible for her to get a cow, milk it, make the cheese and then age it. Although I enjoy seeding tomatoes and onions in the greenhouse, I have little interest or skill at growing much of any other early plant starts.

At the entrance to the farm is a large, high wooden gate. It is solid, tall and imposing. It is not a welcoming gate in any way; in fact, it sends a clear signal that unexpected visitors are not welcome. I have known Leda and Matt for a few years and I still feel intimidated when faced with an eight-foot-high and twenty-foot-wide wooden gate with a sturdy steel slide bolt holding it closed.

The drama that results in sliding that two-foot-long steel bolt and releasing the gate is well worth the apprehensions. The driveway into the farm slopes down quickly toward the house, the greenhouses and the packing area. When the bulky gate swings wide, the farm is apparent in one glance. It is a small farm but full of activity. I walk down the driveway toward the house. Near the entrance to the house is the Kubota, a large orange-colored tractor used to till the gardens and haul supplies. A small, enclosed trailer sits nearby. The trailer is pulled behind one of the trucks to deliver plants from north of Seattle and down past Portland, Oregon. The newest edition to the small fleet is parked opposite the house on the driveway—a large thirty-foot panel truck. This newest delivery truck changes the feel of the place, I am sure. No longer is this a cute greenhouse company delivering a few plant starts in the back of their pickup truck.

I find Leda in her house. She always seems to know when someone is arriving on her porch. Certainly the large, bulky gate helps, as well as the necessary pre-visit phone call, but even still, she just knows that you are about to knock on the door. From the moment she opens it, the conversation begins fluidly. Leda is neither petite nor shy. She is full of body and spirit. At least when I am visiting she is moving constantly, and talking all the while to keep up with her movement. Even when she takes a moment to sit down on the porch with some iced tea on a nice summer day, she still appears to be in motion. I enjoy it.

Matt is Leda's husband. They are quite different. He is quiet and pensive, with a constant sly smile on his face. His wife's expressions vary dramatically, from total excitement and joy to frustration and sadness. All the while, Matt sits nearby with that sly grin, occasionally offering up a few choice words to add to the conversation.

As it is the last week of March and the weather has moved from the chills of the end of winter to the first springlike days, I need to get vegetables started in my gardens. I could seed everything I need in my own small greenhouse, but I enjoy this adventure through the expansive greenhouses of Maury Island.

Before we have finished a complete conversation in the house, Leda is headed out of her home toward the greenhouses a couple hundred feet away. I trail behind quickly, with Matt casually pulling up the rear. His presence is not really needed but he tags along nonetheless. Leda is talking the entire time she walks, extolling the virtues of a new plant and simultaneously handing out gossip about other growers. I certainly comment on her opinions, but this is more of a soliloquy than it is a conversation.

There are five greenhouses on her farm, one row of three side by side with a small alley at one end where two more begin. The main alley is connected to the driveway and to the packing shed, and we march down it and quickly see the five main doors to each house. Whereas the greenhouses look imposing when seen from the road above, upon entering them it is more dramatic.

Different greenhouses contain different kinds of plants— tomatoes, brassicas, flowers and other vegetables. This week is one of the busiest of the year. Most of these plants were seeded late in the winter after the coldest weather had passed. Now, six or eight weeks later, they are ready to be delivered to nurseries and garden stores.

In the houses are her workers tending to the plants. Most are interns from Japanese agricultural colleges. These students study at their universities, come to the United States to

take coursework and hone their English language skills and
then are placed in farms for fourteen months before returning to Japan. They are serious, committed to becoming farmers
and very hard workers. Today I see three Japanese interns—
two women and a man—along with the mother of one of the
interns, who is here visiting. She expected to be on vacation
touring the area, but was quickly bored with being a tourist
and decided to come back to the farm and work for a few days.
I am amused and entranced by this older Asian woman, who
is busy transplanting alpine strawberries, looking as if she has
been here for years.

In rapid fire Leda takes me through the greenhouse, down
one row and up the other, pointing out the plants that she likes
and that she thinks I will enjoy: red Rubine Brussels sprouts,
"Mignonette" alpine strawberries, phygelius. She has an opinion on each and every variety: "This kale cooks up beautifully;
stunning fragrant flowers on this nicotiana, sweet berries but
very small. . . ." I attempt to soak up as much information as
possible, but realize that I am forgetting half of what she says
as she says it. Pulling out my iPhone and recording her com-
mentary would feel forced and ridiculous, and so I attempt to
absorb as much as I can and with luck I can fill in the rest
later. What always strikes me when I come down to visit and
chat with Leda is that, though I have been growing plants for
thirty-five years and I have always been rather confident in my
abilities, when I am here I realize there is still a great deal for
me to learn.

Once she has given me a general tour of the greenhouses,
Leda hands me three large, empty plastic flats and hurriedly
exits, giving me instructions to fill the flats and then find her
in the house when I am finished. In a moment the energy of
her nonstop banter comes to an end and I am left with the
large greenhouses, the three Japanese interns, one of their
mothers and the quiet whirl of the overhead fans. They speak
English, but very little, and have no interest in chatting with

me, their attention focused on the tasks they are engaged in. I am reminded of college classes where I spent the term listening to the professor lecture every week, confident that I fully understood the material, only to find on test day that, in fact, I had absorbed little. Hastily, nervously filling in the flimsy blue exam booklet with the rudiments of the coursework—that feeling comes back to me as I try desperately to remember where the Brussels sprouts are located, and was I supposed to plant them out now or was I supposed to ignore those and come back in June to get them? I wander aimlessly up and down the rows, vaguely recognizing broccoli leaves and radicchio and sweet peas. Luckily Leda cannot see me inside the opaque plastic-covered houses.

Within a few minutes, I get my sea legs, if you will, and attempt to prioritize what I need. I am here for plants that I cannot or am not interested in growing myself—primarily brassicas. Although Leda grows peas and beets and salad greens for sale at city garden centers, it is far more efficient for me to direct-seed those in my garden beds. Leda's plant starts make sense for someone in the city who has a small patio containers to fill, but for me, with an expansive garden, it would be terribly inefficient. For plants such as cabbages, broccoli, Brussels sprouts and the like, however, picking up six or eight individual plants of different varieties works great.

In a very inefficient way, ambling up and down the rows, I manage to fill the three flats with a large variety of vegetables, and a few flowers as well. I didn't head down here for hollyhocks, but they seemed rather irresistible once I was in the greenhouse and could see a hundred flats of them. I took a moment to imagine where all of these flowers would land— some in Seattle, some on Vashon, a few down to Portland. With a great deal of optimism I conjure up the image of hundreds of the mature hollyhocks, tall and majestic, in full bloom against garden walls up and down the coast. More likely maybe half will actually be planted out and grow to maturity. The other half will be impulse buys at the local grocery store by an optimistic dreamer, who will leave it in the back of his car till it dries out or forget to actually plant it, or perhaps even get it home and plant it and then in midsummer forget to water it while it fades to a quiet death.

I pick out a full three flats—Brussels sprouts, red cabbage, broccoli, alpine strawberries, radicchio—both Castelfranco and Red Chiogga—collards, red Winterbor kale and too much Lacinato and, of course, I fall prey to the lure of the hollyhocks. I settle up with Leda outside the packing shed. Each flat is worth one beautiful ripe Dinah's Cheese. I now owe her three. She keeps an open and casual account for me—when she needs cheese for a party this summer she will stop by the farm or have me drop a couple off for her. When I say casual, I mean that there isn't a written log. Neither of us is casual about it. Both of these farms are successful because we watch every sale, and keep it businesslike. Leda is the master of the casual-businesslike.

I head up the inclined driveway, pull back the steel bolt and open wide the long gate to head back to my truck. There is defiantly a feeling of distinction inside the compound and outside. It is a complete, small community within the perimeter fence. Not in a creepy, Waco kind of feeling, but rather you simply can't see other people from inside and Leda and Matt's young son can run around playing without any cares. There is ample food to eat and the entire property feels controlled and complete. The full extent of the farm is cultivated and utilized: chickens on the hill, greenhouses below, growing fields surrounding both for the summer vegetable season and a second house on the opposite corner where the young interns live. It is difficult to imagine a reason to leave the farm, except when Matt loads the long semi truck with flats of plants and drives off the island to deliver.

I head out through the sleepy main street of Dockton, drive back to the crossing and head into Vashon. The drive along the water is ideal. The Dockton Road is located actually on Vashon Island and would be more aptly called the Road to Dockton. It hugs the side of the outer bay, a narrow road barely wide enough for two cars in either direction. The road is a few feet above the beach. When it is low tide, it feels like a calm drive; when the tide is high and lapping the bulkhead holding up the road, it is more alarming. At night it is dark, the road not lit except for ambient light from the city across Puget Sound. The road curves and follows the shape of the island and, oddly, only a small part of the road has a guardrail. But on this March afternoon the sun is bright, the tide is partly out and the vista is magnificent. And the end of the waterfront drive I head up the hill to my farm, located on the top of the island.

My farm does not have an imposing gate at its entrance. The drive into the farm is unmarked, easy to miss and indicates little of what lies down it. When I come up to the driveway, I roll off of the paved county road and head down a bumpy, pot-hole-filled road of sorts. I don't know if I keep it in ill shape to discourage visitors, or because I am too cheap to pay the price of constant upkeep for a thousand-foot gravel road. Three-quarters of the way down, the overreaching trees end and the farm comes into view. In an instant most of the farm is apparent: the barn adjacent to the road, the creamery just after the curve, the Cookhouse visible above the hedge and the pastures surrounding all. The Log House and the gardens are not visible until I pull up at the far end of the tall hedge at the end of the driveway.

I carry the three flats over to the gardens in the ill-fated hope of planting them out this afternoon. Although it is chilly and still technically winter, the sun is shining brightly. I rather lamely convince myself that planting now runs the risk of the plants drying out in the sun, and so postpone my simple task.

The next morning I assess the gardens, the weather and the starts. The clouds have come in, the temperature has dropped a bit and its perfect for working in the garden. An afternoon of cool overcast weather will give the tender starts time to settle in before there is a chance of their wilting in a warm afternoon sun.

The new vegetable gardens are situated just south of the Log House. Three years ago they were completely transformed to make them more permanent, easier to tend to and more accessible to visitors, especially during the wet winter months. The prior vegetable gardens were simply an area of the farm where I had taken the tractor with a rotovator attached behind, tilled the soil, laid out some paths and planted starts or seeds. The benefits to planting a garden in this way is that it is very easy to get it started—an afternoon of tractor work and it is ready to go—and it is movable and flexible. If the site is not ideal, it can be relocated next season with little trouble. The downside is that the boundaries are fluid. The edges are the sod that borders the tilled earth, and they are dynamic. Throughout the growing season—and grass grows nearly year-round in this climate—the grass is pushing its way into the adjacent garden. It is almost as if the goal is to encourage the grass. Right next to healthy, vibrant rhizomatic grasses is freshly tilled, weed-free soil, just beckoning it, daring it to spread those rhizomes into the welcoming tilth. The result is a constant struggle keeping the verdant sod from encroaching into the delineated garden—and the grass wins; the garden shrinks in dimension throughout the season.

I had had years of this losing battle with the *tapis vert* surrounding the kitchen garden. A solution was needed; I may have gone a bit too far.

Three years ago I tackled the challenge in a method that was a bit casual, but in the end was quite useful. On the opposite side of the Cookhouse I had installed years earlier four long, low concrete raised beds. They were performing nicely, holding in the herbs and raspberries and currants while providing distinct areas of cultivation separated from the surrounding grass by permanent concrete. They also provided a convenient place to sit—the concrete was low enough to be close to the plants and strong enough to support a party full of guests.

I took a scrap of paper and sketched out a full kitchen garden made up of similar concrete raised beds. I wanted ample growing space to accommodate a full portfolio of annual vegetables, perennial vegetables such as asparagus and adequate room for permanent fruit plants such as strawberries and blueberries. A couple of extra beds saved for flowers was desired as well. Without much calculation the full garden was determined to be three beds deep and ten wide for a total of thirty beds. I handed this flimsy scrap of paper to my regular contractor for him to assess. I'm thankful he has worked with me through a variety of unusual jobs and has little or no judgment as to the legitimacy of my desires. He did, however, pull out a large tape measure from his truck and begin to lay out my future garden.

I had overstated my need for space, it seemed. Once Stuart laid out the full extent of my garden desires I realized I was overzealous. The potential garden area reached far into the brush on the southern flank of my farm, passed through two large mature trees and was without question too large. The size of the individual beds was based on the existing four beds. They are twenty feet long and five feet wide and six inches thick. The new garden is ten beds across and three beds deep. Stuart convinced me that if I shortened each bed by two feet in length, the entire garden would be six feet shorter in depth. Further, when we began to lay out the full garden I realized that thirty beds was far too crowded and repetitive. To solve this, I had Stuart leave out two beds in the center, creating a large square of open space surrounded by twenty-eight planting beds.

With the beds reconfigured, the dimension of the final garden fit within a reasonable area. Sadly, the two mature trees— one a Jonathan apple and the other a chestnut—had to be cut down and removed. Realistically, both of the trees had been badly damaged and pruned over the years and were not worth saving. It was still a difficult decision. Both trees were most

likely more than seventy years old—it is hard to imagine that
they could have been saved, they were both slowly dying—yet
they were also regal and full of history. Both had been planted
deliberately, I can presume, by one of the early homesteaders
of the property. I must confess that I can contrive a minor history around these two trees and others like them. Before the
Second World War, the homesteading family bought a number
of trees from a local nursery with plans and dreams and expec-
tations of feeding themselves with the nuts and fruits from
these trees once they became mature. What makes this imagined scenario the more interesting is that both of these trees
that I had removed were *standards*.

Today nearly all fruit trees, and some nuts as well, are
grafted onto rootstocks that are either dwarf or semi-dwarf.
The upper portion of the trees are specific to the individual
variety—Granny Smith, Honeycrisp, Comice, Bartlett and so
on. At the base of the tree, the upper varietals' stem is grafted
onto a rootstock of another form of that tree. The upper portion is grown for its specific fruit, with unique characteristics
of flavor and color and taste, and the lower portion is grown
for its ability to not freeze in the winter, its ability to tolerate
wet conditions and also for the height and size of the eventual
tree. The smaller semi-dwarf and dwarf trees are now desired
because of two primary considerations. The first is their production of fruit relative to the amount of space they occupy.
Surprisingly, because the smaller trees can be planted closer
together, they can produce more fruit per acre than the larger,
now-obsolete standards. The second consideration, however,
is paramount—the smaller trees produce earlier than their
larger relatives. Whereas the dwarfs can be mature and in full
production in four to five years, standards might take ten years
minimum and more likely fifteen to reach their full potential.
Although the standards are beautiful trees due to their large
scale and, in the case of apples, wide spreading habit, the varieties of tree fruit are unexpectedly fashionable and changing.

It is not only women's clothes that change from year to year, but also which fruits are in demand and which are considered passé and of last season. A couple of years ago everyone wanted a Pink Lady—a new apple variety that has a pale pink skin as well as a lovely flavor. Seckel pears were de rigueur for the homesteader four years ago as well. Chocolate persimmons are still having their time in the sun, as are doughnut-shaped peaches. It is the nurseryman's goal to keep people wanting new varieties, and the green grocer's as well. With a tree that takes four or maybe five years to produce fruit, the fashions can be relatively quick. If we all had to wait a minimum of a decade to enjoy the fruits of our labors we would be less likely to change our preferences.

Those homesteaders I imagine of six or seven decades ago only had the option of large, slow-growing trees to plant on their farm here. What is remarkable is that the farmer of that era did not even necessarily ever enjoy the fully mature trees that he planted—I was the one who enjoyed those broad canopies of rotund, rigid branches holding up a canopy of light pink delicate open flowers of the apple and yellow spring flowers of the chestnut.

The apple flowers I was certainly familiar with when I first moved to this farm, but the chestnut in bloom was new to me. The tree put out flowers in name only. They are not floral in scent, nor what one would generally characterize as a flower, but rather are long strands of perhaps six inches in length sprouting from the thin final branches, each strand encircled with small, short yellow spikes. When they would first appear it was an appealing scene, I must admit; but then a few days later those bright yellow, vivid wands would be much more dull and brownish, and very quickly would fall to the ground around the chestnut en masse, carpeting the otherwise mowed lawn. In those early days here I was much more concerned with lawn mowing than I am now. I drove a riding mower around in circles for hours most every weekend in the first few years, believing that having a yard similar to the neighbors' was a reasonable and desirable task. At this point, more than two decades into owning this farm, we quickly cut the grass with the brush hog attached to the back of the tractor, the primary goal to spend as little time as possible to achieve adequate results. Keeping up with the surrounding suburban lawns now carries no great allure for me.

This has been a long, roundabout way of saying that I put a great deal of thought into those two stately, mature trees, before I had Stuart rip through their wide bases with his chain saw. In less than two minutes, seventy years of slow growth was abruptly ended. The trees were cut down and the branches, leaves and trunks lay in a large expansive heap on the ground. Even with adequate thought ahead of time, it was a sad moment for me. I didn't want to make a capricious decision, but I also didn't want to hold on to the nostalgia of the trees over a realistic assessment of their condition. The reality is that I have planted many beautiful trees here at the farm over these twenty years, I expect to continue planting trees and I, too, will leave a legacy after my stewardship has ended on this plot of earth.

The ground of those two mature trees is now given over to the garden. The twenty-eight beds are ample for growing most anything I could ever need to feed myself and the guests of this farm. One bed is filled with asparagus, another with blueberries, two more are loaded with flowers—lilies especially—a couple more with strawberries and then the remainder are used for vegetables.

The fertility of these beds can be credited entirely to the compost that we use to enrich the soil. Thankfully, this is a dairy farm, and cows are notorious for their prodigious production of manure. At least I am thankful that there is ample compost when it is needed in the spring for the gardens. In the winter, I am not so thankful.

During the rainy seasons, the cows spend a large percentage of their time in the barn. Cows are rather unaffected by climate but they do not appreciate rain in their faces. So they have a large, expansive barn for waiting out any rainstorm.

Here in the Pacific Northwest that is most days of winter. The result is a great deal of manure building up in the barn beneath their hooves. We add an equal volume of straw daily to keep the cows clean and dry. By the end of the season, the floor of the barn is two feet higher, with the continual layering of manure and straw building up a thick carpet.

When spring arrives, the paths dry up and Jorge can drive the tractor into the barn and haul out this mass. The bucket of the tractor can easily scrape down to the hard-packed soil below and pull up the manure and straw matting. Back and forth Jorge will drive from the barn, through the gates, down the road and through the orchard to a large open space near the gardens. Here he will pile bucketload after bucketload of this precious cargo. This is not a simple forty-five-minute task, but rather one that will continue for hours. When I walk through the barn before he starts, it appears as though there is only a small volume to contend with. This is deceiving. Even if it is two feet deep, over the span of a few hundred square feet that means a great volume of material. From my office I can hear the tractor passing back and forth over and over, the sound of the bucket dropping as the manure is unloaded onto the ever-larger pile next to the garden.

By the end of Jorge's Sisyphean task, the barn will be empty once again, ready for the next fall and winter, and two large manure piles will stand. The ratio is ideal if we have done our job correctly—50 percent wet, nitrogen-rich manure and 50 percent dry, carbon-based straw. With that balance, the piles will quickly begin to heat up, steam rising from the top of each, indicating the heat created by the breakdown of carbon. Within the bulky piles are unfathomable volumes of thermophilic bacteria feasting on the carbon, their respiration producing vast heat—enough to steam the moisture in the pile.

Through the summer and into the fall, Jorge will routinely
return with the tractor and flip the piles. The bacteria need
oxygen to exist and without it the piles turns to an anaerobic
mass of soggy manure and straw. Without access to air, the
bacteria will die, the heat will cease and the vital mix of carbon
and nitrogen will languish. Jorge takes great care to make sure
the piles are not too large, for fear that the center of each pile
cannot get access to adequate air supply, essential to the creation of our needed compost.

This yearly process of hauling out the barn each spring
and maintaining the large compost piles near the garden was
started when the barn was erected four years ago. Now the
raised beds are nourished by the earlier annual additions of
compost, a small pile of finished compost ready to be utilized
for top dressing this coming summer, a larger pile of nearly
completed compost and an even larger series of compost piles
fresh from the barn, still steaming with the combustion of billions upon billions of bacteria feasting on the rich nutrients
of the detritus of our dear Jersey cows. I get a tremendous
sense of satisfaction from the process. It is complete and whole
and entirely mutually beneficial. Throughout the wet winter
months the volume of manure is large and it is unceasing in
its occurrence. Everywhere I turn there is more manure—the
cows are not particular about where they leave it. This is
frankly disheartening in the wet season. It is on my boots, on
the pathways and on the pastures in overwhelming volume,
at times. To see the final compost pile of rich, loamy soil many
months later almost makes the dread of the wet winter months
palatable.

The beds were well augmented with that fine, finished compost last week and the empty beds are ready for the young
plant starts from Leda's. I plant out the starts, a full bed of
cabbage, another of Brussels sprouts, I am a bit overzealous on
radicchio and devote a half a bed to the bitter Italian greens.
I am aware that at best I will eat a fraction of all that I plant

this morning, but I plant more in the hope that I will be a more sophisticated eater by the time that the plants mature. Springtime is about hope and optimism and possibilities, not about realities. I really don't enjoy radicchio all that much, but I want to be the kind of person who does. When the height of summer arrives I will munch on fresh carrots and the just-ripened cherry tomatoes and without question will devour every last blueberry, but in the fall I will take my sturdy garden fork and pull up the bitter greens and send them to be composted. I have a simple palate—sweet things, primarily—but I cherish the hope of spring. Without that optimism—some would say reality—this garden would be blueberries and strawberries and flowers. Beautiful, certainly, and without a doubt enjoyed; but pushing boundaries is essential and welcomed.

There is the possibility of some sun this week, so I water the plants when I finish. They are still too fragile to make it without some assistance. In another week or two I will not worry, but today they get all the care they need.

The individual pots have small white plastic labels with the variety printed on one side and Leda's farm name printed on the other. I use them to tag the plants but I slide them into the soil right next to the concrete wall of the raised bed, the variety name side pointed out, the farm name hidden from sight. I do this for two reasons. The crows that also call this farm home love to swoop down and pick out the bright white labels and drop them askance, leaving me with little idea where they originated. I am not really sure why they do it—to annoy me, or because they think they are something edible, or simple because they can. It may be all three, but the result is I am dismayed by it. When I place the tags very tight against the concrete, they seem to have a harder time grabbing them with their pesky beaks.

The reason for slipping the labels into the soil with the farm name against the concrete is more difficult to describe. I am perfectly capable of growing broccoli or cabbage or lettuce starts. I have a greenhouse with benches and heated pads and an ample supply of pots and flats and such. It isn't particularly difficult or in reality particularly time-consuming. It is, however, more convenient to trade with Leda. I slide the tags in to hide the fact that I am buying plant starts. It is very amateurish and humiliating. Suburban moms buy plant starts at the supermarket, drop them in the garden and then exclaim that they grew a vegetable. I want to be better than them, even if in reality I am not. I doubt that I am fooling anyone, not even the ubiquitous crows overhead, but I still deliberately flip those tiny white labels every time.

The plant starts are all safely in the ground, watered, tagged and left to begin to settle into the tidy raised beds. All is hopeful at this point; there are no weeds, no bugs and my exuberant optimism is evident.

With the plants from Leda's safely in the ground, I can turn to the onions and shallots that I have started myself. Having something to plant out from my greenhouse helps me feel a bit like I am still a farmer, if only in this small way. The hard, black, angular onion seeds that I planted in the neat, tidy rows a few weeks earlier have now sprouted. Each seed sent up a tiny, thin, bright green stalk. If I bring my head down to the level of the flat and look across it I see a miniature diorama of a farm. The rows are straight and parallel, the crop growing from the top of the furrow, a valley between each row of deep brown moist soil. It appears as though a miniature tractor drove down this small square of ground and plowed the soil, opening up the furrows and dropping the seed and covering it; planting this crop of tall green plants.

I leave the confines of the greenhouse with the two flats in my hands, one flat balanced in each open hand, my foot gently sliding open the glass door, thankful that I was a waiter for many years carrying precarious trays of food and drinks. When I get into the garden on the other side of the Cookhouse, I set down the flats and begin to lay out the long raised bed.

There will be four long rows running the full length, spaced equidistant from each other. To achieve the straightest rows I use a line between two stakes. The taut string is stretched down the length of the bed a couple of inches above the soil. The onion seedlings are amazingly strong and resilient. I can grab a clump between my thumb and forefinger and pull them from the flat, their long, wispy roots trailing. Then a quick pull and they are separated, each individual plant three inches of bright green stalk and three inches of root below. One by one they are planted into the soil, using the stretched string as a guide. The tool to plant these wispy bits of onion life is a dibber, truly one of my favorite tools. The one that I have used for years is made by the Sneeboer Company of the Netherlands. It is a short tool, just a foot in length, the handle made of wood, the dibber itself made of cast aluminum. The working end of the tool is shaped like a missile cone, pointed at its peak and then sharply sloped back to the point where it attaches to the handle. The cherrywood handle is not straight like a hoe or a shovel but rather curves back in a gentle, human-friendly way. The tool feels alive, like an extension of one's hand. Looking at the dibber, I always want to smile; there is a personality to it, and an amusing personality at that.

The task assigned to the dibber is to create the holes for the onions in the soil. The missile cone with the sharp point opens up the soil quickly and effortlessly and is just what is needed for the onions' long roots. There is little need to exert much effort in this task; the weight of the dibber pushes open the hole, at least in my loamy, light soil. One hand grasping the ergonomic cherrywood handle and creating the hole, with my other hand I can pick up one of the individual onion seedling and drop it in the awaiting hole, quickly backfilling the hole with the neighboring soil.

There are those who add an additional step. They clip the roots back to a uniform inch or perhaps two when they pull the onions from the flat. It takes little effort and it is tremendously tidy. The onions, rather than trailing lengthy errant roots, transform to an army of identical soldiers, all of the same length. This does, however, just feel a bit off to me. I want to retain as much of the roots as possible in the hope that they will contribute to a healthier and more productive plant down the line. It takes a bit more effort to get the entire long root into the conical hole made by the dibber, but it is certainly possible.

Throughout the morning the process continues: creating the hole with one hand, the other planting out the onion, on down the stretched line. When one row is finished, the line guide is moved over a few inches and the process continues until the bed is full. Each and every year I am confounded by the volume of seedlings in the flat. There appear to be perhaps a hundred, maybe two hundred seedlings cheek-by-jowl in the black plastic flat, and then when they are separated, many more appear. Lying on the edge of the concrete raised bed are suddenly four hundred individual seedlings. In the cool of March it seems annoying and baffling and I am always tempted to finish planting half and then chuck the remainder into the compost pile next to the garden. I manage to control my inherent laziness and finish out the entire flat. Today's lunch includes onions from last year. They are tasty, and needed and valued throughout the winter and spring when few fresh vegetables are in the garden and the storage bins in the Cookhouse are filled with little but onions from the past growing season.

By lunchtime I have found a home for all of the nascent onions. The original seeding soil, empty of seedlings, is all that remains on the base of soggy newspaper in the black plastic flat. A quick walk to the compost pile and a flip, and it is all emptied on the large pile of cow manure mixed with bedding straw. If I flip it just right, the newspaper lands faceup on the side of the deep brown mound. Although the paper and the moist soil were in the greenhouse for weeks, the faded images of the supermarket vegetables remain visible. The bright carrots and lettuce and cucumbers are still apparent from their advertisements deep in the winter when little remained in my larder except the storage onions and garlic and shallots. That grocery store insert is one of my few reminders and connection to the outside world of year-round vegetables independent of climate and distance.

The task completed, I return to the Cookhouse to make lunch for myself and Ben, who is working in the barn. A small pot of basmati rice is started, and then an onion from the bin is peeled and halved and cored and finely diced. It is still in good shape, the root has not begun to sprout; there is not a green center, as there will be in another month. These onions were harvested last summer and brought into the Cookhouse then. There are more than we can eat before they begin to sprout or rot. Every day I cook one up, enjoy the sweetness and freshness that was captured from last summer. While the rice finishes steaming I heat a large sauté pan, add a small walnut-sized lump of lard from the cooler and turn on the flame. The lard easily melts, the smell gutsy and porklike. Then I add the diced onions, and moisture from the stored onions spatters in the hot oil. From the cooler I pull a small piece of roast beef, a leftover from last night's dinner, and dice it as well. The flame is reduced to slowly cook the onions and when they are translucent and cooked I add the beef, just to warm it. The rice is finished in its covered pot next to the sauté, and it is added to the large pan as well. In a few minutes the rice with the beef and the onions is finished and seasoned and dished up for myself and Ben. Not an exciting lunch, but a comforting one. I could have added a dried chili or perhaps some chopped garlic, but little else remains from last summer. If I had a guest here I would have gone to the herb beds and picked a bit of chives or chervil to garnish the bowl, but today it is about simplicity and the comfort of the normal. Ben and I chat a bit about cheese and the cows and the garden. I am hopeful in March. It is the beginning of the season, the grass is green and will start to grow soon, the mud will start to dry up and the garden has just begun. Soon we will have kale and cabbage and broccoli to add to the lunch, but today the onions are sweet and tasty and enjoyed.

The season is changing. The days are ever so slightly longer than they were a few weeks ago. The cabbages and the kale and the onions have begun to grow in the garden now that it is April. We have started to harvest asparagus from the full bed of crowns planted four years earlier. And the frogs have arrived. Just to the west of the garden is a large wetlands area. Perhaps a full acre in size, this circular area contains a seasonal pond at its center and large water-loving trees around its perimeter. Tall willows grow quickly from the wet ground, alders fill in as well and volunteer hawthorns complete this barely penetrable thicket. Throughout the winter months the center is filled with water; it is the lowest point on the farm and the pastures funnel rainwater into this area. By late summer it is dry, the water drained out by the heat and the lack of rainfall. In late spring, however, it is still marshy and moist. And it is inhabited by hundreds, perhaps thousands, of Pacific tree frogs, living feet from the Log House.

At this time of year, the small—perhaps an inch long— bright green frogs begin their mating. Although I have never witnessed the mating itself, I have heard the calls of the males to their potential female suitors each and every year. These tiny male amphibians produce a sound that exceeds their stature many times over. At early evening the chorus is at its most dramatic, but it continues through the early mornings as well. Many times during the two decades I have attempted to describe this to friends living in the city. None could truly understand without being present in the two- to three-week season. However, the ubiquity of the cell phone has given my exaggerations credibility. Now at the end of March and the beginning of April I can leave my Log House and walk out near the pond, hold up my cell phone and have friends listen to the cacophony that is the *ribbits* of these minuscule frogs. If I am talking loudly, they also tend to quiet down for a few moments in response, only to return to their apparent yelling at their female counterparts. It doesn't really sound sexy to me, but since the females lay ample eggs each and every year, it must do the trick.

These Pacific tree frogs are a harbinger of spring. When their boisterous exultations are apparent through the early April nights, I know spring is near.

With the onset of the tree frogs and the beginning of spring, I realize I must make a decision concerning the beehives. Every year I purchase three-pound packages of bees and a queen for each package from a local supplier. Strangely, I seem to have been less successful in recent years in keeping bees and collecting honey than in my early years on the farm. I expected to improve in my beekeeping abilities as my experience increased. Sadly, the opposite has been the case.

With the great hope of springtime, I call the supplier and order three of the packages once again to pick up in the middle of April. The cost of the bees far outweighs the value of the honey that I can expect to collect through the warm seasons, but I continue on, ever optimistic of a great year. I enjoy the process: the installing of the bees, the lighting of the smoker, the opening of the hives through the heat of the summer and then the extraction of the—generally—meager honey harvest. It is not a financial decision, but rather one of passion and hope, and I easily give in and reserve the bees.

With spring's arrival the potatoes for fall must be planted. These ubiquitous members of nearly every garden are not planted by seed, but rather from potatoes saved from the previous year's crop. I return to the Cookhouse and pull out the large plastic tote that contains the remains of the potato harvest. Gone are the best, most well-formed tubers. Some of the spuds are dried-up hollows of their former glory. But enough remain in the bottom of the container to guarantee a great harvest this year.

I look for the small, walnut-sized potatoes. After their long months of storage, those that are viable have already sprouted eyes and tender tendrils. The lengthening sunlight of spring and the increased temperature in the Cookhouse signal these small bits of life to awaken and begin to grow. I carry the plastic lug out to the garden and begin to plant out the best of the bunch. Sadly, there is a bit of selection that needs to happen. Not only do a few of my favorite varieties remain, but also a great deal of the lesser varieties that were not chosen for dinners through the winter months. The tendency is to plant everything that is left, with a result of more and more unpopular varieties filling the long garden beds.

The purple potatoes are removed and sent to the compost pile. I tried them for a few seasons. I enjoyed them, certainly, but they just felt too much like a novelty item. Their best feature was the color of their skin. I carefully pick though the bottom of the lug and find an ample amount of Yukon Golds, fingerlings and russets. All very pedestrian, but tasty and proven to please me throughout the dull days of December.

Jorge was kind enough to dig two deep long trenches down the length of two adjacent beds. They were left open, the soil piled on the side. Now that the hard work is finished, I can easily walk down each row, dropping in the sprouted seed potatoes. A bit of soil covers the brown bits of potato and the work is done. As the plants begin to sprout and grow, more and more of the soil will be moved from the piles to the bottom of the trench. By midsummer the soil in the beds will be level, the plants growing wildly in the loose, rich earth.

The next plants to be seeded are the squashes, both winter and summer varieties. Whereas the tomatoes are seeded in soil blocks, the squashes are seeded directly into four-inch pots. Squashes grow quickly and effortlessly, sprouting in a few days in the temperate spring weather, and are ready to be planted in three to four weeks. I pull out the faux-bamboo trunk filled with the farm's seed collection and pull all the squashes. Quickly the table is filled with nine varieties: Black Beauty for your basic zucchini, Tromboncino for a long summer squash, Magda for a Lebanese variety, and Costato Romanesco, grown primarily for squash blossoms. For winter squash my favorite varieties are Brodé Galeux d'Eysines for its mottled rind and delicate pale pink coloration; Rouge Vif d'Etampe as its counterpoint, bright orange and deeply segmented; Long Island Cheese as a meaty American stand-in; and then two smaller-sized winter varieties—Delicata and a classic acorn. I am certainly open to new varieties, but rarely venture forth; I enjoy these nine. I know they will grow well and produce amply and cover all the culinary needs.

In the greenhouse the stack of four-inch pots is laid out, together with a stack of flats and a bag of potting soil. One by one the pots are filled with the light, fluffy soil, then placed in a flat, four pots by four. On the counter in the Cookhouse I lay out the seed packets, along with the tags and a magic marker. Back and forth I traverse, writing the name of each variety on the labels, then taking the seed packet and the labels out to the greenhouse, a few steps outside the back door of the Cookhouse. Then I plant the seeds, stick the labels in the pots and return to the Cookhouse. Any remaining seeds are returned to the packet, and then I continue on to the next variety. It is a tedious and inefficient mode of planting but it makes certain that the pots are not mislabeled. It matters little, as the eventual squashes are so recognizable and different from their fellows, but still this process gives me a sense of order. Within a few minutes the flats are on the benches with seeds in the soil and labels stuck into the small pots. I can then bring in the watering hose with a gentle spray head on it and soak the soil thoroughly. It is satisfying to see the tidy rows of pots, certain that in a few months' time long, trailing vines and tendrils and obtuse squashes will run over the sides of the beds and into the paths beneath.

Once the squashes are completed I pull out the seeds for cucumbers and melons as well. They too are planted directly into small pots on the flats. Only a couple of cucumbers varieties are selected: a green slicing one and a lemon cucumber, sadly termed a *novelty* cucumber. The lemon cucumbers are my favorite without a doubt. Shaped and colored like a lemon, they never have the tough skin and bitter flavor that a long green standard cucumber often can. The melons selected are of just two varieties as well: a Spanish white sugar melon and the French Charentais melon. Both have only a fifty-fifty chance of ripening during our cool growing season, but the payoff is great when the summer is adequate. Luscious, ripe, and dripping juice, the two melons are worth planting even if most never will be eaten.

On the aluminum benches in the tight greenhouse are the three flats of summer and winter squashes and now the two flats of cucumbers and melons. Alongside these new plantings is the flat filled with tomatoes that I'd planted in February. This flat contains ninety-six one-inch-square cubes, each with a single tomato seedling.

Throughout the cool days of March I check in on the tomato starts. Underneath each flat is a heating mat set to keep the soil at seventy degrees. Without the added heat it is unlikely the tropical tomatoes would germinate until much later in the year. Slowly, one by one, small green sprouts pushed up and out of the dark brown soil of the soil block. As I was rather generous with the seeds, numerous sprouts erupted from the blocks. Once they are three-quarters of an inch tall, I will identify the sturdiest one from each block and pull out the remaining, weaker sprouts. Littered on the floor of the greenhouse will be the detritus of the selection process. Bill's Tomatoes are doing well, the cherries too. The Pineapple and Persimmon germinated nicely, although the Cherokee purple never emerged in any of the soil blocks that were seeded.

———

In the first week of May, the tomatoes are vital, fully leafed out and a couple of inches tall. A few are still just an inch tall, but will catch up with the others by the time they are planted out. Each now needs to be moved into individual four-inch pots, the same size used for the cucumbers and melons and squashes. As I did earlier for the others, I load up many flats with the four-inchers, each filled with the fresh, fluffy soil from the bag of potting mix. When the floor of the greenhouse is chock-full of these flats, then I begin to plant the tomatoes in the pots. It goes quickly, using one hand to create a small hole and the other to pick up a block and push it into the awaiting soil. Just one of the flats holds ninety-six individual tomato starts when in the sixteen-inch-square flat. When they are planted out, six flats will be needed. Doesn't sound like much, but the benches will be quickly filled with the flats, especially with the squashes and melons and cucumbers already hogging the space.

The great mystery of the soil blocks becomes apparent when they are transplanted into the larger pots. For eight weeks these individual soil blocks have sat cheek-by-jowl. The soil is moist and continually watered. The roots of the baby tomato plants are slowly filling each block. The roots do not, however, jump to the next block. Today when I go to pick up each block to drop it into the awaiting pot, the block will come apart easily and effortlessly. One would think that after two months of roots growing in this rich seeding soil the result would be one large mass of roots, creating an intertwined network throughout the flat. In fact the roots grow to the edge of their respective block and then stop. Not sure why, but I enjoy it. I thought it was that the roots wouldn't grow when they were exposed to the air, but there is no gap between each block, no air for the roots to reach. It remains a mystery to me, but a pleasant one.

Repotting the tomatoes into the four-inchers is a pleasurable task, but this year it has a darker side. Growing Bill's Tomatoes has moved from a simple act of raising tomatoes that

I enjoy eating, to carrying on a legacy. I worry that I will forget to water these sixteen young seedlings, or might otherwise allow them to die in the greenhouse. It is an odd bit of gravitas to place on such fragile young plants. With my hands in the warm soil, that gravitas is balanced with the joy I receive from thinking about the great soul who started these tomatoes and passed them on to me.

The planting has taken me through the morning. The sun is shining and I am optimistic, hopeful of a great garden this year. So I hop in my truck and drive again to Leda's farm on Maury Island to pick up more starts, specifically pepper plants. Peppers are not that different from tomatoes, horticulturally speaking. They need heat to germinate, they are annuals producing fruit in their first year and they are slow-growing if they don't receive a great deal of heat. I should be able to grow them, but I have had numerous troubles in recent years. The seeds will not all germinate, and those that do will be weak and spindly and often will die three or four weeks later. My guess is that I am too cheap to heat the greenhouse in the late winter and early spring except for the heating mats under the flats of germinating seeds. Whatever the reason, I now rely on Leda to grow my peppers. Hers are beautiful, vibrant and decidedly not dead.

I drive down the winding road to Tramp Harbor, trace the outline of the cove as the road heads to Portage and then down through Maury Island to Dockton. It is rare for me to head down to Maury and I am pleased every time I do. Tramp Harbor is especially beautiful; the tide has receded greatly, revealing the rocky beach. Where Vashon and Maury come together at the isthmus is especially shallow, so even a moderate low tide exposes a tremendous reveal of beach. Except for the ferryboat ride to and from Seattle, I am oddly not connected to the water, since I live on the top of the island. My life revolves around pastures and tall Doug firs and cows. Rarely do I experience the sand and the beach and the tides. It is this brief drive perched on the edge of the harbor that reminds me that Vashon is indeed an island.

As I pull back the long steel bolt and open wide the gates to Leda's farm I can see her in the distance in the greenhouses. I head over to her, and her expression is welcome and shocking all at once. She demands a hug, and further demands a full embracing hug, not one of "those silly little things you usually give me!" She punctuates her demand with a loud cackle. Although she insists on knowing all that is going on in my life, quickly she begins to fill me in on the travails of running a greenhouse business and I am lulled into her stories, thankful I don't have to talk any more about my personal life.

After a few minutes she takes me to the greenhouse containing all the peppers. Row upon row of peppers fill one side of the long greenhouse. I grab a flat and rapidly fill it with bell peppers and cayenne peppers and jalapeños. She tries to interest me in her favorites but I resist, sticking to my guns— only red bells and a couple of hot chilies. Although the idea of spending the afternoon with Leda and Matt is enticing, I force myself to exit, hoping to get more tasks accomplished at the farm through the afternoon. It is easy for me to spend an entire afternoon sitting with them in their house or in summer weather on the porch, hearing tales of garden stores, friends and other island farmers.

The peppers will be planted in the greenhouse; none will be planted out in the garden beds. The greenhouse assures me that the peppers will ripen fully and produce the most fruit possible. They could live in the field, but a cool summer would greatly limit their production. I find a small area in the greenhouse, add some compost and plant out the sixteen eight-inch-high plants. The greenhouse is filled with the benches that outline nearly all the glass walls. In a four weeks' time all of the starts now on the benches will have been planted out into the garden, the benches removed and the greenhouse will only house these peppers planted out today, and tomato plants as well. Throughout the summer and fall, the greenhouse will have no benches, only plants growing in the soil. Not in pots, but in the actual soil of the greenhouse. By Thanksgiving the plants will reach the roof of the small greenhouse, providing peppers and tomatoes until the temperature drops below freezing.

SEVEN

Summer Arrives

Summer has just begun to take hold. It is mid-June, the days are at their longest of the year, but the temperature is far from the highest it will get. The plants in the garden are beginning to take hold but seem to be slow in growth. I want exuberant growth from these tiny plants—the sun is shining, and the ground is still moist from early summer rains. What I am given instead is tepid growth. Each week the cucumber plants are a bit larger, the winter squash vines are beginning to hit the edges of the raised beds, but everything is far from robust.

In the beds near the kitchen door are four vibrant currant bushes. I planted them four years earlier, too close to each other, not expecting their grand mature size. Now I have to either trim them back through the summer or change my path slightly to avoid brushing into them as I try to pass by on my way to the creamery. It is a small problem to have— plants growing too large, producing too much fruit—but still an annoyance of sorts. First world problems, as they say.

The first two plants are Pink Champagne currants, the second two are red currants. They qualify as shrubs, certainly not as trees. All of the long, straight branches appear to emanate from a central branch of the plant. They appear to be bushy, thick Sputniks that settled in my tidy beds. Their leaves are bright green, almost chartreuse when they first appear, and then settle down into a more mature hunter green. These bright, nascent leaves must be quite tasty to worms, as they have been known to decimate my plants in years past. I must correct that. To decimate would imply that 10 percent of the leaves are eaten. In fact, perhaps 10 percent are left; 90 percent are consumed.

Two years ago on my way out to the milking parlor I noticed that the worms had in fact arrived and had begun their eating of my verdant shrubs. Although I noticed, I didn't feel any great need to deal with them at that early morning hour. I was on my way to tend to the cows and a few worms seemed inconsequential to the robust and many-leaved currant bushes. Midday I passed by again and noticed that the shrubs did in fact seem a bit less leafy—but it still didn't seem worth worrying about. It wasn't until midafternoon that I began to be concerned. I found Jorge and asked his opinion, just to make sure that I wasn't imagining something that wasn't there. He confirmed my suspicions: the worms were swiftly destroying my currant bushes. We both stood there side by side in disbelief. As it happened, Jorge had also noticed the small number of worms chomping through the leaves a few hours earlier when he had arrived at the farm. By midafternoon we both realized that half of the leaves were missing and by nightfall the remainder would be consumed if nothing was done. I chose a fast-acting pesticide from the local hardware store. This resort certainly was not my preferred choice, but given the imperative to kill the worms quickly, it seemed appropriate.

This year the currant bushes have attracted no such worms. The result is especially healthy plants producing copious amounts of fruit. Three weeks ago the long, straight branches began to produce small tender bracts, each with multiple flowers. The blossoms were tiny and delicate and seemed inconsequential; hard to believe that they would lead to bounteous fruit. And now, these four oversized shrubs, barely contained by their concrete bed, are laden with currants, both pink and red.

I wonder why I planted these four specimens. I had little idea what I would do with multiple quarts of the small, sour fruit. I thought of black currant syrup and thought of making kir: mixing a sweetened syrup from the fruit with white wine and enjoying it on a warm summer evening on the porch. I planted red and pink currants, however, not the black currants needed for the sweet syrup of Dijon. I believe the black currants were unavailable at the time, being the chief culprit of the spread of the white pine blister rust. I settled with the red and pink, expecting to find a use for the eventual fruit by the time the plants produced.

Thankfully, the currant bushes took a few years to produce enough fruit for me to worry about. They did in fact follow the classic plantsman motto of: Sleep, creep, leap. The first year, they simply remained in the soil throughout the growing season, with little to show in the way of growth; they truly slept. The second year they appeared to grow a bit, yet nothing remarkable; they crept. As it turned out, the third year was the great worm infestation which does not have a handy word in the trifecta motto. And the fourth year—this year—these four currant bushes have grown tremendously; they've leapt. It took me four years to find a use for the now-formidable harvest of small, sour pink and red berries. We now pickle them.

Originally my mind went to making currant jelly in the French style. The fruits are prolific and easily picked and it just seemed an easy approach to sweeten them and prepare a jam or jelly. And then my mind returned to a photo in a large tome on my shelf: *Culinaria France*. In this encyclopedic volume describing the many food products of France, there is a page devoted to currant jelly, specifically: Bar-le-duc. This sweet, fruity delicacy has a provenance going back to the fourteenth century and I trust that it is especially tasty even though I have never sampled one of the tiny jars of preserves. What kept me from attempting to mimic this regal sweet was the photo on the page in the *Culinaria*: a robust Frenchwoman painstakingly seeding the tiny fruits with the quill of a goose, one by one. My patience level is tremendously low and the thought of individually removing tiny, tiny seeds from a tiny fruit without disturbing the flesh seemed highly unlikely to jibe with my character. Although I have raised geese in the past, I presently only keep chickens and was worried that using an ordinary quill from a rather pedestrian member of the poultry family would doom my endeavors even more. I determined that pickling the fruit with their seeds intact was the best use of my voluptuous harvest.

The fruits hang from the bushes in racemes: tendrils that fall from the branches with many of the fruits delicately attached. This makes for some simple picking. All that is needed is to cup the two-inch-long racemes with the fruits attached in the palm of your hand, then gently close your fingers to enclose the fruits and pull down, releasing them into your palm. The fingers are opened over a waiting bucket and then on to the next draping tendril. The only challenge is getting to the brightly colored fruits before the birds do. With my lack of precision in timing, each raceme tends to be missing one or two of its fruits due to the eager gullets of the awaiting birds. Enough remain, and a full bucket is easily accomplished.

As the picking is not an exact science, pits of stems and unripe errant fruits arrive in the kitchen together with the best of them. It takes little to clean the bounty. When they have been washed a bit and cleaned of debris, I pour the bucketful into a tidy plastic container and turn my attention to the pickling solution. On the range I heat a volume of vinegar ample to cover the currants, together with enough sugar to sweeten. Just a bit of salt can't hurt either. Red wine vinegar would be atrocious, but white wine vinegar or even cider vinegar would suffice. If the vinegar is too hot—too acidic—a bit of water to calm it down is needed. The sweet vinegar mixture is brought to a boil, to incorporate the sugar, but also to cook the currants ever so slightly. They are in fact ripe, but I want them to be just a tad bit more tender, and the heat of the vinegar just after it is boiling suffices.

Once the vinegar has come to a boil, I pull it off the heat for a just a moment and then pour it over the awaiting currants. This has a bit of drama: the hot, steaming liquid quickly flows down through all the tiny crevices of the spherical fruits, and bubbles quickly rise up as the air escapes from the bottom of the container. The smell is intoxicating—hot steaming acidic vinegar filled with sweetness and now, quickly, the scent of the ripe, red and pink currants. I stand over the mixture, breathing in the pernicious steam, my nostrils flaring open from the acid, enjoying the sweet burn.

I allow the pickled currants to cool on the counter, covering the container and placing it in the cooler to cure until I need them. I like this process because in a few minutes I can deal with a large volume of currants. I have things to do today: cheese to make, cows to milk, lunch to be enjoyed. Although I enjoy making tedious jam or a process-laden tomato sauce, a simple, quick way to convert a fresh summer fruit into a delightful product that I can enjoy throughout the winter is a godsend.

With the currants safely picked and processed, I can return to the garden to tend to the other crops. I wish that I could state that the kitchen garden is neat, tidy and free of weeds. In reality it is none of those things. I let it go too long this year without my attention. My interests have been elsewhere this summer and the garden seemed to deal well with my abandonment. Now that it is summer, I realize that I was mistaken. The gravel paths are exploding with weeds, and the paths out of sight in the back of the garden have become carpeted with low-growing invasive weeds. The center open space has been fully populated with flowering dandelions and the like. Every day that I avoid the garden tasks, more seeds explode from the heads of the productive weeds, landing onto the path and continuing the cycle. I want the problem to go away without my effort and attention.

I send Jorge out to the garden, taking him from necessary tasks in the field and with the cows. In many ways he was the worst choice for help and in others he was the best. He rarely questions my judgments and is not afraid of spending time on a tedious task. He does, however, have less strict environmental standards. After a few hours of attempting to eradicate the paths from the weeds, I decide that Roundup is the best alternative. My quick estimation is that spraying the gravel paths with an herbicide is a necessary evil. The weeds can be controlled before they continue to reproduce wildly. The paths will never be planted again with any kind of crops and we can be highly selective in where we spray—the beds filled with vegetables are separated from the paths by the concrete curbs. It seems like an appropriate decision.

Jorge wholeheartedly agrees. He sees no problem whatsoever in spraying herbicides to begin with, and if it can save him some effort he feels it is worth the money to buy the chemicals.

I consult with Ben, who without question has higher environmental standards than either Jorge or myself. I admit to leading him to the answer I wanted, but he still feels that it isn't such a bad idea, although his only caveat is that I buy a different brand of herbicide than the trademarked Roundup from Monsanto. His logic is that if one has to utilize glyphosate as an herbicide, at least I can keep from giving money to Monsanto.

I agree with his logic and head to the hardware store in town. At this point I see no problem with our collective decision. I am confident it is a pragmatic decision based on real-world challenges, and one that was vetted among myself and two employees. I find a large two-gallon container of a concentrated Roundup-like product and proceed to the checkout stand to purchase it. It is then that I realize I don't really stand behind my decision. The line is short, just a couple of people, but those in front of me have tedious, slow purchases—small piles of different plumbing parts, each with a different barely legible price tag.

I'm not in any hurry myself, except that I am standing

near the entrance of the popular store, carrying a bulky large container of the noticeably ill-thought-of herbicide. I want to quickly buy the poison, have it put into an opaque sack and hustle back to my truck before anyone can spot my poor decision. As the checker slowly works and chats, I am shifting from one foot to the other, my eyes affixed on the front door, contemplating someone walking in who knows I have a small farm dedicated to health and sustainability and the stewarding of my land, and them seeing me here with a billboard announcing my laziness and lack of resolve against using herbicides. With luck I make it through the minutes-long ordeal and make my purchase without being discovered. I do however, realize that I don't have complete confidence in my decision, and that I am embarrassed by my sloppiness. If I had kept up with the weeds all spring I wouldn't have had to resort to such questionable solutions. If I could simply devote a couple of days this week to pulling the weeds by hand, then I wouldn't have had to spend that anxious time in the hardware store. But I didn't, I resorted to the easy way, so that Jorge could spray the weeds and rid the garden paths of the ubiquitous weeds.

I pass the jug to Jorge, who quickly begins to dilute the concentrate and spray the carpet of weeds that litter the paths. By tomorrow morning the paths that he has hit will be brown with weeds beginning to die and decay.

———

As the weeks of June morph into July, the weather progresses. It is sunny and hot and the skies are clear blue, and in the garden beds are blueberries and strawberries and zucchini and cucumbers. Although these plants are thriving, my attention must move to both pulling out the spring plants and the introduction of the fall plant starts.

In one of the side beds are long rows of salad greens: lettuces and arugula and bok choy and the like. They were planted in the cool days of April and May and thrived for weeks. We picked some and forgot about others; the speckled trout's back lettuce was tasty, the first of the bok choys were great, but the bugs got the rest. At this point in the season, all have bolted. Out of the center of each plant a small stalk has erupted, created a seedpod to fulfill the destiny of these plants. The arugula was the first; it is always the first to bolt. Its only competition is cilantro, another tender green that is more concerned with its legacy than with its present use as a leafy food. The flowers and their eventual seeds signal the end of the usefulness of everything in this bed and they must be removed. With a small garden fork they are easily levered out, their roots dense and complete but shallow. The wheelbarrow is quickly filled with the flowering detritus and rolled over to the enormous compost pile next to the garden.

I write this in a passive voice not because it sounds very graceful but because I am embarrassed that I am not actually forking out the old plants myself. I should be doing it, as I should also have spent the spring keeping up with the weeds. In fact, I now spend my time driving to the city to deliver cheese, and to sample cheese in grocery stores, and to work at the computer doing the more abstract efforts of running a farm. My days are filled with answering emails about the farm business far more than they are spent weeding the garden beds and planting out garlic or winter squashes or tomatoes.

If I were to be more honest, I would write that Dustin cleaned out the garden beds of the spring plantings and began to introduce wheelbarrowsful of finished compost back into the soil. To my great luck, a few months earlier Dustin and his partner moved to the island, buying a beautiful house a few minutes from the farm. He was working in landscaping in the city and was looking for more work closer to his home. After the debacle with the weeds and the Roundup, I obliged and set Dustin to tackle the garden.

Dustin represents to me the new generation of folks interested in food, its cultivation and preparation. Just thirty years old, he missed out on learning from his family as to the ins and outs of canning and growing vegetables. His family had long since lost the passed-down knowledge of living off of the land.

The result is sad on one hand, but glorious on the other. Dustin is thrilled to be at the farm here, soaking up information like a sponge. Everything is new and exciting and worthy of interest.

This afternoon he rips out the bolted lettuce and bok choy and arugula, fills the beds with compost and then begins to plant more starts.

The idea of tending a garden makes more sense around this time of year. At the beginning of the year the farm is pretty much a blank slate: the garden beds have few if any weeds, the soil is moist from the winter rains, the pastures are bright and green, and through the spring months the gardens are filled with plants with few problems, few pests, and what few weeds that manage to grow are easily eradicated. And then the temperature rises through the early summer weeks and the rains cease and the garden, and the farm in general, become more complex and need more attention, more tending.

―――――

The most apparent part of the farm that needs attention is the pastures. April and May and June are their best months. There is ample rainfall to keep them lush and green and growing. The cows can barely keep up with the flush of fresh grass. I am lulled into thinking that this will continue throughout the year even though I am well aware that the grass will run out at the end of the summer, burned by the heat.

Here at the middle part of July, the corner has turned suddenly on the lushness of the pastures. There is still grass remaining, but the cows can now eat faster than the grass can grow. The result is the need to begin rotational grazing of the cows and the need also to begin cutting the pastures.

The weeds have no competition; the cows are not interested

in their bitter, tough leaves and stems. The soil is still adequately moist to provide sustenance for the weeds, and with that and the heat their growth is dramatic. If not cut, they will flower and bloom and spill their seed throughout the pastures. Many of these weeds are invasive; they could easily take over all of the pastures in a matter of a few short years. The best method to eradicate these unwanted plants is to mechanically cut them, removing their ability to send out seed. It won't kill them, but it will keep them from reproducing.

This magical day—when the weeds begin to appear above the lush grass—is my center point of the year; it is the height of summer. Earlier, the pastures looked like a sea of bright green spears of grass, glistening in the morning dew, swaying in the afternoon wind, and were a soft blanket to lie on in the sunny afternoon. And then one day the pastures are a mix of stiff stalks and wide deep green leaves with flower stalks rising to the sun. Thankfully, Ben and Jorge recognize the importance of cutting these weeds and attach the finish mower to the back of the tractor. The height of the cutting can be adjusted by raising and lowering the four independent wheels that lift the expansive cutting deck. We raise it up to its highest to keep from cutting into the soon-to-be-precious grass and begin the annual cutting.

This bright orange mower that trails behind the John Deere tractor is large, perhaps six feet across, with three expansive blades that turn in tandem. It would be well suited for a large suburban yard. But to entirely cut these ten acres of pastures is a slow and tedious operation. Either Ben or Jorge will drive the tractor each day for a week, putting in three or four or five hours per day between morning and evening milkings to guarantee that all of the weeds have been cut down.

I used to do this myself in the early years and I miss it. It is a pleasant task. You drive the tractor up to the pastures, set the power takeoff, or PTO, to engage the mower, downshift the main gears to the lowest settings and set the throttle high.

The result is the tractor moving very slowly, but the PTO rapidly spinning, driving the blades fast enough to cut the heavy weeds. Once the controls are set, you can take your feet off of the clutch and brake and simply steer across the green pastures. Conveniently, tractors have a rigid throttle, allowing for an easy cruise control, if you will. It is a time to daydream and watch the swallows that dive behind the tractor trying to capture the insects that are brought up from the mower. Back and forth they swoop, in and around the back of the tractor, with unbelievable precision and speed. I think of grand ideas and distant plans and nearly fall asleep on the long legs of the pasture, before I have to turn and start back down the next leg.

Now that Jorge and Ben are here to do the task, I can be down at the gardens, helping out in the beds, pulling the spring plants, doing a bit of weeding and planting the new fall plants. The tractor is the background beat. It is an incessant sound, the whirl of the high-speed PTO and the mower blades as they cross the pastures. I can see many parts of the upper acreage from down below, but not all in its entirety, so every few minutes I see the small tractor cross my line of sight. But the sound easily pierces through the few trees separating the upper and lower portions of farm. It is the sound track of the height of summer and I enjoy it.

———

A month later, and summer has progressed beautifully. What was once warm and sunny is now genuinely hot. We wait all year for these few weeks that are just now starting. Here in the Pacific Northwest there is a mentality of contentment with the mild climate of this region, while at the same time envy for the heat and duration of the summers of the rest of the nation. For a mere two to three weeks we have parity with the warmer regions of the country, and this time—mid-August—is that season.

As I walk up the north road of the farm, through the canopy

of overarching trees, past the entrance to the cheese cave and then on to the upper pasture, I am struck by the quiet. It is eerily silent. This is my customary walk in the late afternoon. The cheese making has been finished for the day and the cows will not be milked for another couple of hours. It is a free time; there are no demands on me for at least two hours. I slowly walk, with a deliberate step, through the gates and up the road to the pastures. The cows are not visible yet I expect they are sitting down idly on the far edge in the shade granted by the large willows near the pond. I know instinctively that with the perimeter fence they are contained within the limits of the farm and yet I am not sure where they are located. All I can hear is the crackling of the dried leaves and needles and twigs beneath my feet as I walk up the hill. It is odd—even the birds have taken a break during this heat spell.

Once I complete my ritualistic walk of the upper pastures, I head back down slowly, deliberately, until I get back to the barn and then to the Cookhouse and the gardens. I feel like an old man, walking with such thought and slow progress. I can imagine a time when I am eighty years old and my entire year is filled with this pace, not just the few heavy, hot days of mid-August.

Whereas the pastures have been rapidly drying out and little activity is apparent, the gardens are the opposite. Walking down the main gravel path between the two beds at the entrance to the garden is difficult. The vines of the pumpkins and squashes have reached nearly across the full run of the gravel. They stretch out and reach with their tendrils, for what I don't know. I doubt they know. It is their nature, to reach and blindly delve with little thought or reason. I enjoy watching their progress, day by day, farther and farther across the gravel path and then across the large open gravel square in the middle of the garden.

On two opposing faces of that square are the flower beds, each planted thickly with lilies and the hollyhocks from Leda and scented geraniums and lavender and poppies and dahlias and sweet peas. Today at the midpoint of the hottest summer month the lilies are at the apex: full of bloom and tall and riotous. The white lilies have their silken petals curled full back in bloom, the stamens bulging out in their vulgar sexuality. The more subtle sweet peas shyly fill in below them, climbing up any branch and stem they can find, their highly scented blossoms filling the quiet air today. I walk around the concrete flower beds, brushing up against the overfilling lavender releasing its full scent of soap and elderly women. I want to remember this day; to hold it in my memory for when in the depths of February I will need this image. In a few months it will seem like an unbelievable dream that a multitude of flowers could all be blooming on tall green stalks full of life. I take a few photos of the lilies and dahlias with my iPhone, a sad attempt to use technology to help me hold on to today's feeling. I will thumb through this album in January or February and the images will be flat and lifeless. Certainly I will look at the photo of Stargazers or coral dahlias and be reminded that summer held my attention in mid-August but reality is a hollow memory. Only with the heat and the bright sun and the warm gravel and the bees buzzing overhead can this scene be convincing.

In the far bed are the garlic plants. They were planted in October last year and spent the winter slowly growing in the cool winter weather and rains. In the early spring they sent up tall green stalks and now, at the end of their cycle, they are complete, dry and full and pungent. I easily pull up each of the garlic plants and lay them on their sides. The individual cloves have all swelled sufficiently and the outer surface has moved from green and subtle to dull brown and dry. The afternoon sun will dry them further and tomorrow the tops can be cut and the heads can be collected and brought inside for use through the winter. They will be oily and green and full of garlic flavor when used early in the season; by next spring many of the cloves will be hollow and vacant and the few usable cloves will be bereft of the pungent nature that they have today.

Next to the garlic bed are the two beds of potatoes. In the early spring the small seed potatoes were planted, and through the early summer the potatoes sprouted and sent up tender green plants. And now those plants have flowered and then fallen, the plants spent from their exuberance of growth. These formerly full, verdant beds are bedraggled, wilting plants. Beneath them, however, lie the tubers that will carry us through the fall and winter months. On the surface a few are visible, their dull brown skins nearly identical to the loamy soil surrounding them.

One of the great benefits of these raised beds is that they are never walked on; the soil is never compressed by the weight of human traffic. The soil remains light and airy, conducive to rapid, healthy plant growth and also to easy harvest, especially of belowground crops such as potatoes. Normally a garden fork would be the weapon of choice to attack such wilted vines, but a gloved hand or two can be adequate in such easily worked ground. With three large plastic containers—the modern equivalent of the bushel bucket of yore—by my side, I reach into the soil and pull up the remains of the plants. The roots easily sever as they are pulled from the soil, and in the process they release the tubers and open up the soil.

The potatoes are three varieties, a mottled Yukon Gold, a smaller fingerling and a robust russet. The russets are large and vulgar and will be used as bakers. The fingerlings are waxy and rich and will make be the best mashers and the Yukon Golds have the great scale and color and taste for a simple boiled potato. There is an ample crop to get the farm through the winter with weekly meals of these spuds.

I used to believe that the best foods to grow yourself were those that were unquestionably better than the store-bought equivalents. Heirloom tomatoes that could be picked fully ripe on a hot summer afternoon and eaten while still warm from the sun. Pastured eggs from chickens allowed plenty of room to roam and grass to eat. Or salad greens grown quickly in rich moist soil, cut and rushed to the kitchen before they fade in any way.

What I have found over the years is that all of the items grown or raised on this farm have a quality unmatched by the industrial foods they vaguely resemble. These fine spuds lifted from the rich, loamy soil are exceptional. I can raise them to my nose as they come from the ground and they smell of potatoes, of the soil, of the earth. It is one of the most beautiful smells of the year. It is hot and sunny and dry outside and yet these weighty bits of the earth are cool and subtle. I easily fill the three lugs with the underground bounty from the beds and carry them back to the kitchen.

My twenty-eight concrete raised beds were established for the Cookhouse dinners. When I served a weekly meal to twenty hungry diners fifty weeks of the year, there was a demand for a hefty volume of vegetables year-round. Now that the Cookhouse dinners have been eliminated, with this farm's primary function the raising of Jersey cows and the production of farmstead cheeses, there is little use for such a large volume of produce, with the exception of this fine feast in a few weeks' time.

Year by year since the end of the Cookhouse dinners, the ration of beds devoted to vegetables versus those devoted to flowers and small fruits has diminished. Each spring I plant another bed or two of lilies or sweet peas or irises. There is now room for a bed of thornless blackberries, or perhaps next year I will devote an entire bed to antique English roses. I still plant easily double the number of onions that I could possibly consume myself, the same with potatoes and tomatoes; I am slow to react to a changing demand. I enjoy the look of a dozen perfect cabbages all lined up precisely on a grid, even if I only eat two.

My thoughts on the nature of this farm have progressed throughout its existence. For years I would raise three or four hogs, slaughter them in the fall, store them in the freezers and then slowly serve them to the guests who sat at the long Doug fir table. I would take the proceeds from those dinners and pay my employees—then just Tyler and Jorge. In turn they each would head to their local neighborhood grocery stores and buy pork or beef to feed their families. Oddly, that made perfect sense to me for half of a decade. And then one day it occurred to me that those who work for me should enjoy the meats and vegetables and fruits of this farm's largesse.

The end of the dinners freed up a tremendous volume of meats especially. The production of vegetables was curtailed, but we still keep three pigs and every year slaughter a cow. When there is a surplus, and there always is, each of the employees receives a share of the pork or beef after it is butchered. The largest share is always reserved for myself and the farm for parties and such, but enough is left to keep the employees from buying meat elsewhere. The same is true with the vegetables. Those who assist in the making of tomato sauce, or picking the peppers, or harvesting squash take enough home to make milking in the wet winters or cutting pastures in the heat of summer more bearable. Honey is always too precious for me to allocate it to Ben or the others. It is one of the few items that I can consume freely through the winter, exhausting my supply. Seeing Jorge's three young sons camped out on the concrete ledges of the garden beds, attempting to eat every ripe strawberry they can find beneath the dense canopy of leaves, pleases me immensely every bright summer day.

———

Just north of the potato beds, a few feet outside of the garden, are the beehives. I moved them here this spring so that they could get the full sun in this choice spot. They have responded in kind, creating good colonies and excellent honey. I still am not the best beekeeper, but I have faith once again in the future of my hives and in my abilities. For a few years, the hives would limp through the season, barely producing much honey, their existence tenuous as best. With their new placement and my new optimism, they have rebounded, and I am reminded of that on this sunny afternoon. As I sit on the edge of the concrete border of the potato garden, running my hands through the soil for any last errant nubs of potatoes, the bees are flying in and out of their hives. They are not interested in me in the least—their goal is the large bed of fennel in full bloom a few feet away from me. The fennel is tall and grandly healthy, with a nearly unlimited source of bright yellow pollen for the busy, eager bees. They make the trip back and forth over my head, their tiny legs weighted down with the saffron-colored dust from the fragrant flowers.

When the potato beds have been emptied of their produce, I continue my afternoon in the garden. The cucumbers are spilling over the sides of their beds in the same manner as the squashes, a multitude of long green slicing cucumbers and small yellow lemon cucumbers hiding beneath the shading leaves.

With most of the bees fully engaged outside of their hive, eagerly drawn to the pollen of the fennel, I decide to take part of the afternoon and extract some honey for the dinner. I don't have a full afternoon to spend with the hives but I want some of the luscious, golden honey available to Tyler. I grab the smoker and the veil and gloves from the front porch of the Log House and assemble them near the hives. I head to the far shed and collect the centrifugal honey extractor and carry it over to the porch off of the Cookhouse. I cleaned it well the last time I used it, so I'm ready to go. The gloves and veil I quickly throw on, and with a bit of dried leaves and grass from the garden I get the smoker started. Not enough to spend much time at the hives, but enough smoke to find a couple of full frames of honey and pull them out.

The bees are well occupied in their sunny pursuits and appear to notice little of my intrusion. Two weighty frames are quickly found and pulled from the hives with my cumbersome gloved fingers. I walk them over the short distance to the extractor, scrape the thin wax cappings off of the individual cells filled with honey and lock the frames in the extractor cage. There's little physical effort required of me. The well-geared crank spins the cage rapidly, the honey spun from each tiny cell, where it collects quickly on the bottom of the stainless steel extractor. On such a hot, sunny day the honey is very liquid and responds quickly, rolling down the sides and now out the valve on the bottom and into a waiting bucket.

It is a crude method of harvesting honey, but it's all that I have time for today. I return the spun frames with the empty cells back to the colony quickly, with the smoker barely breathing any of the calming smoke from its tin spout. I get a small amount of honey, maybe a couple of quarts, but certainly enough to get us through the next several weeks. Later, after the dinner, I will return to the hives and do a proper harvest when I have more time.

When the hives are all back in order, I head back through the Cookhouse and stop in the greenhouse. On the roof of the small glass house are windows that open. When the heat increases sufficiently inside, small oil-filled pistons expand, pushing open the glass windows, allowing the heat built up inside to escape. Even with the four panes fully opened on this sunny afternoon, the greenhouse is sweltering. The only things remaining in the greenhouse are the pepper plants and a couple of tomato plants. All of the starts and the benches were long since removed, the equipment returned to the attic above the milking parlor and the starts planted out in the garden. All around the glass house are the thriving pepper plants, obviously enjoying this intense heat.

Jorge has made a small irrigation trough that runs along one side of the small room, across the width and then back up the other side to the doors. He sets a hose into one end of this shallow channel and runs the water, allowing it to flood down the full length, watering his cherished peppers. They have grown well and produced large quantities of their respective red fruit. The bell pepper plants are short and remarkably carrying bulbous, weighty fruit in varying stages of ripeness. The cayenne and other hot chilies are tall, lanky plants nearly reaching the roof of the low house, many slender red chilies draping down from the full length of the plants. It is difficult to stand in the small space for very long; the heat is overwhelming even with the windows open on the roof and the doors open wide. The intensity of the heat is compounded by the smell of the peppers. The air is filled with their spicy heat.

I finish my slow walk around the farm, reveling in the intensity that I find, yet aware that it is transient. In a few days or weeks the weather will crest and return to its customary moderate warmth. Today it is quiet and calm, the plants soaking up the heat of the sun, the cows resting in the shade of the trees and the eager bees the only sign of activity on this hot summer afternoon.

EIGHT

Preparation for Dinner Begins

Seventeen months ago Andi gave birth to a beautiful bull calf—Boy—just a few weeks after Dinah gave birth to Alice. I was originally disappointed, preferring a heifer instead. A few days after the birth of Boy, I decided that, instead of selling off this beautiful young calf, I would keep him at the farm for beef. He was castrated a few days later and sent off to live with the herd of Jersey females here on the pastures. It was a questionable decision. I want to produce the highest volume of milk from the cows that I have. In order to do that I need to reserve all of the pasture for the cows that either are in milk presently or will come into milk when they have their calf. Boy was never to contribute to the milk supply; he would only cost me money as he ate through the expensive winter hay and grazed on pasture that should be reserved for the females.

I did want fabulous beef for the Cookhouse table and so I decided to keep him and fatten him up over the months. The year and a half have come and gone and although we could keep him here on grass for another year to fatten him up further, it is time to slaughter him. Soon we will be going into winter and he will need to be fed more costly hay trucked onto the island from Eastern Washington. It is time.

It is not the best time to slaughter. It is September and the weather has been warm after the heat of August. Cool, or preferably cold weather would be preferable, as there is little if any chance of flies laying eggs on the exposed carcass while it is hanging and also the cooler weather helps chill the meat down. If I had a very large walk-in cooler with an overhead rail that could hold a steer, it wouldn't be an issue, but with only three pigs slaughtered every year and at most one cow, there is hardly the need. Timing the slaughters in the dead of winter is best. If we were slaughtering a pig, I would certainly wait until winter, but a cow is less of a worry. Pigs are difficult to butcher unless they are very cold; the pork fat is too fluid at greater than forty degrees. Cows are much less fatty than hogs and I can quickly break down a steer carcass into large primal cuts even if it is not completely chilled and get them into a cooler if need be.

The advantage to slaughtering on a warm, sunny day in contrast to a wet, winter day is that there is a great absence of mud. Kurtwood Farms is indeed a farm, a rather tidy farm indeed, but with thirteen cows living here, a great deal of manure and mud appears throughout the winter months. In the summer the manure quickly dries and breaks down, in the winter it accumulates rapidly. To add to the challenge, the constant churning of the soil and water by the hooves of those animals, each a thousand pounds, produces thick mud bogs on the cow paths.

The morning chores have been finished, with the exception of the feeding of the cows. Ben earlier cut the cows, dividing Boy from the others and putting him into the large lower fenced paddock. This paddock is near the Cookhouse and can easily be accessed by the tractor. Once Boy is separated, the rest of the herd is fed on the upper pasture and they quickly leave the area.

The procedure for slaughtering a steer is in essence no different than that of slaughtering a hog. Steers are easier to move than hogs. It can be a bit difficult to get just one pig in a great position to slaughter; a bucketful of grain will entice them over to a nice level dry spot, but more than likely it will entice all of the hogs jostling for grain. The cows are much more used to human contact and can be easily isolated and led to where they need to be. The downside to that is that I have a connection to the cows. The pigs—I can't even tell them apart. The cows—I know them by name, even the steers that will never be milked and that I don't have that much contact with. They were bottle-fed for a few weeks. It is hard to forget that time.

But once I have the rifle in hand, that connection quickly falls away. The rifle is locked away in the Log House. I respect the gun and its power. I am not scared of it, but am aware of its place in the slaughter of the farm's animals.

Once Boy is isolated from the other cows, I drop a flake of alfalfa from the barn on the ground just in front of the locked gate leading up to the pastures. Boy casually walks over to the gate to investigate the hay. It is not the usual setting for feeding, yet he can't ignore it. Quickly he drops his head down to the hay, placing his head in a perfect position for me to shoot him. In a moment the gun goes off, the bullet enters his skull at point-blank range and he immediately drops to the ground. His death is instantaneous as the large-caliber bullet enters his brain.

As I move aside and leave the area to return the rifle to the Log House, Ben moves in, opens the gate and quickly cuts the throat of the steer with a sharp scimitar knife. As he cuts through the jugular vein, the bright, vibrant red blood pumps out onto his knife. I am reminded of the term *sang de boeuf*, French for "beef blood." It most commonly refers to Chinese ceramics glazes that were later imitated by European potters. It is a deep, dark red color, nearly purple and always glossy. In early Chinese ceramics it also often puddles at the bottom of the classic bottle vase shape, giving the illusion of the vessel coated in the thick, deep blood of a slaughtered steer. In the thick puddles the color appears almost black, yet still retains it deep ruby color.

The blood pumping from Boy's still-beating heart is indeed *sang de boeuf.* Although the heart continues beating, there is very little other movement from the steer. The slaughter is calm; the shot rings out and the steer drops and is dead immediately.

When the heart has ceased, the gates are opened wide and the tractor is driven over to transport the body in the bucket of the tractor to the Cookhouse. Boy is large, his legs long and sprawling. Rigor has not started to take over the carcass and the short drive is not graceful.

I drive the tractor to the west side of the Cookhouse building, where the steel gambrel hangs from the roof beam of the Cookhouse porch. Boy is now in the raised bucket, his hind legs just underneath the hanging gambrel. Ben quickly trims the hide off of the heels of the steer, cuts into the Achilles tendon and inserts one end and then the other of the gambrel into the space between the tendon and the leg bone.

The gambrel is raised with the seven-to-one block and tackle with far less effort than the weighty carcass would appear to require. Ben and I together can raise the hundreds of pounds with a bit of work, but nothing near what would be needed without the miraculous engineering of the block and tackle.

With Ben working one side and myself working the other, we systematically remove the hide from the hanging steer. We start at the top of the animal, high on the rear legs, pulling it down past the central body, over the shoulders and off of the front legs. Gravity is a welcome assistance as the hide is removed like a tight sweater. This is pleasant work. There are sections of the body where the hide is easily removed, others where it is much more difficult. The legs, backs and sides are the easiest—the hide can be pulled off with little need for a sharp knife to assist. In the large central section it is possible to *punch* the hide off— you slam your fist into the hide where it connects to the body. Relatively thin membranes connect the hide and physical force can dislodge it.

The front chest of the carcass is different. It is at the brisket that the hide is tightly adhered to the body. It is only with a thin, sharp knife that the hide can be removed. At the end of three-quarters of an hour the entire hide is off of the carcass and on the concrete base of the back porch of the Cookhouse. The hide is wet from being sprayed with the hose to clean off any mud and blood from the kill an hour earlier. It appears to be heavy, certainly, but when I start to pick it up to move it out of the way, I am immediately shocked. What appears to be twenty pounds is more likely close to seventy five. It also has helped keep the heat in the animal. With it removed completely from the hanging beast, the meat begins rapidly to cool down.

What is hanging from the high beam of the Cookhouse porch now little resembles the live, walking animal of ninety minutes earlier. After Ben removes the head, the carcass resembles meat more than beast.

The process now changes to gutting. With a sharp knife I cut into the center of the belly, as high as possible on the animal, pulling the knife down as far as possible, stopping at the firm bone of the sternum low on the chest of the inverted carcass. As the cut progresses down lower and lower, opening up the cavity, the interior contents begin to push against the chest more and more. Cows are ruminants, with a complex system of digestion to process their diet of primarily grasses into protein. The abomasums, the reticulum, the omasum, and the rumen, I know the names, certainly, but when these large, weighty, bulbous stomachs come at me I have little interest in identifying them. They are all filled with half-fermented grasses, and I am confident that the tip of my knife cutting into any of them would elicit a mess of stomach acids and noxious grassy gases that I have little interest in experiencing. The goal is simply to get the heavy, unwieldy stomachs out of the belly of the beast and into the bucket of the tractor to send to the compost pile.

The guts of the cow are attached to the spine by the hanger, the tasty muscle that will be the basis of our lunch in a few minutes. With a great deal of pushing and shoving and careful cutting with a sharp-bladed knife, the guts are eventually released. Just before that, I pull the tractor with its forward bucket just under the waiting carcass. With a final cut, the guts very ungracefully fall into the awaiting bucket. Then the tractor can be pulled back from the scene and driven to the compost pile. By this time of the year, the compost is no longer wet and heavy, but rather it is beginning to look like its final product of dry, friable soil. The guts are unloaded onto the ground next to the pile, and I then drive the tractor to the other side of the pile and begin to mound the nearly finished compost onto the awaiting stomachs and intestines and organs. The offal must be well covered so that the dogs will not attempt to dig them out—the organs' scent must be tremendously attractive, even to my already overfed canines. Of all the additions to the compost, such as old vegetables and fruits and discarded plants from the garden, the addition of moist animal guts is the most amazing. In a matter of days they will quickly be digested by the worms of the vibrant compost pile. When Ben returns in a week to flip and turn the compost, little will remain of the unwieldy, heavy guts and stomachs. If I had any worry as to the health of my animals I would refrain from adding these parts to what will end up being the soil of my garden. I am fully confident that Boy had no parasites or diseases, and the heat from the breakdown of the compost can only further contribute to killing any possible pathogens.

It is late in the afternoon and the carcass is hanging from the gambrel off the ridge beam of the Cookhouse porch. Byron sits nearby, guarding the meat, under the impression that it is entirely for him. He is not protecting the hundreds of pounds of beef for me, but rather because he is convinced that he will consume the entire weighty bulk of steaks and bones himself. He is narcissism personified.

The temperature has begun to cool off this afternoon and through the night it will cool the beef adequately. Certainly an evening in the thirties would have been preferred but this temperature will suffice.

The tools are put away, the blood hosed off the concrete, the tractor washed down and returned to the barn and the heart and livers wrapped and put into the freezer. As Ben and I are finishing up, Dustin arrives for work, unaware that Boy was going to be slaughtered today. He pulls up in the driveway in his vintage Ford truck with the dusty blue paint job and Oregon plates, then walks around the Cookhouse to find the beef hanging and Ben hosing the blood off the concrete floor. It is an arresting site, I am sure, and Dustin stops suddenly, his eyes wide, and then comes in close, fascinated by the beast.

I have slaughtered many animals—pigs and cows and chickens—here in the past decade. It has become part of my life now. It is only when someone walks around that corner and sees a large dead animal hanging that I am reminded how unusual this seems. That does strike me as somewhat sad. Most of us eat beef or pork most every day, and yet can spend our entire lives never observing the slaughter and butcher of the meat that will become our dinner.

Dustin has come to help in making tomato sauce, however, not for the slaughter of Boy. Once Ben and I have finished cleaning up, I move into the Cookhouse to work on the tomato sauce. I send Dustin out to the garden to pick all of the ripe tomatoes he can find. And I get busy setting up the kitchen for the processing of the tomatoes.

Up in the attic of the Cookhouse are boxes of tools and supplies needed to live off of the land. Over the years I have slowly collected most everything necessary to process the fruits and vegetables for the winter. One of my favorite tools is the Victorio strainer.

I found it at the local thrift shop a few years back and have appreciated it ever since. It was made in the sixties and still works great. The main body is cast aluminum, but not the modern cast aluminum that is thin and dull and cheap. This mechanism is finely made and built to last.

The strainer looks very much like the old-style hand-cranked meat grinders. The main body is a horizontal tube a couple inches across and six inches long that contains an Archimedes' screw that pushes the fruit from the opening on top to the front end. On the rear end is a large hand crank that turns the screw. On a meat grinder, the meat would be pushed to a rotating blade and then through a die pierced with a series of holes. The strainer, however, doesn't need to chop the fruit, but rather pushes it through a funnel perforated with many small openings.

Dustin has begun to return to the kitchen with bucketsful of ripe tomatoes. The Sun Gold tomatoes have produced hundreds of small cherries. The heirlooms, the Pineapples and Persimmons are also well represented. In a third bucket are ample Taxi and Early Girl tomatoes. Those last are disturbingly consistent in their size and shape and color. The heirloom fruits are a motley mix of colors and sizes and ripeness; some are grotesque in their uniqueness and shape. The Taxis and Early Girls have the benefit of years of hybridizing and their consistency reflects it.

Bringing up the rear are the Bill's Tomatoes. Large, lobed, heavy and the ones that are fully ripe are deeply red. Their skins are thin; those ripe specimens feel as if the entire contents of the long, pepperlike fruit will fall out of the delicate skin if I'm not careful. They are monstrous compared to the delicate Taxis and the tiny cherries. I prefer them for the sauce.

While Dustin goes back and forth from the Cookhouse down the sidewalk to the garden, I put on a large pot of water to boil and bolt the Victorio strainer to the wooden counter. The water will be used heat up the tomatoes and make them easier to pass through the strainer.

Also on the range is the large, wide rondeau to cook down the tomato sauce after it comes out of the strainer. Its base is warped and bent, the aluminum discolored from much use, but it will easily hold the sauce made this afternoon.

By the time I have mustered everything necessary and the water has come to a boil, Dustin has finished bringing in all of the ripe tomatoes. Boxes line the counter, filled with some beautiful fruit and some that should have been picked a week earlier. We begin to line up a simple assembly line to process the many tomatoes.

At the first stop in the line, Dustin empties the boxes of tomatoes into the deep sink at the far end of the room. There he washes the fruit, ridding it of errant dirt and mud. He cuts off any rotten parts of the most ripe specimens. When a tomato is clean, he drops it into the large stockpot on the right side of the range.

I am standing in front of the range and after a few moments I fish the tomatoes out of the water with a Chinese wire strainer and drop the steaming tomatoes into the large hopper on the top of the strainer. I start turning the crank and the screw within the aluminum body begins to push the now-mushy fruit through the system. At the other end of the small mechanism two products emerge. From the end of the perforated funnel emerges the dry mash of seeds and skin that don't pass through the holes. The sauce falls to an awaiting bowl beneath the fine holes of the long straining cone. As the two containers fill, I quickly reach over and empty them: the finished sauce is sent to the rondeau at the far left side of the range, the dry mash to the bucket on the floor beneath my feet, headed to the pigs.

The process is amazingly efficient. Not particularly tidy, yet dramatically fast. In a couple of hours the many boxes of tomatoes are empty, and the sink is soiled with mud and pebbles and errant leaves. The boiling water has a few lost cherry tomatoes deep in the bottom, long overcooked, the water fouled by the many tomatoes that have passed through. The strainer sits exhausted on the counter, tomato juice and seeds and skins littering the counter and the floor, as well as my shoes, my pants and my shirtfront. On the stove is the large, wide pot with a few inches of the precious tomato juice, now slowly coming to a simmer. While Dustin and I put the kitchen back to order, the tomatoes will continue to reduce, the steam escaping over the afternoon, the level in the pot reducing and the contents getting ever thicker. When I shut off the flame, the sauce will not in any way resemble the tomato paste of those tiny cans in the supermarket, or the jars of omnipresent spaghetti sauce either. It will more closely resemble a thick version of tomato juice. While it slowly bubbles and steams, Dustin and I package up the Victorio strainer, placing the individual parts back into its fitted sixties cardboard box and hoisting it up to the attic for the next sauce-making afternoon. While I am teetering on the ladder to return the box, I grab a couple dozen quart-sized mason jars that are scattered about the low ceilinged storage space. The ebb and flow of the canning jars indicates the season. In the early winter, only a couple of chipped or dirty or perhaps just ugly jars remain deep in the corners of the small space. The vast majority of the farm's collection are filled with jams and jellies, chutneys and sauces, poached plums and honey, and either line the steel shelves in the Cookhouse or have been given away as gifts or traded for other preserves with friends.

Through the winter and early spring, I will head to the rack, find a jar of tomato sauce or blackberry jam, pop the sealed-metal lid and greedily spread the jam on my morning toast or begin to prepare some pizza sauce. When the jar is empty, the lid, the ring and the jar are washed and dried and sent up to the attic. They come up the ladder one or two at a time and are casually left just inside the small opening, my laziness apparent. As spring turns to summer the steel rack downstairs empties, the less popular green tomato chutney is all that remains, the overcooked plum preserves as well. Upstairs, the floor of the tight space is littered with a sea of empty jars and their lids, casually placed, shoved back toward the corners as the next jar comes up.

Until now, in late September, when the process reverses course and I head up the wobbly ladder, teetering on the top step—*"This is not a step"*—ignored by myself and all others. And then I reach in and grab a couple dozen jars and bring them down to the kitchen and begin their usefulness all over again. I like this flow, this ebb. I imagine a time-lapse film, the jars all congregating on the floor of the attic and then quickly diminishing, and then filled with brightly covered contents, and then clear glass once again and so on. Back and forth, back and forth.

Today a couple dozen will suffice. They are brought down to the dishwasher in the kitchen and sent through the high-temperature machine, quickly sterilizing them of any possible bacteria they picked up in their sabbatical above. From the drawer of the sideboard, I find a couple boxes of new lids and rings used to seal the canning jars. The old lids are bent from prying them open and only intended for a single use. The rings tend to get a bit rusty and bent from their journey up and down the ladder, back and forth to friends' larders and in and out of the refrigerator after the jars are opened. They are replaced as well.

The dishwasher does a fine job of both cleaning and sanitizing the jars. It heats to 185 degrees, steaming the jars for a few seconds to kill any bacteria, whether friend or foe. Just to be sure, I send them through a second time. It is a large commercial dishwasher and the cycle is all of four minutes, so a second time seems prudent. When I grew up canning with my mother and my grandmother, we would go to odd lengths to guarantee sanitation—boiling water in cake pans on the stove and putting in the inverted jars together with new lids and rings, then leaving them to dry on cake cooling racks positioned over tea towels. It all felt rather odd, but I cherished the ritual. Botulism was the great worry.

I remember my mother speaking of botulism in hushed tones, indicating that it was all around, always looking to appear, striking down children left and right from raspberry jam made in our little kitchen. It seems unlikely that such ever could have happened, but botulism is a legitimate concern.

Its great uniqueness is the ability of the bacteria to reproduce anaerobically. Most bacteria need air to thrive, yet botulism does not. This makes for its great love of the sealed canning jar, left for months on the shelf, slowly breeding danger for the dining table.

There are certainly remedies—high-temperature cooking of the most likely vehicles for the pathogen, namely tomatoes, green beans and asparagus. The sad reality is that such treatment would most likely guarantee the most overcooked tomatoes, green beans and asparagus possible. Great quality is the reason we do our canning ourselves. If I wanted overcooked vegetables, I would head to the supermarket and by a can of theirs.

What both relieves me and also scares me is the incidence rates of food-borne botulism in the United States. A very high percentage of all outbreaks occurs in Alaska, in foods of traditional aboriginal peoples. One of the prime culprits is the muktuk: whale skin, harvested and eaten from a beached whale. I am confident that is not a likely problem here on my farm.

But other leading states with occurrences of food-borne botulism are Oregon, Washington and Idaho. This has me much more concerned. Either there is botulism in the soil in this part of the country or there is a great love of muktuk here. I will continue to spend some time sterilizing my jars and lids and rings in the high-temperature steam of my dishwasher. I also tend to enjoy asparagus and green beans fresh from the garden and it never occurs to me to can them for later consumption.

Dustin and I continue, lining up the clean jars, lids and rings, and monitoring the simmering tomato sauce, the stereo blaring disco music behind us, its quick beat useful for keeping the process going. When the sauce is sufficiently reduced, or when my impatience is sufficiently grown, I shut off the flame and allow it to cool for a moment. And then we ladle the steaming-hot sauce into the quart jars. We take our time, making sure not to dirty the rims of the spotless jars with errant sauce. One by one the jars are filled—twenty in all, it turns out. Then we place a new, fresh lid on each jar and a ring as well. The rondeau is washed in the same high-temp dishwasher and the aluminum comes out stained by the high acid of the tomatoes.

I have a piece of equipment on the farm that makes the next step easy and efficient. On the low shelf beneath the counter is the largest stockpot imaginable. Made of stainless steel, with a three-quarter-inch-thick base, riveted steel handles and tall sides, it is immense. It is too large for one burner of my large stove and must straddle two burners. Originally I bought it for cheese making, but now it is used in a multitude of chores, especially for canning.

I pull up the weighty beast and place it on the stove with a resounding thud. Into it Dustin and I gently place the twenty quart-sized jars filled with the deep red tomato sauce. The pot holds all of the many jars in one layer on the bottom; there is no need to stack them or process them in two batches. And then I use the teakettle to pour warm water over the awaiting jars. It takes a few trips with the robust kettle to fill the stockpot to a level an inch above the seven-inch-tall jars. When done, it reminds me of archaeological artifacts from a galleon found buried deep in the sea. I peer over the tall sides of the steel pot and see the shiny lids all lined up on the bottom, covered in water, ready to be discovered in centuries to come from their underwater tomb.

With two flames licking at the sides of the vast pot, the water slowly heats. It takes most of an hour to come to a simmer and then to a boil. Dustin tires of the exercise and returns home, leaving me to watch the pot boil.

It does, in fact, come to a boil, and then I can set the timer on my iPhone for forty-five minutes, keeping the flame high enough to ensure the constant and consistent boiling, the bubbles sneaking up and around the twenty jars. At times bubbles escape from beneath the filled glass containers with such ferocity that the jars bobble and bounce around, jostling each other in their underwater confinement.

At last the time allotted comes to an end, the alarm goes off and I can kill the double flames on the range. After the sound of the gas is stopped, there is a moment or two when the water continues to boil, as if by magic, the clacking jars making a few more sounds before it all goes still and quiet.

With a set of tongs, I reach into the steaming water bath and gently grab the metal ring of each jar and lift it out of the water, over the high rim of the pot and onto the wooden counter next to the stove. With great fear of dropping the precious cargo, I slowly go back and forth until the pot is empty, save for the still-hot water. The counter is now filled with the lot of hot jars.

The tomato sauce within the glass confines appears deeper in color now, more ruby than when it was ladled into the cool jars. After a short time, I attend to each jar, tightening up each ring that is now looser than when first screwed on. And then the magic happens. Each jar in unison, randomly, emits a clear and distinct sound. The thin metal lids move from convex to concave, making a popping sound, guaranteeing their seal. Over the course of the forty-five minutes cooking in the water bath the contents expand, holding each lid in a convex form, and then as the contents cool on the countertop the volume slowly shrinks, until the lid changes its form and becomes a concave dimple on the top of the jars. It is reassuring and magical.

By morning the jars will be fully cooled. Half will be relocated to the steel shelf on the side wall of the Cookhouse, a few more will be sent to Dustin for his help and a couple more will be given to friends.

The next morning I walk the short distance from my home to the Cookhouse. The beef was left to hang through the cool night outside, hanging from the gambrel. Byron gave up his watch early in the evening, confident that it would be undisturbed in the evening hours. He follows me down the stairs of the Log House and out the front door, quickly running out to confirm his confidence.

Raising hogs and cows is important to me, I love the taste and the health of meat raised on this farm, and I believe in the process. I must confess, however, that I would prefer to look over at the end of the Cookhouse as I come around the corner of the Log House and see that some sprites have sneaked onto the farm during the night, broken down the beef into primal and then subprimal cuts, wrapped and labeled the cuts and stored them in the freezers for me. Alas, no such fantasy is apparent, as the carcass is where we left it last evening.

Ben is in the milking parlor finishing up the morning milkings. I can hear the whirring of the vacuum pump in the attic and the dull thud as the milking bucket hits the concrete. I head into the kitchen and begin to get ready for the beef.

All the countertops are cleared and wiped down, the dining table too. I sharpen the large scimitar knives, the boning knives and any others than might come in handy. An extrawide box of plastic wrap is pulled down from the attic, a couple of permanent marking pens as well.

The Cookhouse was, inadvertently, well designed for moving large slabs of meat from the gambrel on the porch to the center of the kitchen. The tables that form the counters in the center of the room all have casters on their bases and can easily be rolled about. The doors leading from the kitchen to the vestibule and from there outside to the porch are all double French doors, identical to the main entrance, and are amply wide to accommodate a rolling table and its cargo.

Ben and I follow a simple procedure. The doors are all opened and the long, wooden-topped table rolled out to the porch adjacent to the hanging side of beef, the casters locked in place. We lift the front legs—hanging toward the ground—onto the wooden table. It takes a bit of doing to wrestle the unwieldy and weighty beast, but it swings freely from the ropes attaching it to the high beam of the building.

I release the ropes from the boat cleat bolted onto the side post of the building and slowly let out the rope, gently lowering the carcass onto the table. Ben assists by guiding the few hundred pounds of beef, making sure that the ground beneath is not the final resting place for Boy. In a quick few moments, the ropes are all slack and the full weight of the beef is on the table. The gambrel is released from the tendons of the hind legs, the ropes are pulled back up and out of the way and the beef is ready to be moved into the kitchen for butchering.

I enjoy the cinematic qualities of daily life and this next moment is one of the more cherished. The gurney loaded with a large body is wheeled down through the two sets of double doors into the large room of the Cookhouse. It is difficult not to see this as wheeling a hospital patient from an ambulance outside to the emergency room. A bit of deep red blood dripping down the side of the gurney, a bit on my hand, and the effect is complete.

Ben and I attack the carcass aggressively, systematically. The head has already been removed, the tail as well. Inside the Cookhouse we remove the four hooves with an electric reciprocating saw. Already the vast size of the project is quickly shrinking.

The beast must be divided into six primal cuts—three from each of the two sides. The shoulder, the loin and the leg are how each side is divided. From those six large sections the smaller steaks and cuts are revealed.

We start by releasing the saddle from the rest of the carcass. The saddle is made up of the two legs, together with the hips that join them. With a cut straight across the lowest point of the spine, the weighty double leg unit separates from the rest of the cow. Concentrating on the saddle, Ben and I divide it into two smaller pieces, with a cut down the middle of the saddle. What results are two large, heavily muscled legs, each with its hoof removed.

The leg is a relatively simple cut to break down further. The

cuts are primarily the bottom round, the eye of round and the
top round. Each are bulky, large cuts of varying toughness. The
eye of round is the most tender and smallest, from the center
of the leg, and the top and bottom round are from the outer
muscles of the leg of the cow, and are less tender.

Each of us has one leg in front of us and a sharp, thin boning
knife in our hands. I approach the breaking down of a leg as
letting the muscles tell me where to cut rather than imposing
my ideas upon the muscles. They have a natural tendency to
fall into these three large pieces just described. I can almost
slide my palm between the roasts; primarily sinew divides the
cuts. The knife cuts the connective tissues and sinews, not the
muscles.

With a bit of tugging and pulling, and rotating the leg many
times during the process, I succeed in freeing the three large
pieces from the thick strong leg bone. They are neither tidy nor
resemble the images in the butchery book that sits open on the
long table behind me. They will, however, be delicious and true
to this farm.

I spend little time cleaning the roasts. I am well aware that
Tyler will spend the time removing silver skin and sinew when
he tackles the roast in a few weeks. Remaining on the table
is the bulk of the animal. Ben and I each begin wrapping our
respective roasts, completely covering the bulky, fresh meat in
the plastic wrap, each tagged with the date and the cut with
the permanent markers. Throughout the afternoon Ben and I
plod through the large task at hand. Slowly the large hulking
carcass disappears, on the long table opposite plastic-wrapped
beef lies in tidy rows and on sheet pans in the oven are trays
of beef bones roasting for beef stock. The smell of the roasting bones, large bits of beef remaining on them, fills the air. It
smells like a large roast beef is soon to come from the range to
grace the table, when in fact only dry beef bones are cooking.

By late afternoon we have finished breaking down Boy into
large cuts of meat. We are somewhat rushed and the final cuts

are large—each enough for a dinner for twenty folks in most cases. The skirts are cut into smaller amounts so that I can quickly grill up a bit of beef for tacos and the like, but most of the beef is kept in full roasts and steaks. When four o'clock arrives, I quickly fill plastic totes with cut and wrapped beef and load them into the back of my truck. Ben finishes cleaning the kitchen and breaking down the last remaining pieces before heading out at five to milk the cows and attend to the afternoon chores.

There is one chest freezer at the farm but it is not large enough to hold all of the beef from the slaughter and butchering of Boy. It holds a great deal of pork from the last pig, together with bags of tomatillos and fava beans and currants harvested from the garden. In the baskets of the freezer are freeze-dried cultures for cheese making and ice packs used to ship cheeses across the country. The odd container of Ben & Jerry's Chunky Monkey ice cream fills out the icy freezer.

Thankfully Vashon retains of bit of 1950s American culture to remedy my frozen-food storage problem. In the small town of Burton is a general store with meat lockers.

I live just outside of the town of Vashon, located in the center of the island of Vashon. It is essentially the only commercial area of the island. In Vashon are two grocery stores, a lumberyard, three banks and a credit union, many restaurants, the movie theater, the public library and a large selection of small stores and services. Only a handful of other retail businesses exist outside of the central business district of Vashon. Sandy's store is one of those few.

Burton is located south of the town of Vashon on the Vashon Highway. It is another ten minutes south of the farm by car and well worth the drive. Whereas Vashon town is completely landlocked and has no connections to the water surrounding the island, Burton is just a block from the water and reflects that connection. A large marina is just a short walk from the center of the tiny town, and beautiful south-facing sandy beaches are a short walk on the other side of this beautiful spot. The inter-section—and there is only one—is where Sandy's is located. Housed in a turn-of-the-last-century two-story building, the store on street level, Sandy's residence above, this general store commands the corner of this sleepy hamlet. Across the street is a four-room hotel with a dining room, the other corner has a gallery and next to that is a coffee cart, its parking lot filled with the locals of Vashon drinking coffee and catching up on the island's gossip incessantly.

It is a miracle that Sandy's has persevered. Although Burton is a far more beautiful town than Vashon ever could be, it has been largely forgotten by the island residents. Fifty years ago there were many small general stores dotted around the sparsely populated island. All have closed shop except for this exceptional one.

The store is expansive by tiny neighborhood bodega stan-dards. Rows of canned goods and cereal and household sup-plies fill the room, but in a sparse manner unheard-of in a modern supermarket. There is no musical sound track piped in, there are few if any signs and there is a distinct absence of the din of electronic equipment. With the store's proximity to the marina and many of the island boats, a large part of one aisle is dedicated to floats and tackle and nautical supplies. An oddly thorough selection of table wines is apparent, together with a produce section that reminds me more of my local A&P in the 1960s than the multicultural Whole Foods Market we are accustomed to today.

The most consistent part of this commercial enterprise is Sandy herself. Just inside the front door is a large Formica counter, with the daily newspapers stacked on one end and bunches of bananas on the other. On a worn seat behind that counter Sandy is installed, watching all who come and go through the large double doors of the busy store. She appears to be familiar with every customer, calling them by name, chat-ting with them about their children, their jobs and their lives.

There is a constant conversation in the room, a never-ending patter of gossip and discussions. On most days a dedicated local joins her, sitting on the second chair just to the side of the long sales counter. Occasionally Sandy stands to ring up a sale, giving change to one of the many kids who stop in for some soda pop or a contractor who needs a snack during his long day.

What is hidden in the far back corner of this quaint throwback of a store is a large wooden door that leads to the meat lockers. I had only heard this term growing up, never having actually seen a meat locker until my chest freezer filled up and I needed to find more space to store the bulky beef and pork of the farm.

So I head down to Sandy's, chat her up and she gives me a rental agreement for a small meat locker deep in the store's freezers. She never comes out from behind her station at the front of the store, only telling me the vague directions to find my designated space.

The main entrance to the freezers is a wide, bulky door of unpainted oak. The handle is chromed steel, and snaps into place with a dull thud when the door is closed and sealed. Just behind this quaint and functioning door is a small vestibule. I enter the room, close the oak slab behind me and find a second door resembling the first with a few distinct differences. This door is also made of the clear, quarter-sawn oak common when the building was built, the clasp also of the well-chromed steel as the first. This secondary door does not close tightly, however. There is no dull thud as the weighty door closes into its frame.

Around the edges of this eight-inch-thick insulated door is ice. Not a slight, thin skin of frost as on the windshield of your car after a chilly night, but rather a good solid inch of musty ice. The door is closed in the sense that it is not left open wide, but rather is distinctly proud of its frame. The ice also makes it stick to the edge of the frame, its tin-lined edge covered in ice of a lesser volume than the door.

Alone in the six foot square room, with a bare lightbulb

above me, I question the entire procedure. I am in the back
of a very quiet store, one with no employees except for the
owner, whom I chat with by name but whom I know nothing
of, other than that well-known name. I grab the handle, lean
into it and put a bit of strength into the effort to pull open the
iced-up door. It budges, coming toward me slowly, indicating
potential iced hinges as well. Behind this second door is the
freezer itself.

In front of me is a large, high-ceilinged room, a hallway leading from the entrance and a series of floor-to-ceiling shelves
leading from that aisle and twenty feet to the right. On the left
are stacks of bags of ice, presumably in anticipation of a busy
summer season nine months in the future.

Each of the three shelving units is wide and double-sided.
To describe them as shelves is misleading, as is the term meat
"locker." A more apt description would be dog kennels. On either
side of the ceiling-high shelves are series of three-by-three-by-
three-foot cages, all made of varnished wood and complete with
a hinged door on the front. Each of these individual doors is
labeled with a stenciled tag—the tallest row begins with A,
the lowest labeled D, the first cages from the hallway begin
with 1 and end at the far wall at 8. Sandy told me that the
only lockers available were on the bottom, everyone wants the
waist-level ones, but since I was new I would get one with the
tag of D. I was three in from the hallway, so my locker was D3. I
don't understand the concept of having a floor-level locker until
I begin to find and open my small cage down on the concrete
floor of the freezing-cold room. It is hard to be graceful locating
the label and then prying open the rickety wooden gate. Down
on my hands and knees, searching for the faded red stencil,
most likely tagged during the Eisenhower administration, is a
challenge as my knees freeze up in the dimly lit room.

Once I find my new bit of freezer heaven, I head out to load
up the beef that I brought with me in my truck. I wasn't sure of
the protocol of meat lockers when I arrived this afternoon, and

it isn't until I read the lengthy contract that Sandy handed to me that I realize I need my own padlock to secure my wooden cage. With a bit of joy I find a small, toy padlock on the home supplies shelf next to the shelves of brightly labeled canned goods. Sandy is happy to ring me up for this simple purchase and then I go out to my truck to grab the first of the two large plastic lugs that I had loaded from the Cookhouse counter.

There is a second part of the contract that I was unaware of when I headed down to Burton today. One of the rules is that the meat must be frozen when it is placed in the meat locker. I find this so counterintuitive: I rented this locker to freeze and store meat, didn't I? If I had room in my freezer I would be using that, after all. My likely guess is that there is the danger of blood dripping from still-warm slaughtered deer and elk from hunting trips, freezing in the hallways or dripping through the cages to a neighbor's locker below. Since I have a bottom locker and the beef is not a dripping mess, I decide to risk it, and proceed to carry the first bulky load through the wide front doors of the store, past the sentry that is Sandy, down the far aisle, through the tidy first door and then through the stuck second one and down to my private locker.

I am glad Sandy is chatting with a customer as I pass by the first time, so she doesn't notice the room-temperature load in my hands. I manage to transfer the contents into the floor-level cage, marveling at the roominess of what first appeared to be a tiny space. I expected to need two or three of these wooden spaces until I placed the first load in and realized there was adequate room for at least three such loads.

When I return to my truck for the next load, Sandy shouts out to me—reminding me that everything needs to be frozen. I call out in agreement, assuring her that I am of course following all of the rules. I now have to make the gauntlet one more time, at the same time hiding the flaunting of her rules. Luckily it is a sunny, warm day and the after-school rush appears as the school bus pulls up in the front of the building and a half dozen schoolkids from the neighborhood pour into their familiar store, eager to chat with everyone's grandmother and purchase sodas and potato chips before their walk home a couple of blocks away. Sandy is consumed completely, appearing to know each of their names and families, most likely with an accuracy that comes from running the same store for decades. In reality she sold their parents their after-school treats and in a few cases knew their grandparents from their shopping as well.

I safely get my many pounds of beef into my wooden locker, immediately giving up on any sense of order or tidiness, but rather happy that the locker holds all that I have brought with me. I do hold back the eight-pound bottom round that I will serve at the feast in October, along with some skirt steak, placing them at the front of the misshapen pile of plastic-wrapped roasts so that I can easily find those cuts when I need to defrost them for the dinner.

I place the toy padlock into the tiny clasp on my wooden gate, turn off the bare lightbulbs above the row of shelves and head out through the first icy door. For a moment I panic, worried that in the few minutes I have spent on my knees loading my locker, the door has frozen ever more, locking me in this small-town purgatory. The freezer is deep in the back of the store, the front filled with noisy kids, the owner most likely having long lost her capable hearing, and the chance of cell service unlikely in this tomb of a freezer.

Thankfully, with a heavy push of my shoulder the door slowly creaks open, revealing the small vestibule that looks like a bright, warm, sunny space compared with the frightening dimness that I long to exit quickly. By the time I come out into the store exploding with fluorescent lighting I have calmed down, my momentary anxiety attack quelled as I walk past Sandy, waving and saying good-bye and thank you as if I have known her for decades. She plays her part well, waving back to me, saying good-bye, both of us having no idea who each other is, but happy to live the roles given to us.

NINE

Two Weeks Before; Alice Calves

Alice has grown into a fine cow. She filled out nicely over the past two years, put on weight from her early days of much full, rich milk and then spent the past two summers gently grazing the pastures with the other young calves. Through the winter months she had her fair share of grass hay and alfalfa hay and a bit of grain from time to time. Ben has kept his eye on her in the past two weeks. When Wayne came out to breed the young Alice, Ben marked it on the calendar in the milk room and from that calculated her expected due date. Wayne provides a new calendar each year from the semen company and each insemination date has the date nine months out listed as well.

The expected due date for Alice was a few days ago. On Monday, six days ago, Ben moved Alice from the pastures with the other cows into the small stall at the south end of the barn. In the weeks leading up to Monday, he had brought Alice into the milking parlor after milking the other cows, luring her in with some grain and then allowing her to remain in the stanchion unbothered while she enjoyed a bucket of the grain before her. He wanted her to associate coming into the milking parlor and getting locked in the stanchion as a positive and enjoyable experience well before she had her first calf. He also gently prodded her udder, getting her used to being handled even though there was no milk to be had in this young cow.

On Monday her udder began to show signs of producing milk, of inflating from the small, deflated "bag" to what will soon resemble the large milk-engorged udder of a fully mature cow. Her stance also began to change: her hips looked ever so slightly different, indicating an impending birth.

And so she was moved into the confines of the stall. Many times during the day, one of us would stop in the barn, walk down the alley and look on in anticipation. And each day we would be disappointed.

Jorge took one look on the first day and declared that she was a week off and walked away. He either has great insight into reading the signs of calving, or he is simply more confident than Ben and myself. Either way, he tends to be correct and this cow was no different.

This birth is no different than that of Boy or even of Alice herself. Along the way others have been born as well: Stella, Amanda and Halley were born in the past two years, all with no complications. A couple of bull calves were also born here, in addition to the one that was kept for meat. Even though the birth of a calf is a predictable part of the life of a dairy, it is one of great importance and all of us take interest when a cow in near to calving.

I often wonder what it is like to work at a 350-cow dairy where essentially a calf is born every day of the year. I would guess that it would become rote and repetitive and without joy. There is no chance of that at this humble dairy farm, where the birth of a calf is a joyous occasion, even if it is a bull calf.

After a week of looking in on Alice, she does in fact drop a young bull calf. He is healthy and beautiful, but still a male that we have no use for. Alice is in fine condition and responds to her role as a mother—if only for a day—with gusto. She cleans and dries her young charge and prods him to get up and walk around the small straw-covered room.

The next day Ben takes Alice from the confines of the stall and brings her back to her fellow herd of milking cows.

As this is Alice's first calf, there is no chance of her getting milk fever, the dreaded, deadly condition that threatens to kill every mature cow after delivery. It is pleasing to get a pass, to not have to worry, at least for one time for each cow. When Alice has her second calf in a year and a half, then we will worry and watch her and give her additional calcium to get her through the days following the birth.

For three days Ben and Jorge will milk Alice last, after the other more mature and senior cows have been attended to. Their milk will be poured into the bulk tank and then Alice will be hooked up to the equipment. Through the clear plastic hoses, the remaining colostrum will flow. It is thick and slow to move, a much deeper yellow than the milk that will come in a couple more days. Alice appears okay with the entire process. She has already acquired a taste for the sweet grain in the bucket at the front of the stanchion. Her udders are tender and swollen but will relax after the first couple of days.

The colostrum will be poured from the milk bucket into a bottle with a nipple to feed the unnamed bull calf that is still in the stall. After the first day of feeding this small charge, I calculate what it will cost to feed this beautiful young animal. He easily can consume two to three gallons of milk per day and will need to be fed milk for at least a month and a half before he can subsist on hay and grass alone.

I make a quick calculation and decide to change the farm policy on the spot. That rich, creamy milk that I use to make cheese with is worth twenty dollars per gallon to me. That is the price of cheese that can be made from a gallon of the milk. I realize that keeping a bull calf around, castrating him, raising him up and selling him after two months for two hundred dollars is pure folly.

I decide to sell him immediately. Or rather, I decide to give him away as fast as possible. With the assistance of Craigslist I create a posting announcing the availability of a day-old Jersey bull calf. I include a photo, which I must confess is a generic shot of a day-old calf. They all look the same—fawn-colored hide, tiny ivory hooves, large inquisitive eyes and long black eyelashes. The posting goes online and in a couple hours I have a response. By morning this still-unnamed calf will be loaded into a trailer and headed off to a backyard farm on the island. They will have to buy milk, warm it up and feed him, but the price for the young animal is right and they are thrilled with the prospect of raising him. And I am relieved to keep the needed profitability of this small creamery in line.

_____

It is September and although the cold winter weather and short days are weeks away, I address tasks that need to be done to keep the farm running well. For the past four years I have housed chickens in portable coops with the peculiar name of chicken tractors. These two aluminum coops are low—just two feet high—and five feet wide and eight feet long. The chickens spend their entire lives in these roomy confines. Each morning I roll the lightweight tractors to a new spot of grass. The four walls and the roof are fully secure, yet the base is completely open, so the chickens can peck at the bugs and grass all day. Raccoons have never found a way to breach the secure tractors and the chickens enjoy a home with none of the built-up manure common in a traditional chicken coop. In the chicken tractors are eighteen mature Rhode Island Reds. Each day they are fed a bucket of grain, their water bucket is refilled and any eggs they have laid in the past twenty-four hours are removed and brought into the Cookhouse.

This is a fine system and through the spring and summer months it works exceptionally well. Once the chickens are mature enough to produce eggs, they keep up a fine schedule, producing on average nearly an egg per day. When the days are shorter and the temperature plummets, their production decreases prodigiously. In a standard chicken coop the remedy would be to keep a light on twenty-four hours a day, to stimulate their pituitary glands and to keep them producing eggs through the winter.

As my chickens are housed in chicken tractors that I move all around the farm, it would be folly to string up extension cords and attempt to power up a small lightbulb for my fowl in the hopes of higher production. I have decided, this year, to reduce the flock over the course of the winter and to start a new flock in the spring. The feed is expensive and there is little return in the form of eggs. When all twenty-four birds are laying, there is a bonanza of eggs—easily a dozen a day in the height of summer. It's a good thing eggs are the easiest things to give away to those who work here or to visitors to the farm. And I enjoy eating eggs daily, as do the dogs who call this farm home.

This afternoon I have decided to slaughter eight of the birds, followed by another eight next month and the final eight after that. I could conceivable slaughter all at one time, but I find the task distasteful and eight is all I can handle in one after-noon. Also, as the chickens are still producing, I will still get a fair amount of eggs in these fall weeks before the production completely falls off.

A large pot of boiling water is readied on the back porch, and the knives assembled. I go to work, slitting their throats, bleeding them out and then scalding them in the large stockpot set on the portable propane burner. It is not pretty work—the water is soon floating with errant feathers and chicken manure and the like—but with only eight birds to do, the work goes quickly.

Once the birds are slaughtered and plucked, I bring the eight bald, dead birds into the kitchen to gut them and process the parts. With the cleaver hanging to the side of the chopping block I chop off the head of each, dropping the heads in the pig bucket at my feet. Then with the sharp paring knife I cut into the gut, opening it up enough to reach in and grab the guts with my plastic-gloved hand. The guts of a chicken are stubborn, but generally are all well connected. With a bit of practice, the livers, hearts, stomach, gizzards and trachea can all come out easily. The kidneys tend to remain on the side of the rib cage, but all else can be pulled out with a bit of a tug.

Soon the counter is filled with a wet, messy covering of innards. They are easily divided—the hearts in one small bowl, the large, meaty gizzards in another. The bile sac is delicately removed from each of the tasty livers, and so on. The undesirable bits—the trachea, the stomachs—are dropped into the pig bucket. I wash out the hollow chickens over the sink, grabbing the kidneys for the pigs as well.

In the space of an hour of unglamorous work the counter now has eight scrawny, skinny old laying hens ready to be made into soup or stock. Next to these flavorful if not beautiful birds are the gizzards, hearts and livers, all rinsed and tidy.

I decide that I have had enough of chickens for one day and place each bird inside a plastic bag and find room for them in the chest freezer in the farm shed. As the dinner is just two weeks away I begin to imagine a pasta dish made with all of these beautiful chicken organs. There is enough to feed the twenty folks soon to arrive at the farm and it reflects this season beautifully. The chicken organs have rich and gutsy flavors. The colors are dark and somber, deep browns and reds. I snap a photo with my iPhone of the counter filled with the organs and text it to Tyler.

I drop the beautiful fixings for the pasta-dish-to-be into a few small deli containers and send them to the very full freezer, knowing that they will be enjoyed soon.

With a good scrub, the counter is cleaned of the slime of chicken processing. The pig bucket is emptied into the pig pen trough, the pigs eagerly eating up every bit of refuse from the slaughter of a third of the chicken flock. In a few weeks I will tackle the next eight, but today I am imaging the livers and gizzards and hearts fried up and cooked into a rich, dark sauce. With luck, Tyler is ruminating on the same ideas while staring at the small, clear photo, imagining ways to coax the most flavors for the upcoming feast.

TEN

Four Days Before;
Foraging and Harvesting

October has finally arrived with all its glory. Summer gets all the attention in the garden—it is the time when culturally we expect there to be great amounts of produce from the earth—when in fact it is the fall when the earth gives up its bounty. The light is beautiful this time of year, the weather ideal and an overabundance of food makes it appear as though winter will never arrive.

The dinner is scheduled for this Saturday, a mere four days in the future. All of the prior preparations were merely theoretical. The tomato sauce could certainly have been made just to use through the winter; the cheese in the cave could be brought up and enjoyed when the weather turns cold. But now we have begun to prepare the actual meal. Without question twenty guests will descend on the farm at the end of this week and they have the expectation of being fed. The theoretical has now moved to the practical.

The weather has been both warm and a bit moist from some early rains. With luck I can find some mushrooms to add to the antipasti course. It is not certain that I can find an ample amount but it is likely. I must convince Michiko to assist me. Although the farm has a variety of terrain and trees, it is not reliable for mushroom foraging. A decade ago I cleared a bit of land in the center of the farm and burned the brush that was there. The next April I was most pleasantly surprised to find morels beneath the remaining birch trees. Even with these easily identified mushrooms, I laid them out on the kitchen counter together with a rather decorative 1936 *The Mushroom*

Handbook by Louis C. C. Krieger that I had picked up at the local thrift store years before and spent a tremendous part of the afternoon comparing the delicate watercolor plates with my newly found morels before I tentatively sautéed them and then ate them with caution. By the end of the afternoon I was convinced that the knobby fungi that I found on my farm were in fact *Morchella esculenta*, if not from their drawings in my field guide, then from the fact that they were quite tasty and I lived to sauté up a second batch.

Since that early foraging experience I have had no more sightings of morels on this bit of land. What I do find, however, are birch boletes. Or at least I think they are. Sadly my 1936 guide has beautiful colored plates that are artistic but not exactly detailed. This year I have found no such boletus around the confines of the farm property.

Although I still have that relic of early mycological identification, of late I have turned to a new friend on the island— Michiko. A spry fifty-something Japanese woman of uncommon enthusiasm, Michiko came to the farm by chance a few years earlier. A guest heading to the farm picked up her hitchhiking husband and brought him to join us for dinner. A moment after he entered the Cookhouse he called his wife and she quickly joined us that evening. Since that fateful evening she has consistently stopped by the back door to the kitchen with an abundance of mushrooms. And with her unbridled excitement in tow. At times this occurs when I am by myself having lunch, and at other times when the table is full of diners, unaware of why a Japanese sprite has descended on their dinner. When they realize she is carrying a handful of exceptional mushrooms destined for the dinner table, all apprehension is forgotten. She often is not just quietly carrying those beautiful fungi, but rather dances into the room with such pride and excitement that it is a bit disconcerting. She is all of five feet three inches tall, but she bounds into the room appearing to be a giant among us—exclaiming to all who will pay attention that she has found the largest chanterelle of the season. I guarantee that we all pay her rapt attention.

The uncertainty of her arrivals is exciting, but difficult to plan for when a special meal such as this one is planned. For this dinner I decided to alter our unspoken arrangement and ask her to take me foraging in time for a specific meal. Sadly, I don't have a way to contact Michiko. It is difficult for me to imagine her with a cell phone or an email address: vashonshroom23@gmail.com just seems so very unlike this woman. In all likelihood she does in fact check her email account regularly, post on Facebook daily and text incessantly to her friends from her cell phone. It is entirely possible that I have created a false persona for her, but I actually prefer it that way. She has a bit of mystery to her and I enjoy it. Luckily I do see her often at the local bank branch and make my request of her there. She agrees with less resistance than I'd expected. She agrees to take me out in time to find mushrooms for my dinner. I may have misunderstood, I am not entirely sure when she will arrive, but I am confident she will.

Dustin has come by the farm this morning to help me make tomato jam. He is entirely intrigued: accustomed to jam made from blackberries, or strawberries, or perhaps grapes, the idea of a sweet preserve made from tomatoes gets him to the farm to assist.

We begin by heading out to the gardens, where an entire bed is dedicated to Sun Gold tomatoes. They are cherry tomatoes, yellow and terribly sweet. I never staked them, so now at the end of the season they are sprawling, draping over the sides of the concrete beds and loaded with fruit. Much of the fruit is certainly ripe, but many have languished on the vine in the late-season sun and are distinctly overripe, bursting in half. In a matter of minutes we have large bowls filled with the best of the golden fruit. The bed is still covered in tomatoes, with little evidence that we removed any, despite each of us lugging an oversized stainless bowl filled with tomatoes.

The tomatoes are quickly washed in the deep prep sinks of the Cookhouse, the small yet firm stems tediously removed from each fruit. As with each project that Dustin and I attempt, the kitchen is filled with loud dance music and the constant patter of gossip. Together we measure out the cleaned fruit with oversized two-quart measuring pitchers, dumping the Sun Golds into the warped aluminum rondeau, making a quick mark on a piece of scrap paper for each time another two quarts are filled. When the rondeau is filled and the prep sink empty, we check the tally and calculate the number of quarts of tomatoes and the corresponding sugar needed according to the recipe. The tomatoes are sweetened half with white sugar, half with brown, and always more than seems possible. It is always the point in jam making when I want to look away; to not acknowledge the excess sugar needed to make fruit preserves.

As Katy Perry belts out her latest hit over the speakers, I move the wobbly rondeau onto the range and over the heat. A long wooden spoon is needed to mix the mountain of brown and white sugar with the many firm yellow tomatoes. Slowly the sugars begin to melt, and the tomatoes begin to burst as the pot warms up.

As I continue stirring, Dustin cleans up the counter filled with the many errant green stems, the sink littered with a few overripe tomatoes and the water that is splashed about from the washing. Astonishingly, our chatter has lulled a bit and only the beat of the music fills the room. And then the doors burst open and in walks Michiko.

She had been foraging this morning, and after the long dry spell of summer, the early fall rains have caused the mushrooms to blossom. I am surprised, but also relieved that she remembered that I needed mushrooms for Saturday's dinner. She insists—it takes little convincing, in actuality—that I drop what I am doing and join her. I hand the long wooden spoon to Dustin to stir with as the jam begins to bubble up, then I grab a large paper sack, a knife and a coat. Simply the idea that she insists that I bring a large sack with me convinces me of the ensured success of this venture.

I have never been in a car with Michiko and was not as trepidatious as I should have been. In the front seat of the old, small undistinguished car is her dog. I never knew she had a dog, despite her having been to the farm many times. She never mentioned him and he never has stepped out of the car while she has been at the farm. He is a beautiful deep-black-colored Lab, but smaller than most. He has a peacefulness to him that is intriguing. The term "old soul" immediately comes to my mind. He doesn't appear to be old in terms of age, but he is filled with such calmness that I am charmed. He gracefully slips from the front seat to the rear, hopping over the center console and between the two bucket seats.

And then Michiko starts the car and we begin the drive. I believe that to say that I was scared would be an overstatement. Death or dismemberment was not a likely outcome of the short trip across the island—but it was an unsettling ride.

Michiko's exuberance in life is equaled by her exuberance in driving. A nonstop story in broken English of mushrooms, the weather, foraging, the Fukushima nuclear disaster, meditation, banking and dogs fills the air. Her right foot hits the accelerator rapidly, repeatedly thrusting the car forward in unison with her discussion. The gas pedal becomes the de facto exclamation mark to her riveting story. The steering wheel holds no great role of punctuation, but rather rolls left and right with little regard for the lay of the road.

Thankfully, where we will be foraging is close to the farm and the drive is short, if not uneventful. The car is barely turned off when Michiko is out of the car, has opened up the back hatch to access our bags and knives and we are off down the path. I feel much more comfortable now. The conversation continues uninterrupted, but the terra firma is pleasing and reassures me that I will make it to see the intended mushrooms.

We walk rapidly through the forest, down paths and winding through the trees; she has obviously been here many times over the years and knows the area well. And then abruptly we stop as she looks for the spot where she saw the mushrooms earlier today. She is off by a few feet and it takes her perhaps three or four minutes to find the right entrance into the deep brush of the lush forest and find the exact spot. It is still remarkable, as she lifts up the low-level brush to reveal a small trove of white chanterelles.

These pale mushrooms are the cousins of the more common golden chanterelles. They have quickly sprouted on this coniferous floor beneath the tall stands of Douglas firs and hemlocks in the area. Although the summer has been remarkably dry, a bit of rain in the past few days has caused these small white delicacies to emerge.

Michiko gives me instructions as to how to harvest them, cutting them just below the level of the ground and leaving the least desirable to repopulate the area in the future. Her face lights up with an enormous smile as she leans down to the mushrooms and gently cuts the ones she likes. There are plenty for the meal Saturday even with leaving some behind. I silently question if the limited harvesting is based on their growth pattern or on her sense of keeping equilibrium with nature. It matters little which it is, or it might be both; it feels correct and is easily done.

We move around the area, finding a few more small stands of the barely visible mushrooms. We continue to cut and bag the best of them, filling the bags. When we have completed this section of the woods, Michiko promptly turns around and we are headed back to the car with her ever-obedient dog. My tendency would be to keep looking for more—always that sense of wanting more—but she has no interest in searching through the woods needlessly. We have enough. After a few minutes of walking we are back in the car and on the road and, after a quick, perilous U-turn, heading back to the farm, the accelerator pedal again demonstrating Michiko's endless enthusiasm and joy.

Back at the farm we divide up the cache of white gems. She takes half, and I the remaining half. She explains that these mushrooms, these *Cantharellus subalbidus*, are common enough for her to have complete confidence in their identification. If they were more rare, she would show them to someone with more experience for verification. It makes me realize that my nervousness about my long-ago foraging for morels was justified.

Once she has left the farm, I wrap the white chanterelles in moist paper and place them in the cooler, confident they will be in fine shape for the ensuing dinner in a few days, and return to Dustin and the tomato jam, which is still simmering on the range.

––––––

Wednesday: The weather has cleared from the rains earlier in the week. With the sun shining, the temperature rising and clear skies expected for the next few days I can begin the harvest in earnest. The onions will need the next couple days to dry in the sun, the potatoes just a day or two.

A full bed was dedicated to onions when they were planted out in the spring. Throughout the summer they slowly changed from the slim, wispy strips of green to bulbous, golden globes with the tall, rigid stalks about to go to seed by the beginning of October. Soon after finishing the morning milking I head into the garden and quickly pull up the onions and lay them on their sides on the dirt. My nature is to drop them randomly and haphazardly, with the only regard to leave them one layer deep. When I have used this method in the past, Jorge has come back after me and rearranged the onions so that they are in tidy rows, the bulbs cheek by jowl with the tall stalks withering in the heat lying parallel. No words are exchanged between us, but I feel scolded nonetheless. Now I attempt to line them up myself, knowing that these onions will neither prosper nor fail based on their alignment on the soil in their last days in the open air, but that my relationship with my employee of more than a decade will.

The onions have done better than in any previous year that I can remember. They are rotund, almost obscene in their grandeur, resembling the prize-winning examples at the state fairs where size matters more than anything. Even though I strive for great flavor, I take pride in their volume. Most likely the enormity of these alliums is the result of an abundance of compost in their bed and an ideal summer of little rainfall and adequate heat, but it is easy to fall into the trap of taking credit for their success. Conversely, the cabbages in the next bed that are downright Lilliputian are the result of unknown forces, in no way the result of my inadequate watering and general benign neglect.

In a very short few minutes the onions have been pulled from the ground and are drying in the midday heat. They will be left here for the next days until the outer skins are dry and until I can clip their fully wilted greenery and store them in the kitchen for use throughout the winter months.

Across the garden are two garden beds that were planted in winter squash. The vines trail up out of the beds and down into the gravel paths that separate the concrete beds. A motley collection of squashes were planted in the spring and now as the season ends different varieties are apparent. I unexpectedly find Blue Hubbards, bulbous and weighty, shaped like a balloon that has been overfilled with a surface crenellated and rough. The Rouge Vif d'Etampes scream heirloom squash for the Francophile. Their squat, irregular, garish-colored pumpkin shapes make the standard grocery store pumpkin appear classless and simple. They are the pumpkins of choice for the nouveau intelligentsia of the gardening world. Hidden among the others are Long Island Cheese, a variety that says solid, hearty, American sensibility, sturdiness and practicality. Those squashes are a dull putty color, vaguely pumpkin-shaped but with little to distinguish themselves. The flesh inside, however, makes up for any lack of pretension on their exterior: it is deep orange, firm and full of flavor.

The weather is expected to stay warm and relatively dry for the next couple weeks, and so I plan on keeping the majority of the squashes here on their vines in the cucurbit beds. Those extra fourteen-plus days can contribute to their sweetness of flesh and an increased firmness in the rind. As the dinner is scheduled, though, for this week, I will cut loose two large squashes from their vines and move them to the middle of the large garden to cure in the warm sun. The two that I have chosen are of a variety called Brodé Galeux d'Eysines, certainly the current cause célèbre of those who chase after the latest heirloom varieties. I must admit to falling prey to this squash's charms. A striking presentation sets this variety apart. It is *brodé*, as in "embroidered or embellished." And it is also *galeux*, which I learned so many years ago in French class means "mangy." And this fine squash is from Eysines, evidently a very small commune in Bordeaux, if the Wikipedia listing is correct. Visually these mangy squashes are large and lobed very slightly, almost salmon in color, nearly round in shape and adorned, or embroidered if you will, with warts. I know of no other produce to come from my garden that has these omnipresent bumps covering its skin. And I love that it has them. If the actual flesh of the squash was of poor quality, then all this mangy beauty would be for naught, but in fact it is superior in taste and texture. Firm, sweet, deeply colored and able to be transformed into a silky, full-flavored soup, these two Brodé Galeux d'Eysines are the perfect choice for the soup course for dinner. I cut the stems a few inches long, and release the squashes from the entangled vines, setting them down on the gravel to dry and cure for the next few days. Also on the menu is pickled pumpkin for the antipasti course. I find a Long Island Cheese variety that is smaller than the others and cut it free as well, bringing it inside to for the pick-led pumpkin slices.

I find it sad that the term *pickles* so firmly means pickled cucumbers in our collective culinary minds. I do wish that we could liberate the meaning, opening it up to define pickles as simply a fruit or vegetable or perhaps even a nut that is trans-formed with vinegar. In the hopes of moving this along, I prefer to pickle anything but cucumbers. My choice for Saturday's dinner is to serve pickled pumpkin.

It is a bit unusual, but really shouldn't be. Pumpkins fit all of the criteria of a delightful pickled product: firm, full-flavored, colorful and available in excess at harvest time. Per-haps I like to pickle pumpkins simply because I need every possible method to rid myself of the abundant squashes this time of year.

The Long Island Cheese variety is ideal. As I look at it, it really does resemble a cheese: squat and putty-colored, dull in appearance and weighty. Not sure why the "Long Island" is there, but I agree with the "Cheese" part of the name.

I split the squash in half to remove the seeds. A quick scrape with the edge of a spoon and the moist interior is removed for the pigs' enjoyment. Then the exterior rind is sliced off with a long-bladed knife. What remains is an awkward shape of beau-tifully colored, firm squash. The trick then is to find a block of squash within that odd half sphere to slice into the eventual pickles. Certainly a lot of waste in involved, but the pigs will relish the bits and pieces of culled squash.

When a suitable long, vaguely rectangular block is freed, I take a mandoline to slice the squash thinly and consistently. The mandoline is a kitchen tool of remarkable use, yet sur-prisingly simple to use. Technology has changed in the three decades since I began working in restaurants. At that time the only mandolines were bulky, heavy French contraptions made of steel. Their primary function was to slice potatoes with a waffle pattern for *pommes gaufrettes*. Although I miss the days of classic French cuisine being the *ne plus ultra* of dining, I don't miss slicing potatoes for that beautiful but tedious dish. The goal was to slice the spuds with a crenellated design on one side, then to turn the potatoes ninety degrees, cut the next slice with the same ribbed design, turn ninety degrees again and continue. The result, when it worked well, was a woven pattern of potato chips that were then deep-fried. Beautiful, yes, but terribly tedious. Thankfully they went out of fashion around 1980. The mandoline continues, however. Now made of plastic in Japan for a quarter the price and seemingly absent of that annoying ribbed blade.

With a simple, straight blade, a series of identical slices can be achieved, thinly and easily. In essence a mandoline is a long, flat rectangular board with the sharp blade halfway down the rectangular plane. The vegetable—in this case the pumpkin— is slid down the plastic trough and the edge against the board hits the sharp blade and a thin slice is cut from the squash and falls down below the board. The pumpkin is then slid back up to the top and the run is made once again, until all of the pumpkin lies beneath the mandoline in identical thin slices.

There is a small challenge to the efficacy of the simple tool. It is unable to decipher the difference between the firm, orange flesh of the Long Island Cheese and the less firm, pale flesh of my knuckles. Never have I used a mandoline without losing a thin slice of skin. Today was no exception.

The task of slicing the squash, however painful, is quick. When the squash is prepared and sliced, I turn to the vinegar. I measure out the white vinegar with some water to bring the acid level down a bit. I fill a small saucepan with the mixture and add in some smashed garlic and some large chunks of onion. Some sugar and salt are thrown in as well and then a couple of fresh bay leaves from the trees in front of the Cookhouse. I crush the leaves a bit to release their oils. In the kitchen are a couple of spices—coriander and black peppercorns—neither were grown here, but I think they will add a bit of flavor to the pickles and so I include those in the vinegar mixture on the stove. I turn on the flame and begin to warm the vinegar. In a couple of minutes it will be boiling. While waiting, I return to the pumpkin slices.

I find an ample plastic square container, and transfer the stack of pumpkin slices resembling a deck of playing cards into it. Once it boils, the hot vinegar mixture is poured over the awaiting squash, and the container is covered with its lid. I like to check it a few minutes into its steeping while the vinegar is still steaming. The smell is intoxicating—sour, acid yet, sweet and flavorful because of the squash. It still burns my nose as I inhale deeply, aware that this a part of the process I always indulge in.

Over the course of the next few hours as the vinegar slowly cools down, the pickles will cook and soften slightly, and by Saturday evening the sliced pumpkin with be fully pickled.

Once I get the pumpkin slices covered with the vinegar, I decide to take a break and hop in the truck and head down to Burton to pick up the beef roast stored in the freezer. It is a ten-minute drive, pleasant, as the barely busy Vashon Highway enters the small town of Burton and the speed limit drops to twenty-five miles per hour. Few notice or care, as the traffic is much less than half of that at the busy intersection in the town of Vashon. I pull into one of the many open parking spots on the side of Sandy's general store. As I enter, I realize that I recognized a friend's car parked next to mine. In my hand is the minuscule toy key that will unlock the equally tiny padlock in the freezer. My friend, standing at the counter chatting with Sandy, immediately recognizes me and we begin a short chat, catching up on news of her extended family and gossip of her neighbors from Burton. I am thankful for this brief interruption. Sandy, at her station behind the counter next to the microwave and cash register and stack of daily newspapers, appears to notice my connection to this local resident. I feel my standing in the community of Burton rise immediately. Even though I have lived more than two decades near the larger town of Vashon, I have little or no standing in this tradition-bound community. Within a short walk of this store are the best beaches on the islands, and with them are the beach houses owned by families of long-standing histories. Owning a farm on the top of the island gives me no credibility with Sandy. Knowing her neighbors brings me a modicum of respectability.

Brandishing my toy key ring, I end my conversation and head to the back of the store, nodding to Sandy my intentions as if I have been coming here for decades. As fast as I can, I hustle in, leaving the icy door wide open, grab the leg roast and a bit of skirt steak as well and head back into the bright, warm store. In a few minutes, I am back on the highway heading back to the twenty-first century, my beef in tow.

Pulling the onions from the ground and picking out the squash took only a hour at most, the trip to Burton perhaps another hour. When I have returned to the farm, I place the roast and skirt into the sink to defrost and head over to the line of fruit trees that run from the vegetable garden to the Cook-house and that form the orchard. Halfway down the row and closest to the garden is the quince tree, full of fruit.

The quince was one of the first two trees planted here when I moved to what is now Kurtwood Farms in 1991. As such, it is twenty-plus years old and fully producing. I wish I could say that I had put a great deal of thought into the fruit trees planted at that time, but rather it was most likely on sale at a local nursery and I had always wanted a quince tree and subsequently I planted it. I do remember it being a tall, thin whip of a tree when it went into the ground, much taller than others here. Most likely no one was interested in quince at the time and it spent a longer time at the nursery than the other, more popular fruit trees. Purely speculation at this point, but most likely.

That first winter I did back over the freshly planted sapling with my pickup truck. Not so badly that I killed it, but I permanently gave the trunk a wayward angle. Even with such disregard from myself, the quince has outperformed every other tree on the farm, producing crates of beautiful fruit every year.

The quince, or *Cydonia oblonga*, may very well be my most favorite fruit. Granted, part of that specialness is that it is not terribly well known and that it is impossible to eat fresh off of the tree. Quinces are one of the very few fruits that must be cooked to be enjoyed. There is a great pleasure in the cooking and serving of these beautiful fruits, but also in sharing them with others for the first time. Visitors will often find a quince in the kitchen in late fall, and quickly approach it, expecting it to be a familiar pear or perhaps an apple. When they are close to picking it up, they realize that in fact it is not one of those common pomes but rather an unknown, and stop short in bewilderment. Introducing freshmen such as Dustin to the enjoyments of this favorite of mine is exciting every time it occurs.

The quince tree is similar in appearance to an apple or pear, although the bark is smoother than either of those. The leaves are large and droopy, with a deep green color, and remind me of a lazy hound dog's ears, at the end of fall. The fruits are essentially pear shaped except that they are more like an overweight pear, a bit more robust at the bottom than the trim gym body of a Bartlett. Before they are ripe, quinces have a fuzz or fur that is termed a pubescence, a term that I feel makes this noble fruit sound like a sex offender or such. But when fully ripe that fur disappears and a smooth, nearly glossy, deeply yellow skin replaces it. Although the taste of the cooked quince is remarkable, it is the overwhelming scent of the raw, fresh quince that is one of its greatest glories. It is a scent like perfume: sweet, pungent and full. I am reminded of my grandmother's ever-present lily of the valley, but with a fruitiness rather than a floral nature. Whereas my grandmother's scent could be just too much at times with little variation, the quince scent is never enough for me. When the fruits are first brought into the Cookhouse the smell begins to climb and I expect that it will continue for weeks.

The unique nature of the quinces is that they are extremely firm-fleshed when picked off the tree. Truly ripe, but not in any way tender. The only way to release their flavor is to cook them. With heat, the flesh breaks down into a flavorful mash.

The quinces will be utilized today for membrillo, or quince paste, sometimes known as quince cheese. This membrillo is in no way a cheese in nature, nor would I call it a paste, implying sticky and unctuous. It is in fact closer in form to a French *pâte de fruits*, which you could certainly translate as fruit paste. Maybe *jelly* is an apt description for this delectable treat. The plan is to cook the quinces down with a bit of water and more than a bit of sugar until it is thick and nearly rigid, so that when it cools it can stand up rigid and be cut into squares for the antipasti course of dinner.

I pick a dozen of the oblong, bulbous fruits from the tree loaded with such pendulous fruits. I choose those that have lost their pubescent fuzz, are bright yellow in color and that come off of the tree with a swift yet complete snap of the stem. I fill the crate I brought along from the kitchen quickly with the easily reached quinces. It is hard for me not to be reminded of conversations with lawyers in the past about the concept of the "low-hanging fruit." They were not speaking of harvesting quinces to make membrillo, but rather the tendency of litigants to attack the most likely source of redress in a lawsuit, looking for the best chance of getting paid in a lawsuit by picking those most likely to pay. There are no litigants here, no issues to redress, but rather simply a crate full of fragrant fruits.

It is midday and I want to get started cooking the quinces so that I have ample time for the membrillo to finish cooking today. The quinces are first peeled, then quartered and the cores cut out of their firm flesh. They are tremendously difficult to cut and I worry about slipping with the paring knife and

cutting my hand rather than the rigid fruit. I do find it imperative to remove all of the core, seeds and peel at this time rather
than have those appear later in the final membrillo.

In a few minutes I have worked my way through the entire
nine pounds of quince. I could save the peels and use them
to flavor simple syrup by boiling them in sugar water, but I
choose to send them to the pigs instead. With more free time
I would utilize all the little bits, but today my mind is on the
dinner Saturday and not on maximizing the harvest.

On the shelf under the prep table is an old balance scale
that I bought at an antique store thirty-plus years ago together
with a set of steel weights I brought back from London a
couple of years later. It is a heavy, clumsy piece of technology but one that I prefer tremendously. On one side of the balance is a large welcoming brass pan and on the other side a
flat iron plate to hold the weights. I load the brass pan with
the cut and trimmed quinces and then weigh them by adding
and subtracting weights to the other side. A combined five-
pound and a one-pound weight is too much, I lose the one-
pounder and the fiver is too little. I add a half-pound weight
to the existing fiver and it is still too little to raise the opposing brass of quince. A four-ounce lump of iron is too heavy but
just barely, so I switch to a two ounce and a one-ounce brass
disk and the quinces on one side of the scale rise half way
in unison with the small pile of iron and brass objects on the
other. The weight of the quinces: five pounds eleven ounces.
Certainly a modern digital scale is quicker and most probably
more accurate but it lacks the tactile nature of this favorite
piece of kitchen equipment.

This recipe also calls for equal parts of quince and granu-
lated white sugar, so it is straightforward to pick up the brass
pan from the scale and slide the trimmed quinces off into a
thick-bottomed rondeau and return the pan to the scale. On
the other side the weights remain. It is simple to pour white
sugar into the brass pan until the weights begin to rise and

then balance. Presto, I now have equal weights of quince and sugar.

The sugar is poured into the rondeau with the quinces, a bit of water is added to keep the quinces from sticking and the pan is put over the flame to heat. At this point a great transformation will take place. What were crude hunks of firm fruit with little possibility of being edible will slowly change to a pan of soft, fragrant, sweet, flavorful quince in a matter of time. The color is the most unexpected transformation. The raw fruit is barely yellow with little to distinguish it. With the addition of heat it will change to a lovely rose color and, with continued cooking, to the deep red of the final quince paste. More water may be needed to keep the quince from sticking as it moves from soft pieces of fruit to what resembles rose-colored applesauce. I convince myself that it is imperative to taste the quince often at this point, although there is no such necessity except to appease my desire to enjoy this sweet, flavorful delicacy.

The difficulty of this recipe is in knowing how long to cook this quince puree. The goal is a thick, almost sticky paste that, once cooled, will set into a jelly—rigid and with the ability to be cut. Quinces are noted for their high level of pectin, capable of creating this jellylike consistency, but adequate cooking is still necessary. If it is inadequately cooked the paste will be simply a sticky mess—a tasty sticky mess, but lacking in the rigidity desired. If it is overcooked, then it will begin to gel up in the pan and must be broken up to pour it into a final tray.

After much trial and error, the proper consistency can be found. Pulling out a spoonful and letting it cool is the best method of trial. When it appears complete, pour the deep red warm fruit onto a plastic-lined sheet tray large enough that the entire quince paste will finish at three-quarters of an inch. A bit more trial and error may be needed here as well.

The sheet tray with the cooling quince paste is then left to dry out. If it is slow to firm up it can be placed in the oven overnight with the pilot on but the heat off. By dinner on Saturday it will be firmly jellylike and can be cut into squares for the antipasti course alongside the cheese, pickles and crackers. My last task of the day is to grab the plastic-wrapped cuts of beef from the prep sink, place both in a small hotel pan and then in the cooler to stay cold until they are needed. They are both nearly defrosted, and will be ready for us on Saturday morning.

ELEVEN

Milk, Cream and Butter

This morning the older cows have all been milked: Dinah, Flora, Andi, Martha and 4 x 4. The last one in line is Alice, still new to the whole experience but much more competent than she was in the first few days. This morning her milk is exceptional: there is no sign of the thick colostrum, and the swelling of her udders has abated.

Although the usual procedure during the milking is to pour the fresh milk directly from the milking can into the bulk tank to cool as soon as the can is full, today I am changing that procedure. We need butter and cream for dinner tomorrow and the best way to capture the heavy cream from the milk is by using a cream separator. The great requirement of the separator, however, is fresh warm milk. Hence, I pour milk from the milking can into two large plastic buckets in the milk room. When I have finished milking the six cows, including the young Alice, I will have fifteen gallons of beautiful fresh warm milk.

The separator is in essence a centrifuge. At its core is a rapidly spinning disk that divides the milk's components into heavier and lighter parts. Cream is lighter than milk and can be separated by this rapid spinning.

Prior to this invention the only way to capture the cream was to allow the milk to sit for hours until the heavier milk naturally fell to the bottom of the container and the lighter cream rose to the top. Today I could do this by turning off the agitator in the bulk tank. The refrigeration would continue operating but without the paddle stirring the milk and keeping the cream in suspension. By morning the cream would rise to the top, where it could be skimmed. This works adequately when a sophisticated bulk tank is involved, but on a small farm of a hundred years ago it would not have existed.

A few years ago an older man came to my farm and saw the cream separator sitting in my milk room. I knew how it worked and had used it often, but I never really understood its importance. He explained that he had grown up on a farm in rural Michigan in a very remote area. The farm was too isolated to make it possible to truck the milk from the dairy into a processor every day or every couple of days. If they had had to store the milk for an extended amount of time it would have taken the addition of large costly bulk tanks, something they were unable to do.

When the cream separator came along, it changed the nature of his family's farm. Each morning and evening they would process the milk from their cows, separating the cream and the milk. The milk would go to the pigs, the calves and the farm family to consume. The cream would be chilled, held and then after a few days they would drive it into the nearest town and sell it or use it to make butter that they could sell. The selling of the cream supported the small farm without their having to invest in large costly refrigeration and transportation equipment. It was the reduction of the volume that made it work. The sheer bulk of all of the milk was difficult to cool and store. The much smaller volume of the higher-valued cream could be sold profitably.

I originally owned a large 1940s motor-driven cream separator that someone on the island had given me in order to get it out of their garage. While trying to get it working—eventually I concluded it was missing a pivotal part—I looked into the crafty machines. One of the most amazing tidbits of information was the number of these machines sold in the early part of the twentieth century in this country. Millions of these centrifuges graced the barns and farmhouses of pre–World War II America. This one invention transformed small family farms in the decades between the two world wars. Oddly, few of the original separators remain. A few show up rusted-out at barn sales and the like, but most are missing key components. The reason is that, because they had a fast-spinning centrifuge in them, they were made of heavy, solid cast iron, to stabilize them. When the Second World War approached, those not in use were quickly melted down as scrap iron for the war effort.

I tried out the large donated one, but could never find the missing part needed to utilize it. Instead I went to eBay to purchase a new version of the hundred-plus-year-old technology. Oddly, I found one in Eastern Europe, an unlikely locale. My only guess is that small family farms continue to exist in the former Soviet Bloc countries and that consequently manufacturers remain to supply them. This new Ukrainian model is essentially the same apparatus that Gustav de Laval invented in Sweden in the nineteenth century.

The modern Ukrainian model is efficient, although tedious, and now I spend an hour hand-cranking the machine, watching as the level of the whole milk drops and the large stainless-steel bowls below fill with the skimmed milk and the heavy cream.

The skimmed milk is poured into the now-empty plastic containers and is returned to the milk room to be poured into the bulk tank and chilled down for cheese making. The cream is poured into the vintage glass bowl of the butter churn, to be made into butter for tomorrow's feast.

I assemble the butter churn, screwing the dasher into the motor and screwing the motor housing onto the top of the glass jar filled with the fresh cream. The long black cord is plugged in and immediately the cream begins to whirl around the vintage glass jar.

While the cream is churning on the counter, I head out to the chicken tractor to feed the remaining laying hens, move the tractor to new grass and pick up today's eggs. The tractor is located in the small orchard near the Cookhouse, midway between the Italian prune plum and the Seckel pear. The chickens see me coming and begin to get excited, pleased to be fed the grain that they enjoy. I shy away from anthropomorphizing animals, but at times it feels comforting. It is probably a good bet that they enjoy eating and they connect my arriving and their getting fed. I pull the lightweight coop to its new location quickly and easily. The chickens leave the shadow of the plum tree and head down to the William's Pride apple neighborhood. I pour a small pail's worth of grain through the perforated lid of the tractor onto the hens as they gather where they know the grain will land. The water pail on the top of the tractor is nearly dry and so I unconnect the drain hose and refill it at the frost-free water faucet nearby, return to the tractor and reconnect the hose to fill the small watering bowls in the interior of the chicken tractor.

At the end of the aluminum traveling hen home are the three nesting boxes. The chickens can enter them from their interior space, and I can lift open the individual exterior lids to access the boxes. Each of the three has a base of straw and today each has a few eggs nestled in the straw, laid since yesterday's feeding. One nest has three, another five and the third just two. The eggs are thankfully clean, and a couple are still warm to the touch.

The eggs will be used in the preparation of tomorrow's feast. Eggs are needed for the pasta, the tomato upside-down cake, the béarnaise sauce and will be poached for the egg course of the meal. I have been saving eggs all week.

When I return to the Cookhouse the cream is nearly fully churned. Good thing I didn't get distracted and wander off to another project, ignoring the butter in process on the counter. I drain the butter into a metal sieve, capturing the buttermilk to feed the pigs. When the butter has drained adequately I rinse it under the spray nozzle of the large sink with cold water, rinsing away as much buttermilk as possible. When the water runs clear, the butter is left to drain in its sieve. In a few hours I will form the butter, pushing out the rest of the water and salting the rich, golden final product.

I turn my attention to making the ricotta. This ricotta needed for tomorrow's dinner is not the common variety found in the grocery stores, based on milk, but rather is a *whey* ricotta, based on that by-product of cheese making.

The dividing of the curds and whey from the formerly liquid milk is the essence of cheese making. The curds becomes the cheese, the whey is left over.

The whey has characteristics that make it difficult to simply discard. It is acidic from the introduction of cultures that convert the lactose to lactic acid, and it contains residual proteins. The primary protein, casein, is retained in the curds, but other proteins, including albumin and globulin, remain.

I look at the utilization of the whey primarily as a business decision. I have paid for the land and the development and cultivating and liming of the pastures. The fences and gates and the water lines are paid for as well. A barn was built for the cows, along with a number of smaller structures. The cows are paid for and fed costly grains and hay throughout their lifetime. One of my employees brought the cows down to the milking parlor, milked them, chilled the milk and washed up all of the equipment, all while on the clock. Another employee made beautiful cheese from that fresh milk, spending hours in the process, all at an expense.

And then 60 percent of the volume of that milk I have invested heavily in over the years I should simply pour down the drain? The reality is that almost all of it is fed to the pigs, who thrive on it. I do insist, however, on making ricotta from it when time permits. It is tasty and luscious and rich. And there is a bit of magic to its preparation.

Yesterday I made cheese in the make room. Overnight the cheeses sat in their molds on the draining table, the whey slowly exiting from the curds ladled into those molds. The whey runs down the long stainless-steel draining tables into large white plastic buckets set on the floor. By this morning those buckets are full of the nearly clear, slightly greenish-yellow liquid. The riboflavin present in the whey gives it that telltale color. The taste is slightly sweet and it has an acid edge to it. The lactic acid strengthens overnight and through the day.

By this afternoon the liquid is sour. I bring the three large three-gallon buckets into the Cookhouse and pour them into the expansive, oversized stockpot that generally resides far back on the lower shelf of the kitchen and which is used for making ricotta and for canning. The pot is nearly filled.

I add to the yellow-green liquid a large pitcher of whole milk that I can scoop out of the bulk tank in the milk room. It will augment the volume of the finished ricotta. It is not essential, but if I am going to go through this allocation of time and effort, I would prefer to render the largest quantity possible.

The bulky stockpot straddles two of the burners on the gas range, which I turn up to high, the flames hitting two sides of the heavy-bottomed stainless steel pot. After a few minutes the fats from the rich, whole milk will curdle in the acid of the whey. It looks odd and not appealing but will be fully absorbed by the end of the ricotta-making process.

Slowly, over the course of nearly an hour, the temperature of the whey will rise. It will begin to steam and get a bit frothy on top. The intended goal is to heat the whey and milk mixture to 180 degrees.

While the whey is slowly heating, I turn my attention to preparing the two doughs needed for tomorrow's dinner: pizza dough and bread dough for the rolls. They are essentially the same. Both are basic bread doughs with just a few ingredients: flour, salt, yeast, water, sugar, the pizza dough with a bit of fat added.

When I was twenty-four I opened a small coffee shop in a neglected part of downtown Seattle. Each afternoon I would prepare this bread dough, mixing it in the small stand mixer, then leaving it to rest during the late afternoon and chilling it overnight. In the early morning hours I would form small rolls, allow them to rise on top of the small oven and bake them in time for the early commuters heading into their offices. Served with butter and a bit of jam, they were a very popular item and I kept them on the menu for years. When I started up the Cookhouse dinners, I pulled the old, crusty recipe from my files and began to make these rolls again. At the end of the run of the Cookhouse dinners, the ultimate validation of this simple recipe came my way when Martha Stewart asked me to come to New York City and make these rolls for her on her live television show. Thankfully I had made them hundreds of times and was able to competently prepare them in that stressful situation.

This afternoon I pull out the small stand mixer and place it on the counter, hooking the bowl and dough hook into place. The warm water is added to the bottom of the bowl, a bit of sugar and the yeast floated on top. In the days of the café I would use molasses as the sweetener that would drive the yeast, but today I only have white sugar around and it works equally well. I watch the drab tan kernels of yeast float across the warm water, the shiny crystals of sugar piled on the bottom of the bowl, the yeast begin to agitate and dive to the bottom and then quickly bloom and explode, bouncing up to the surface and in a couple more minutes frothing on the top of the warm water. This simple act of watching the proofing of the yeast, peering over the rim of the stainless steel bowl locked in the mixer, takes me back to the past. The process never changes, never veers.

Once the yeast has proofed, I add the flour, a bit of whole wheat flour for texture and the salt, and knead it until it has formed a coherent ball. The dough is heavy and strains the small home-model mixer. The machine bounces around and appears to walk across the counter. In a couple of minutes the dough is adequately kneaded in the machine and I turn it off, lower the bowl and disentangle the strong dough from the grip of the dough hook. I could most likely use it as it is, but I lightly dust the wooden counter and begin to knead the dough by hand. It is a tactile experience, and soothing and reflective. I have done this physical task many times, each of them essentially the same: pushing forward with the heels of both hands to smear out the ball, pulling it back with both sets of fingers, then turning and folding it over into a ball and continuing the process, stopping every two or three cycles to further dust the counter as the flour is consumed by the ever-smoother ball.

At last I place the dusted and smooth ball into a large stainless steel bowl and set it aside. I turn back to the mixer and start a second batch, the same as the first. While the yeast is beginning to proof, I return to the whey on the range and stir it and check on the temperature, keeping my eye on it throughout the process of making the doughs.

When the second batch is ready, I turn it out onto the board like the first, kneading it well and adding it to the first bowl. A third batch is made, the same as the first two, but with a lump of pork lard added to the slightly hotter water. I let the lard slowly melt, pooling on the top of the sweetened water, before adding the sprinkled dry yeast. The pizza dough will only contain a tiny amount of yeast in comparison to the hard rolls. Over the course of the evening the yeast added to the pizza dough will grow tremendously, enough to give the dough the rise it needs. Even though the hard rolls also have a lengthy all-night rise, they have a normal amount of yeast added to give them a rich, yeasty flavor.

I add a little less flour to the pizza dough during the process as well. The final ball of dough, kneaded by hand like the others, will be slightly wetter, slightly slicker and smell nicely of pork. This third ball of dough will be shaped and tossed in the air and flavored with tomato sauce and herbs and chilies and baked in the hot brick oven outside the doors of the kitchen. The mixer, the bowl, the dough hook are cleaned, the bread dough and the pizza dough are resting in their stainless-steel bowls, slowly beginning to rise in the warm kitchen. I cover them with plastic wrap to keep them from drying out and return to the butter, which has been draining through the afternoon.

The majority of the buttermilk has drained from the fresh butter, but a bit of water and buttermilk remains. I sprinkle the butter with an ample amount of coarse kosher salt and with gloved hands I reach in and grab the sieve full of butter. I knead the errant bits of butter into a large cohesive ball, squeezing out the moisture, incorporating the salt at the same time. Two small ramekins are filled with the luscious butter, destined for the table, and the rest is placed in a stainless-steel bowl, wrapped with plastic and put in the cooler to chill overnight.

All the while I was making the doughs and the butter I have kept my eye on the large stockpot on the range, which was slowing heating up. It is now beginning to steam and is nearly ready. I made this ricotta many times before I finally read up on the technical end of the process. The whey contains the remaining proteins of albumin and globulin, even though the majority of the casein from the milk resides in the curds. The ricotta is produced by isolating the proteins and capturing them. The trick to this is to denature the proteins, a term I have a gut sense of, but most likely the lessons of my chemistry classes of thirty years earlier have long since vanished. In essence the form of the proteins is changed. Two characteristics of this process contribute to this. The first is the high acid level of the whey and the second is the temperature of the whey. Both make the proteins unstable and allow them to be released by the solution.

When the temperature has risen to nearly the requisite 180 degrees, I salt the whey. Honestly, I don't know why. I was taught to add salt at this stage, but I am not confident that it contributes to the process. The final product does need to be seasoned, but it is possible that it could be accomplished later in the process. I continue to add a half a cup of kosher salt to the hot, steaming liquid each time, however.

Sometimes I use a thermometer to check the temperature, sometimes I rely on luck and my experience, but the needed temperature is visible. It is not boiling: that is 212. It is not even simmering. It is that sweet spot when it is steaming and you can anticipate small bubbles before it begins to simmer.

Hitting the intended temperature is important, however, for two reasons. If it is too cool, then the proteins will stay in their original form and will not break out of the liquid. And if it is too hot, the proteins will come out of suspension, land on the bottom of the hot stockpot and burn. If the former is done, it can be reheated, if the latter, there is no solution; it must be discarded and the pot cleaned at the cost of great effort and time.

The magic is the temperature in the middle—neither cold enough to keep the proteins locked up, nor hot enough to cause them to scorch. That 180 degrees causes the proteins to precipitate in the whey. It is entirely as the word describes—it *precipitates*—it is as if it is snowing deep in the pot of steaming liquid; reminds me of a snow globe. You peer down over the high sides of the stockpot into the diorama scene of the yellow-green liquid and then, deep down within, it begins to snow: softly and slightly at first. Then it looks a little cloudy, and finally small specks of white appear.

I continue to stir the pot, trying to keep the bits of white from settling onto the hot bottom and sides of the stockpot where they could stick. Once I am confident that the whey is hot enough and that the albumin and globulin are falling out of the whey, I turn off the two flames beneath the pot and stop stirring.

After a minute or two the whey that I kept in motion with my constantly moving long-handled spoon slows down and comes to a stop. The small particles of ricotta slowly continue to precipitate and then casually fall to the bottom. I will not touch the pot for a couple of hours, allowing it to fully settle and cool.

When I return to the pot, the ricotta has landed on the bottom. I cannot see how much or even if it has, but the liquid on top is completely clear. It still retains that yellow-green of the riboflavin, but it is no longer opaque. I take it on faith that this indicates the absence of the proteins in the liquid.

In a deep sink next to the range, I set up a tall colander. On top of the colander I place a large stainless-steel wire sieve. The colander is there just to support the wide sieve during the draining of the ricotta. In the base of the sieve I lay a piece of washed cheesecloth. Carefully I take a two-quart plastic pitcher and scoop from the top of the stockpot, pouring it into the muslin-lined sieve in the sink. The clear whey runs through the setup, draining into the sink. Scoop by scoop I lower the level of the stockpot until the action of scooping out the whey causes the frail ricotta on the bottom to be disturbed and the liquid that I scoop out is progressive more cloudy with the white precipitation and less filled with the clear liquid whey.

The fine mesh of the cloth stops the ricotta from passing through the sieve. In a few minutes the deep sieve is filled with a slurry of white ricotta, slowly draining through the cheesecloth. As the pores of the cloths fill with the cheese, the whey will drain slower and slower. After a few more scoops with the plastic pitcher it will be barely a dribble from the bottom of the sieve and I will stop before adding another pitcher from the voluminous pot. Over the course of an hour the sieve will drain enough for me to empty the entire contents of the stockpot into the cheesecloth-lined strainer.

The ricotta will drain through the night, the remaining whey exiting through the colander on the base of the sink. It will be white, fresh and bright; smooth and silky and very much different from the more grainy, gritty qualities of the store-bought whole-milk variation.

The stockpot will be less than fresh and bright. Even with

the careful watching and stirring and diligence, some of the ricotta will have stuck to the hot sides and bottom of the expansive kettle. It is not an insurmountable task, cleaning and scraping down the crusted-on milk solids, but it does distract from the enjoyment of the finished product.

When I had first started my creamery here, I intended to save all of the whey from the cheese making and then transfer it back into the cheese vat, cook it and create the ricotta for commercial sales. My first and only commercially intended batch was tragic.

In the vat was forty gallons of beautiful whey, slowly heating by way of the hot water jacket that surrounds the large, robust vat. The make room was correspondingly slowly filling with steam, the small, not particularly well-vented room never designed for steaming-hot liquid. It was a warm summer day when I performed this task and very quickly I had discarded my lab coat and long-sleeved shirt for the thin white T-shirt I wore underneath. Soon I was standing over the steaming vat, sweating profusely, an image of a muscled Italian cheese maker in Naples coming to my mind.

I brought the whey up to the requisite 180 degrees after nearly two hours of cooking and then proceeded to allow the nearly boiling liquid to cool and settle. It was an equally long period before the suspended ricotta settled to the bottom, and then I hooked up a series of valves and elbows and piping and fittings to drain the whey out of the bottom side of the tank into awaiting strainers and buckets and cheesecloth. The release of all that not-cool-enough whey filled the room with even more steam, and the floor filled with buckets of whey.

The resulting ricotta was divine: fresh and creamy and easily salable. Even with my unexpected afternoon of sauna I could envision this daily process. And then I looked into the vat.

The large stainless steel Dutch vat has a double wall of thick steel, with heating elements and water jackets. It is designed to hold the heat efficiently. When I am making cheese the milk will maintain its desired temperature of ninety degrees for two or three hours with no problem. It is a great asset to have a cheese vat well insulated.

When I looked into that beautiful vat of mine, it was completely coated with cooked-on milk solids. I was still hopeful at this point until I took a small plastic scrubber to it, expecting it to fall away gracefully. In fact it stubbornly adhered, refusing to let go of the shiny stainless steel. Water was sprayed in, dairy detergents were used, I enlisted the help of Jorge's wife for an afternoon and finally it was cleaned. The great worry was that the integrity of the pasteurizing could be compromised if any milk films remained. If fresh raw milk was added the next day to make cheese and it was not adequately pasteurized, then it was potentially possible for pathogens to pass through the milk and into the cheese.

I ditched the idea of producing and selling fresh whey ricotta that next day. In a small batch on the stovetop it is a great task; in volumes of forty gallons, less so. Today's batch was well worth the effort and will be enjoyed at tomorrow's dinner without question.

It is late by the time I finish up in the kitchen. In the far sink is the ricotta draining in the sieve; I can hear the whey dribbling slowly out of the bottom, hitting the base of the sink in an intermittent patter. I move the two bowls of doughs to the refrigerator. Both the pizza dough and the dinner-roll dough have risen through the late afternoon and into the evening, filling the large stainless-steel bowls completely, pushing up against the plastic wrap that desperately is trying to contain them. I remember to grab the gizzards and livers from the house freezer, pulling the two small containers and moving them to the refrigerator to defrost. By the time they are needed tomorrow evening, they will be fully thawed.

The sun has long since set and it is completely dark outside; with the bright lights of the kitchen reflecting off the windows, I can see nothing outside. Byron has been asleep underneath the table for hours; Daisy left for the Log House soon after I made them their dinner.

I flip off the lights over the stove and counters, and proceed to dim the lights in the alcove and the bathroom. When the room begins to darken, Byron instinctively wakes up and begins his laborious walk down the length of the dining table, exiting between the end chairs, knowing that it is time to head to the Log House for the night. He looks terribly put out by this demand on his time and energy. I could leave him here all night sleeping on the bright red kilims that are underneath the table, but I know that he insists on sleeping on his lumpy pillow at the base of my bed. I open one of the clumsy French doors and reach over to hit the switch that controls the bright halogen lights focused on the top of the fir table. As I reach over, Byron passes through the door and heads down the sidewalk, through the bay trees and over to the front door of the Log House.

I take this moment to pause. All I can hear in the still night is the sound of Byron's nails slowly hitting the concrete on his short walk and the dripping of the whey as it hits the sink. No sounds come from outside; the cows are long since ensconced in the field, the pigs and chickens are asleep and no cars can be heard heading down the highway just over the tree line.

In a few hours' time, the sun will come up and this room will fill with life. Tyler and Jorge will arrive, the cows will line up to be milked, the wood oven will be lit and the stereo will begin cranking with classic rock. In the afternoon the twenty guests will arrive and the mood and sounds and feelings will increase tenfold. Even though I have served these dinners more than two hundred times, I find it hard to believe on this still, quiet, dark evening. I flip the switch and the halogen lights slowly lose their brightness; the room goes dark and I too head over to the Log House to get some sleep before the big day begins.

TWELVE

Saturday Morning; Tyler Arrives

Byron is a cruel dog. Not intentionally cruel, but his inadvertent actions cause me to believe he is cruel. He spent the bulk of the night walking up and down the staircase of the Log House, periodically stopping for a few minutes to lie down next to my bed with great aplomb, only to return to his incessant stair-walking. The result was that I received less sleep than I had anticipated or wanted or in fact needed. By six in the morning I was relieved that I could get out of bed and head over to the kitchen to begin the day's work. I believe that Byron had picked up on my excitement and anticipation of the coming meal and felt that keeping me from my rest was justified.

Although it's still a bit dark outside, I walk over to the Cookhouse kitchen, open those clumsy French doors and soak in that stillness and darkness inside. None of the coolers are making much noise and the only illumination I can see is the dim light over the front door, the bulb chosen for its old-fashioned charm rather than for its ability to light a path. Once I flip on the lights I quickly begin the day's work. The two bowls full of chilled doughs are removed from the cooler, as are two containers of butter, the beef roast and a large bowl of eggs. The butter, beef and eggs all need time to temper. I turn on the oven as well; the sound of the gas lighting in a burst below is a welcoming sign. I won't need the oven for a few hours but it will help warm the chilly kitchen. I turn on the radio and begin to brew a cup of coffee for myself. By the time the coffee is ready, Jorge is knocking on the doors on the creamery side of the kitchen. He is earlier than usual and I welcome him.

Jorge has worked for me for fifteen years, first at the restaurant as a line cook, and then out here at the farm taking care of the cows. I cherish him and am endlessly pleased that he has continued working for me. I hired Ben when Jorge informed me that he was opening a tiny taqueria on the island. With just five stools and a small stand-up counter, La Zamorana is indeed a tiny spot, but tremendously tasty and successful. Although I was initially worried about how I would replace my trusted herdsman, thankfully the change benefited all of us.

While working at another farm on the island, Ben heard about the availability of work at Kurtwood Farms and quickly came to speak with me. Jorge asked to continue working two days per week, to keep his connection to the farm and animals that he loves. The greatest benefit has been that all of us on this island have someplace to have a lunch filled with flavor and integrity and character.

It is my great fortune to have managed to convince Jorge to work today—not his usual schedule—knowing that he will step in to make lunch for Tyler and myself.

The first task at hand is to scale and roll out the dinner rolls. The dough is firm, chilled and a bit clammy. A stiff *corne,* a plastic handheld scraper is used to release the dough cleanly from the cold bowl. With a bench scraper I cut the large mass of dough into a long tube and then clip off twenty three-ounce portions. With my thumbs and middle fingers I quickly roll each one into an identical ball, repeatedly pulling the outside into the center until the exterior is smooth. After they are placed on a perforated sheet pan they will have a few hours to rise. The second bowl holds the pizza dough and I leave it on the counter to scale later in the day.

In the sink, still draining since last night is the colander lined with cheesecloth filled with the creamy whey ricotta. Last night when I left it, it was filled to the edge, a wet slurry filling the sieve. Eight-plus hours later it has drained and shrunk down in volume. I pick up the four corners of the moist cheese-cloth and lift the heavy ricotta out of the strainer. With a bit of twine, I gently tie off the ball of ricotta, leaving a long lead of string. I hang the weighty ball of still-very-moist ricotta from the shelf hanging above the counter. Underneath is a small bowl to catch the incessant, slow drips of whey.

By this afternoon when Tyler will need the ricotta it will have drained sufficiently to use.

The sun has come up enough by now to illuminate the out-side. I want to get the fire started in the wood oven as soon as possible so that I can be sure of the high heat needed to cook the pizzas well.

The pizza oven is located just outside of the kitchen building, ten feet from the back door. I built it with a friend's help a few years ago. Although my original intent was to have an oven for baking bread, it gets far more use baking pizzas or pita bread or roasting meats and vegetables than baking loaves of bread. The base is made of four courses of cement blocks in a square six feet across. On top of that weighty base is a hearth of cast concrete reinforced with steel rebar. The concrete hearth is topped with fire bricks laid dry to form the base of the oven. More fire bricks form the dome of the actual oven itself. The shell of the oven is brick, and covering the bricks is a thick layer of cast concrete, in places six inches thick. At the front of the oven is a constricted opening. Although the oven chamber is two feet high in the center, this opening is merely ten inches high; the width of the chamber is three feet across and yet the width of the entrance is eighteen inches. The result is a nearly closed chamber that holds in the heat yet does allow for air to be drawn in to feed the fire and provides an egress for the smoke. The entrance is also adequate for me to move pizzas or trays of meat or vegetables in and out as needed.

I must admit that it wasn't until I began to build this oven that I learned the basic concept of the wood-fired bread oven.

The basic procedure is to build a fire in the center of the brick chamber, burning wood for hours throughout the day. Over these hours the heat from the fire is transferred to the thick concrete and brick hearth beneath the fire, and to the thick dome above the fire made of bricks and concrete. Over the course of the day this mass—the thick, heavy concrete and masonry—absorbs the heat of the burning fire. After a few hours, the fire is allowed to slowly burn down to coals and then those coals are allowed to slowly burn down to ash. When the fire that was started early in the day is finally ash, what is left is pulled into the ash bin under the hearth and the bricks are swept clean.

Now the raw bread dough can be placed onto the hearth, deep in the oven by means of a peel, the door at the front of the oven closed, and the masonry that absorbed the collective heat of the hours-long fire will radiate that heat back into the chamber. It is a slow, even and full heat: ideal for baking bread.

This oven, however, is rarely used for baking bread. Generally it is used to bake pizzas, and that is what will start tonight's meal. For baking pizzas there is a difference in how the oven will be used. Instead of allowing the fire to burn down to ash over hours, I will keep it going and leave the fire in the chamber while the pizzas are baked, pushing the lit fire to one corner after it has burned in the center for hours.

The wood comes from this farm. When I moved here, most of the thirteen acres were covered in trees—cherry trees, birches, hawthorn, Doug fir and a few noble madrones. The madrones have not been removed. Most every Doug fir has remained as well. As many hawthorns, cherries and birches as possible have been pulled in order to plant pasture for the dairy cows. The result is stacks of logs in many corners of the property that are ideal for burning in the wood oven. The best stack of wood is from the removal of the mature apple and chestnut trees when the garden was put in. The chestnut burns hotter than any of the other wood, the mature Jonathan apple nearly as well. If I had to go out and buy wood I would most likely think differently about using the oven. People who come by the farm for a dinner love the pizza and want to build one of these ovens in their backyards in the city. Although I certainly would welcome them to have a way to bake great pizzas and bread, to me the amount of wood that would need to be harvested to bake a few pizzas seems to be wasteful. I can justify it because I need to clear these trees to keep this very growing herd of cows in grass.

With a few easy minutes of work, the fire is lit and slowly starts to burn. Through the morning and on into the early afternoon I will walk past the oven and throw another log on the fire, slowly heating that large, heavy mass of masonry so that by four-thirty this afternoon the hearth will be near seven hundred degrees, with a fire roaring in the corner of the oven, nestled on a bed of red-hot coals.

I stand in front of the nascent fire, watching it quickly grow. Like clockwork, I can see Tyler heading into the farm down the driveway, driving a bit too fast for seven-thirty on a Saturday morning. I am not sure what time of day he would be calm and cautious, as he comes around the first curve, past the barn, takes the second curve and approaches the kitchen, but his speed does feel unlike the early morning calm of a few minutes earlier.

Tyler is full of energy at every hour of the day. For years he was a line cook and chef at restaurants in Seattle and Portland. Just over thirty years old, married and with a young son, he is like many of the cooks I have known over the years. He started working in kitchens while in high school and has never left. His arms are now covered in tattoos, his politics are liberal and he lives the fast pace of a line cook.

Tyler sets his priorities for the day. Those items taking the most time are begun first, and those that take less are held for later in the afternoon. The two items on the menu that he puts his attention to first are the soup and the braised beef. Both require some initial preparation and then will spend quite a bit of time slowly cooking. Tackling them in tandem will give him the ability to accomplish both tasks before noon.

I had pulled the large beef roast out of the refrigerator when I first came into the Cookhouse and by the time Tyler has arrived and begun, it has started to come to room temperature, making it easier to work with. The roast that I pulled from the meat locker is a bottom round roast, from Boy's slaughter. It is a great cut to braise. As a well-used muscle on the cow, it is inherently tough and would not respond favorably to roasting. The extended time of the slow braising will bring out the flavor of the beef and a rich sauce to accompany it will guarantee that any potential dryness can be lessened.

The roast is about eight pounds and is still wrapped in plastic. Tyler discards the plastic and places the large piece of beef on the cutting board. It is still a bit wet from defrosting, and he quickly grabs a paper towel and wipes it dry, along with the wooden butcher block. He flips the meat and turns it and folds it this way and that, looking for a way to approach it. You might say that he is letting the beef speak to him. Possibly, but more likely he is simply deciding how best to cook the roast. His decision is to cut the piece of meat into two equal pieces and tie each of them into a tight, long, cylindrical roast. The roast is an odd shape and his goal is to cook the meat evenly by creating roasts of equal thickness and shape. Tyler is also looking to the plate that he will assemble hours in the future.

He takes a few minutes trimming and cleaning the meat, removing any silver skin or sinew so that all that remains is the muscles of the leg. He rolls each piece, finding the best way to create the eventual cylindrical shape, and trims off that which veers from his design. Those bits of trim are quickly placed into a small copper saucepan he keeps by the side of the chopping block. From the small shelf above the counter he grabs the small roll of cotton twine and cuts a long length. With a studied dexterity he begins to tie each roast. He chooses to make a continuous series of bands of string encircling each roast, each band an inch apart down the length. The string is looped around the raw beef, cinched up tight and then he moves onto the next loop. In the matter of a couple of minutes each roast has seven tight bands constricting the meat. With a sharp paring knife from his bag he trims the loose ends of each knot, a short bit of string left on each. All are the same length, an obsessive but unnecessary detail.

Tyler stands back and admires his handiwork. It is impressive. The vague and uncontrolled shape of a floppy, cold piece of meat has been transformed into two controlled, identical roasts. Each is well salted. First a few generous drams of salt are picked up between pinched fingers and sprinkled over the length of the roasts. When enough has been used, he rolls each roast in the salt that has fallen onto the chopping block, pushing it into the flesh of the beef with the pressure of his palms. What remains is a counter nearly free of salt and two very well seasoned roasts.

From below the counter he pulls a heavy, flame-colored Le Creuset pan. Oblong in shape and high-sided, it is one of the largest made by the traditional French producer. It is easily lifted onto the gas range and the fire lit beneath it. A lump of lard from the cooler is spooned into the deeply stained dark interior of the orange pot.

When the lard has melted and is sizzling hot, each roast is lowered into the awaiting fat. Even though they were dried, they sizzle and pop. The flame is on high and the meat sears quickly. Tyler allows each side to get crusty and stuck to the bottom of the heavy pan bottom. The room fills with the gutsy smell of strong meat. The hot lard is pervasive, the nearly burning beef as well. A bit of smoke begins to collect in the large, rectangular steel hood hanging above the range.

While Tyler is flipping and rotating the roasts, I head out to the milk room and grab a pitcher full of milk from the bulk tank. Jorge is just finishing milking the cows and the milk is not yet cool. I return to the kitchen and hand the rich, creamy pitcher of milk to Tyler. He pours it directly into the French cast-iron casserole, causing a great reaction. The milk immediately begins to boil as it hits the hot oil, large bubbles of creamy milk mixed with the pork fat and the bits of crusty beef from the searing. In a moment the bubbles subside and the pot finds its balance.

He takes a moment and lifts each roast with the tongs hanging from the front of the range, moving each one around a bit to deglaze the pot with the milk, bringing up any more bits of flavor that might still be stuck on the bottom of the pan. When he is content that the milk has done its first duty, he finds the large ovoid iron lid and seals the roasts in the steamy chamber.

With a bit of a heft the flame-colored pot is slid into the oven below, cooking at a slow, low temperature to gently braise the beef roasts in the rich, creamy milk.

Tyler now turns to begin the soup course. I have brought him the squash that I would like him to use—the large, pink, netted Brodé Galeux d'Eysines. It is an imposing beast—a scraggly stem, warts covering the outer rind and it is slightly misshapen. As he did with the beef roast, he spends a few pregnant moments looking at it and turning it around on the cutting board before picking up the largest knife at the farm and splitting it in two. With a large spoon he scoops out the seeds and interior flesh; the pigs will enjoy that before the day is over. With a smaller chef's knife he methodically goes around each half sphere and slices off the pinkish rind. On a thinner-skinned squash perhaps a small peeler could accomplish the task, but this rind is deep and firm and the knife is necessary. Once the squash is adequately cleaned, he dices it into chunks each an inch to an inch and a half across. Soon the small circular cutting board is filled with a tidy pile of the deep orange-fleshed squash. In the space remaining, Tyler prepares to skin and slice two large Copra onions. Just picked a few days earlier, they are easily peeled, pungent and fresh. The slices are thick, no need to cut them into small, fussy dicing. Both the squash and the onions will cook for hours and completely break down before they are later pureed for the eventual soup this evening.

Below the counter lies a large rondeau. It is made of aluminum, is high-sided, sixteen inches across and warped from years of use. It arrived here at the Cookhouse from a cook who had been working at a restaurant that closed down. As is customary in the restaurant business, the employees in those last few days of operation steal everything not bolted down. Or locked away by the soon-to-be-bankrupt owners. Every time this rondeau with the crooked base is pulled out to cook a soup or braise some greens, I am reminded of its pedigree. As I have been both a member of an hourly restaurant staff and also an owner for many years, I understand both sides of the custom. I don't judge it too much, and enjoy the use of the heavy pot, but I haven't forgotten either.

Into the quickly heated pot Tyler throws a large lump of butter. It quickly melts and spreads out across the aluminum base. Into that hot fat the onions are added, the moist, fresh onions popping as they come into contract with the melted butter. A few shakes of the handle on the pot's side and they are coated and begin to cook down. In a couple minutes Tyler will add the large firm chucks of squash. They are dry and make little reaction in the hot pan. Slowly the squash begins to break down from the heat. The onions continue to sweat and cook. The bright orange cubes get pushed around and their edges lose their sharpness in a few minutes. When the squash has begun to soften, Tyler adds water, filling the rondeau to just cover the squash.

My tendency is to make everything as rich and as flavorful as possible. Early on in my career, if a recipe called for one cup of butter I would add an additional half cup, convinced that would make the pie or cake or cookies that much richer or better. Experience has taught me that that is primarily false. There is such a thing as too much butter or chocolate or cream.

Tyler has far more restraint. I ask him why he doesn't cook the
squash in milk. This is, after all, a dairy, and fifty feet from
the kitchen is a bulk tank filled with thirty gallons of beautiful
fresh Jersey milk. It would make sense to start the soup from
a base of that milk. He patiently, once again, informs me that
it is not necessary. The flavor is in the squash and to a lesser
extent the onion. The substitution of milk for the cooking water
would also have two potential problems. It might, and most
likely would, curdle. As the water in the milk evaporated from
the long cooking time, it would change into a curdled mess.
Even if it didn't curdle, the resulting soup would taste primarily of cooked milk. Nice, if that was the goal, but we are looking
for a clear taste of the Brodé Galeux d'Eysines squash. And so
water wins over milk.

The water comes to a slow simmer, surrounding the bright
orange chunks on the back burner. Through the morning hours
it will slowly cook, Tyler occasionally picking up a spoon and
stirring it, the tender chunks completely breaking down by the
time we have finished lunch.

While Tyler is finishing up the cooking of the soup, I grab a
set of keys from the ring hanging in the kitchen and head up to
the cheese cave. It is a short walk, out of the kitchen, past the
wood oven, past the creamery, around the barn, through the
large double gates and up the north road to the upper pastures.
Just before the crest of the hill I can see the entrance to the
cave. Throughout the summer the weeds have been growing in
the large stones that form the entrance; now that it is October
the weeds are large and leggy, draping over with their heavy
seedheads, crowding the walk down the gravel path to the door.

I unlock the first heavy wooden door, turn on the interior
lights, walk into the vestibule and close the door behind me.
The bright, sunny fall day is quickly left behind me. The air
has dropped twenty degrees in the quick walk down the path
to the door and into the first small room of the underground
vault. Outside it is a warm seventy degrees this early in the

day, and by late afternoon it might reach seventy-five degrees or higher. The cave will remain the constant fifty degrees, never changing from season to season. The air is also moist. It doesn't feel humid, as a suffocating summer day can feel. It is humid yet very cool.

With the same key I unlock the second weighty door. The dead bolt turning in the chamber and clicking open is greatly exaggerated by the acoustics of the room. The second door has swollen a bit from moisture and I need to push it open forcefully to gain entry.

I come into the cave throughout the year, checking on the cheeses, flipping them, brushing them and adding and subtracting cheeses from the shelves. It has become a common occurrence, walking down the boulder-lined entrance, unlocking the two doors and entering the dark, concrete room. And yet, it always impresses me when I open the second door and walk in. The temperature is startling, the humidity is as well and the space—the tall, barrel-vaulted concrete vault. Other than here, I don't enter spaces such as these often. It is the quick contrast that increases the surprise. There are certainly other beautiful spaces—high-vaulted churches, intimate warm libraries, vast industrial floors—but generally there are lengthy entrances, slow transitions from the exteriors to the interior spaces. Here in this humble cheese cave it is a nearly instant transition from the seventy-degree grassy pasture with bulky bovines to the cool, damp concrete room smelling of sweet, aged cheeses.

I close the second door behind me with a dramatic thud and begin to search for a cheese to serve at dinner. This is a fairly simple task, as the cheeses are arranged in chronological order—the oldest closest to the door on the top shelves and the younger cheeses continuing down the shelf and toward the back of the cave. As I want the most nutty, deep and firm cheese tonight, I go for the first shelf and the highest board, where there are the five cheeses that I made eighteen months earlier. All were made the same day and presumably are identical in taste. I do want the nicest-looking cheese, so I pick one whose sides are straight and true and whose ends are flat and level. The rind is beautiful, mottled and clear. I reach up and grab the eight-pound wheel and then go back through the two doors. In a moment I have returned to the bright, sunny day that I left behind two minutes earlier. The doors locked, the cheese in my hand, I walk back down the north road, through the double gates and head into the kitchen to inspect the cheese.

It was eighteen months ago that I made this batch of cheese. This Francesca's Cheese is five inches high and eight inches across, with a distinctive mottled gray rind. It is in fact many colors that appear to be gray in toto. The rind is covered in a multitude of different molds and spores that were rubbed down daily and weekly over the eighteen-month period. There are parts of the rind that appear to be black and some nearly snowy white, and every shade of gray in between those two extremes.

I haven't been making this cheese for very long—maybe three years—and I am still quite nervous, apprehensive about breaking into a new one. They are by and large all quite tasty, but there is still the possibility that even with great, fresh milk and nearly two years of aging, it may still lack any distinctive flavors, or be terribly salty, or have an absence of flavor altogether.

I set the cheese on the counter, knowing that I will know in a few hours how it will taste. Throughout the day it will tease me, not telling me how tasty or off-flavored it is until I finally cut into the wheel.

———

In a few hours' time, pizzas will be served, each with a bit of tomato sauce. Tyler goes to the shelf on the side of the Cookhouse and grabs two of the jars of tomato sauce. The bright rings are spun off and the tin lids easily pried up. The sauce Dustin and I canned is far too liquid to use on the pizzas, so

Tyler pours the contents into a medium-sized copper pot and begins to heat the sauce gently, bringing it to a simmer to slowly reduce through the day. Over the course of the day he will add scraps of chopped tomatoes, onions and fresh herbs as well, so that by the time he begins to roll out the pizza dough, the sauce on the back of the range will be rich, thick and filled with the concentrated flavor of this summer's tomatoes.

While Tyler begins the tomato sauce, I scale the pizza dough. It was removed from the refrigerator early this morning and has begun to warm up to room temperature but has barely begun to rise. I pull the clammy dough from the bowl and cut it into eight pie-shaped pieces. They are quickly formed into round disks, just three inches across. I place them on a full sheet pan dusted with flour, then dust the tops of the disks as well, covering them with a towel to keep them from drying out as they rise through the afternoon.

On the range next to that simmering sauce Tyler sets the small copper pan filled with the meat scraps from the cleaning of the beef earlier this morning. He fills the pot with water and lights a gentle flame beneath it. This pot too will slowly simmer through the day. Immediately he adds the trimmed pieces of onions from the soup to begin to flavor it. By the late afternoon, he can strain the small pan. The liquid will form the base of a meat stock for the making of the pasta sauce, and the very-well-cooked beef scraps will be a treat for the two canine members of the kitchen team.

Once the roasts are slowly braising in the oven, the tomato sauce begun and the soup cooking on the back of the stove, Tyler can turn to the two starches he is responsible for: the noodles and the crackers. Both require similar procedures and he prepares them in tandem. The first is the black pepper crackers. The crackers are made from a terribly simple recipe. The ingredients are all-purpose flour, some fat, some liquid and a bit of leavening, salt, and black pepper. They will be combined quickly in a food processor. The processor that we have here in the Cookhouse is a Robot Coupe, the professional version of the domestic food processor. It is large, weighty and astonishingly simple. Absent are the buttons and labels of its home cousins. The Robot's only options are off and on, and that one function is enabled by clicking the large, clear lid completely shut on the opaque plastic bowl. The design is redolent of the French 1960s when it was designed. Few changes have been made to this sturdy workhorse of restaurant kitchens the world over. The Robot also has a cultural function as well as the ability to chop, mix and puree. Although the name may signify a specific brand of processor, the name is used to mean any food processor in a professional kitchen. It has therefore become a gatekeeper, if you will, into acceptance into the trade. If on your first day as a young cook in a kitchen, the chef tells you to grab the "Robot," it is an instant test to see if you have ever been in a professional kitchen before. To make it more difficult, the word is always pronounced *row-bow* and never *robot*.

My reason for keeping this dated piece of equipment in my kitchen is less to judge youngsters than because it is a work-horse—always strong enough to do the job. And it is a tell, a signifier, that this is a well-equipped kitchen.

Tyler adds the short list of ingredients into the bowl for the crackers—the flour, leavening, salt and fat—and slowly pours the liquid—in this case milk—into the opening in the lid as the machine is running. When there is ample liquid the dough will form a loose ball, and he cuts the motor and releases the lid. By hand he grabs the dough, finishes forming it into a compact ball, flattens it a bit and wraps it in plastic wrap to rest. The entire procedure takes but a couple of minutes.

He moves on to the pasta dough. It is a similar procedure, but one done with more precision and by hand. On the maple-block counter he measures out the all-purpose flour needed, passing it through a *tamis* to sift it and catch any errant bits. It will resemble a tall, round, snowy mountain on the wooden table. With his hand he pushes down the summit, creating a crater surrounded by a large circular levee of flour. Into that well he cracks the fresh, pastured eggs from the chickens just outside the Cookhouse window. The ratio of eggs to flour is well established—in this case it is eight cups of flour to twelve whole eggs. The balance in this ratio is not only between wet and dry, but also in the nature of the moisture added to the dry flour. In the case of the noodles Tyler is making for this evening's dinner it is 100 percent whole eggs. The other extreme of that would be 100 percent egg yolks—no whites whatsoever. It is certainly an option, albeit a luxurious one. More than twice as many eggs would be used and many egg whites would presumably be wasted. Certainly I could make a batch of meringues for dessert, but I find them tedious and dull.

The yolk-only pasta would be luxurious not only in its wastefulness, but also in its taste. The color of the final noodles is bright, golden, saffrony. The texture is equally special—smooth and tight. The traditional use of an all-yolk noodle is a *tajarin*, a typical pasta of Piedmont that is an extremely finely cut noodle. And one that is also very rich, smooth and fine. When the whites of the eggs are substituted with yolks the percentage of fat increases dramatically in the pasta, creating a richer noodle. Occasionally we do make such festive noodles, but today is not such a fete. The pasta dish is made of chicken gizzards and hearts and livers with bread crumbs and butter and onions. There could be no dish more peasanty, more rustic than this one. All-yolk noodles would be a juxtaposition with little or no merit.

Into the well of flour with the levees, Tyler cracks the eggs. They are very fresh and beautiful. Some were taken from the chicken coop this morning, the rest during the past few days. The yolks are deep orange, characteristic of eggs from pastured chickens. The yolks are strong, their outer membrane ample to keep the shape of the golden spheres. The whites have a texture both fluid and firm. They are healthy eggs. I like to look at this scene and marvel at the beauty: on the table is a ring of fluffy white flour—a nest, if you will. In the center of that nest are the eggs, all the bright orange yolks visible. It is not just that the colors and the shapes are beautiful, but also the symmetry of it all—the eggs are cradled in a nest—a bird's nest, if you will.

Once the eggs are all cracked, the shells in the bucket headed for the pigs, Tyler takes a large silver dinner fork and begins to break the yolks with a bit of precision and intent. The sharp tines of the long fork easily break the yolks and the rich, golden yolks run. Slowly he begins to whip the eggs, mixing the whites and yolks until they are incorporated together. Next the fork will nick the sides of the flour levee, a bit of the flour coming into the well of eggs, all the while the fork whisking the eggs. Slowly, bit by bit, the flour is incorporated into the eggs. The levee may accidentally be breached by some errant whisking, but it is easy enough to close that hole before the still-liquid eggs flow out onto the counter. After a few minutes the task has changed from adding flour to the liquid eggs to adding more flour to the pasta dough that is forming in the center of the ring of white flour. When the fork is no longer helpful it is retired, but not before the tines are firmly rolled on the floured counter to push out the bits of dough stuck between them. The fork can then be replaced with a bench scraper.

My first job in a kitchen was as a *stagiaire* in a patisserie in Paris while I was in college. I spoke inadequate French for the job, but I learned ample nonetheless. Many basic tenets of a French kitchen have stuck with me in the intervening thirty years. One such idea is the use of a bench scraper. It is a ubiquitous tool in any pastry kitchen or bakery. It should be as ubiquitous in a home kitchen. In that fiercely run French pastry shop on the Rue Jean-Nicot, the counters were constantly scraped with the sharp edge of the straight blade. No bits of dough or crumbs or errant pieces of fruit were ever to be wasted. It was imperative that the counters were tidy, with all foodstuffs saved. It is hard to forget those lessons.

The bench scraper is a simple tool. It is rectangular, perhaps five inches in width and four inches tall. On one of the long edges a wooden or plastic handle is attached, and the other long edge is sharpened slightly. It is not designed primarily to cut, but rather to scrape. If it is kept perfectly flat and never dented, it can scrape every possible bit of flour or pastry from a wooden counter. If it is adversely treated and has a bit of a bend or knick, it will gouge an otherwise beautiful counter, ruining it in a quick motion.

For assisting in the making of pasta dough, the bench scraper is ideal and essentially obligatory. At this stage, there is a large round mixture of eggs and flour. It isn't uniform, nor is the flour fully integrated. A good proportion of the original flour still remains, with bits of sticky eggs and flour stuck on the wooden counter. The scraper can come along the sides and under the dough, lifting the mixed dough, the bits of egg and the dry flour, further incorporating the wet and the dry.

This process of pulling the errant pieces, bringing them up and folding them into the dough continues. Tyler slowly and consistently works the dough until it is uniform, until the counter is clean and all that may remain is a bit of flour. The dough will no longer be sticky, not adhering to the counter, but rather firm and smooth. Excess flour may remain, or more flour may be necessary to finish the dough. The original ratio of eggs to flour is a basic starting point for the final pasta, but the weather may be different, the eggs larger or smaller, the flour moister or dryer. Each or all could affect the amount of flour needed to bind with the volume of eggs originally cracked into that well. Tyler has made noodles many times in his career and knows enough to add or subtract flour as need be. I doubt he thinks about much of the process; it is a tactile process primarily.

The fork has been retired, and now the bench scraper as well. The maple top is cleaned; no bits remain. Now Tyler kneads the dough by hand. Forcefully he pushes down hard on the firm ball of dough, folds it over on itself, pushes down again on the resulting ball and so on. A bit more flour might be dusted to keep it dry, as the kneading will bring out more moisture in the pasta. For a few minutes he will continue this physical match with the dough, the wheeled table bouncing back and forth with the action of the kneading. The stainless-steel bowls that are on the lower shelf below the wooden top bang into each other in unison to the rhythm. I myself give up too early when I am making noodles. I always think it is good enough, the dough smooth enough, when in fact I am simply tired and worn out. Tyler has more endurance. The cook who worked here before him, Joel, a hulking god of a cook, could knead a large ball of pasta dough even longer. His noodles were the most refined of anyone's here.

Once the pasta is considered amply worked, it is wrapped in plastic to keep it from drying out, to allow it to relax and to hydrate the dough. A dry crust would be disastrous—if the outer part of the dough were to dry out it would make rolling and forming the noodles difficult if not impossible. Also, the kneading gave the dough a great deal of elasticity. If it were to be rolled out immediately the dough would repeatedly shrink back, returning to its original shape as you tried unsuccessfully to roll it thin. After a time the long strands of gluten developed during the kneading will relax, allowing for a more successful forming of the final noodles. The dough also needs to hydrate; that is, the moisture needs to infiltrate the entire dough. Time redistributes the moisture throughout the ball evenly and completely. If one were to cut open the ball of dough at the beginning and then at the end of the rest this would be easily apparent. The early dough shows a dry texture with inconsistent texture, the later dough a consistent texture with moisture throughout.

The hydration also makes it appear as though moisture is being added. What was a dry, stiff dough when wrapped in the plastic is a pliable, moist dough an hour or two later. Most likely the dough is now too moist—too little flour was added during the forming of the dough. The result would be a need to add additional flour during the rolling of the dough to keep it from sticking.

I did have an earlier cook at the farm make pasta dough in a completely different manner. He mixed eggs and flour with a higher proportion of flour than today's ratio. When he brought it together it was crumbly and dry and he did not knead it. Rather, he gathered it together and pressed it into a shallow stainless-steel pan—a small hotel pan. The eight-by-twelve-inch pan held all of the rough, dry dough. It resembled the crumbly topping of an apple crisp, bits of dry flour, bits of egg and flour, some mixed, some not. The idea that this could result in a beautiful final noodle was laughable. He pushed it all down into the bottom of the hotel pan with his fists, wrapped the entire hotel pan in plastic wrap and left it to sit for a couple of hours. When he returned to it, the dough had hydrated like the hugely kneaded varieties. In this case, however, it had moistened up to the point where it was now a stiff yet pliable dough.

While Tyler begins another task, I start on the dessert for the evening. Although it is the beginning of October, it is only quite recently that the large heirloom varieties of tomatoes have ripened in the garden. The smaller, cherry tomatoes were ready a few weeks earlier, but there just wasn't enough continued heat to push a lot of the large, bulky varieties to ripeness until now. I want to celebrate those heirlooms tonight with the dessert. I have chosen a tomato upside down cake with tomato jam to finish off this meal.

I originally got the idea a few years ago from Paul Bertolli's book *Cooking by Hand*. I must correct that. Bertolli had the idea, and presented his recipe in his book. I read it there and now make it. I do wish that I could take credit for it, but honestly I cannot. I may have changed it slightly, but Paul gets the credit.

What I like about this cake is that it tricks people who eat it for the first time. It looks very much like the pineapple upside down cake that we all grew up with as children: a couple of inches high, nine inches across, a golden, buttery cake that is inverted after baking to show the pineapple rings with, often, maraschino cherries in the pineapple centers, with a healthy amount of sugary syrup pouring down the sides of the cake from the top. This cake resembles that entirely except that the pineapples have been replaced with half-inch-thick slices of meaty tomatoes, with red cherry tomatoes standing in for the absent maraschino cherries.

I may be overstating my case, but I think this cake is the best argument for eating locally. It is not necessary to import pineapples from the tropics to present a delightful, tasty dessert, when in fact our own gardens, here in the temperate continental United States, contain beautiful, sweet fruit. This is not just an apt intellectual argument but also a fine gustatory argument—it is tasty.

The cake is a simple butter cake leavened with baking powder. I start by grabbing a couple of nine-inch metal cake pans and lining them with waxed paper. Flipping the pans upside down on the counter, covering them with the waxed paper and opening a pair of scissors wide, I trace the outer edges of the pans with the open dull blade, tracing the large circle onto the waxed paper. It is not a difficult task, but it is one that I relish. Maybe my mother showed me originally how to do it, maybe my grandmother, I don't remember, but I do remember learning this simple technique more than forty years ago. I most likely have my iPhone near me while I am making these cakes today, and the farm iPad is on the table as well. It is a modern, technological life I now lead. I am now in middle age and my life has certainly changed since the late 1960s when I started making cakes. This simple physical task—dragging the dull scissor blade around the edges of the cake pan—brings back that time immediately. It is a tactile memory, one that I enjoy every time.

Once there is a dim circle scratched out on the paper, I close up the extended scissors and cut out the circle. With a bit of butter on my index finger I quickly smear the butter around the inside bottom of the cake pan—just enough to anchor the waxed paper—then I place the liner down smoothly in the pan.

I mix the brown sugar and some of the beautiful farm butter in a small saucepan, melting both together to create a sugary syrupy base for the fruits. When it bubbles and boils, I take it off the flame and pour half into each pan, watching it as it spreads out over the paper, the excess butter breaking from the hot sugar-butter mixture and filling the bottom of the pan. It doesn't look very precise or tidy, but it will be beautiful in the final cake.

While that cools and the butter begins to firm up, I return to the kitchen garden and select the tomatoes for the base of the cake. I am looking for tomatoes that are large, but not too large; firm, but ripe. I find a couple of large aptly named ripe Pineapple varieties, and then a couple of large, ribbed Marmande that look good, and three smaller yellow Taxis to fill in the cake. A small handful of Sun Gold cherry tomatoes and a few Sweet 100 cherries will be used as well.

All are quickly washed in the kitchen and the large fruits are thickly sliced. I only want the center slices from the tomatoes. From each of the tomatoes I can get at most three slices but more likely just two. The smaller Taxi tomatoes are also sliced for their prime central section. The cherries I cut in half easily, using both halves equally.

The bits unused—the tops, the bottoms, the sections trimmed off—I hand off to Tyler working next to me on the other worktable. He quickly cores them and chops them roughly and adds them to the tomato sauce slowly simmering on the back of the range, destined for the wood-fired pizzas in a few hours.

One by one I set the large slices of tomatoes into the brown-sugar-and-butter base in the cake pans. The sugary syrup holds them in place nicely. Once the largest slices are set, I place the gradually smaller slices next to them tightly. As the pans fill up, I pick from my table full of pieces to find a fitting puzzle piece of fruit. The smaller cherry tomatoes provide the diminutive size to finish out the puzzle.

I turn to make the cake base. The butter is weighed out on the old balance scales kept on the shelf under the worktable. The butter is certainly not pressed into convenient rectangles each of a quarter pound as they are in the supermarket. The farm butter is more aptly described as a large three-pound amorphous ball of golden butter. As an aside: Why is it that butter is always referred to as a "cube of butter"? Possibly it is just how it is packaged here on the West Coast, but I have never seen either a quarter-pound "cube" or a set of four sticks in a one-pound package of butter that resembles a cube. A quick bit of checking, and I now know that the three-dimensional form of a rectangle is referred to as a *right-angled parallelepiped*. It is now apparent why we use the much easier, though inaccurate, term *cube* to describe a block of butter.

The scales make it an easy task to measure the needed butter, and it is added to the bowl of the small stand-mixer. A rigid paddle is added to the mixer and I begin to beat the butter. Although the butter was pulled from the reach-in cooler early this morning, I want to use cool butter. Warm butter has the possibility of overwhipping and could begin to break if it is too warm. In my early days of baking I would leave butter in a mixer briefly, feeling that a great deal of whipping did not change the structure of the butter. I was grossly mistaken. Butter responds dramatically to whipping. It incorporates a tremendous amount of air within the fat and increases in volume as a result. Because some of that air will be collapsed by the incorporation of the dry ingredients, it is imperative to introduce as much lightness as possible in this early step.

The air bubbles are necessary for the leavening of the final cake. Although baking powder will be added as the leavening agent, baking powders do not *create* air holes in the batter, they only can *enlarge* air holes that are already there. It is for that reason that we want to create the largest quantity of air pockets.

Once the butter begins to lighten in color, I slowly add in the sugar called for in the Bertolli recipe. The crystalline structure of the sugar also aids in cutting into the butter and making it whip more. We want the butter and sugar to be evenly distributed at this stage of the cake-making.

While the butter and sugar are in the mixer, I have a few minutes to sieve the dry ingredients. On the wooden table I place a large sheet of waxed paper and a *tamis* on that. Into the round wooden sieve I pour the all-purpose flour, the salt and the baking powder. I lift the wooden *tamis*, tap its side gently and the dry ingredients pass through onto the waxed paper.

Once the butter is light and fluffy and ivory-colored—the standard descriptions in every baking book for decades—I add the cool eggs. I don't want any chance of heating up the butter mixture, so cool eggs are always best. One at a time they are dropped into the mixer's bowl as the paddle is slowly running. I pick up two opposite sides of the waxed paper and create a flume, directing the dry ingredients down the length of the waxed paper and out the narrow opening and into the waiting mixer. I can raise or lower the opening to speed up or slow down the flour.

The electric mixer does quick work incorporating the dry ingredients and the egg, sugar and butter mixture. It is a stiff batter. I must taste it raw, fresh out of the mixing bowl, even though I am very familiar with it from past baking. It is sweet, buttery and rich. The butter quickly begins to melt on the tongue, coating my mouth. I could eat the entire bowl.

The challenge is now to distribute the stiff batter equally among the two cake pans lined with tomatoes. I also don't want to disturb the well-placed fruits. The answer is to ladle out the batter spoonful by spoonful. With a large soup spoon I drop spoonfuls onto the waiting tomatoes. It is at first glance not very equitable. Once the entire bowlful has been transferred to the two pans, I can take the back of the large silver soup spoon and smooth it out, leveling the peaks and valleys of the golden, buttery batter. A firm rap of each pan on the counter to settle the cakes, and they are put in the oven.

The cakes bake in the middle shelf of the large gas oven. I did need to negotiate with Tyler for oven space and he agreed to remove his roast for part of an hour, to slowly simmer on the back of the stove while the cakes bake. The oven is quite hot, at four hundred degrees, and the lumpy-looking surface of the cake quickly begins to flatten out and rise.

Although I love this tomato cake, I want just a bit more for dessert this evening and decide to make a few butter cookies as well. Gilding the lily, perhaps, but I will enjoy them even if no one else does.

It is a simple recipe—just butter, all-purpose flour, sugar and a bit of rice four—but it is still a delightful cookie. I always looked for the most competent pastry cooks to work for me. Those who made desserts that had too many ingredients and garnishes and frills were attempting to hide their youth and inexperience. Those who made me a simple lemon tart or shortbread cookie, or custard, understood technique and ingredients.

In the small stand mixer, I thoroughly beat room-temperature butter with the slight sugar, then add the sifted flours. The strong paddle incorporates the ingredients effortlessly. With my hands I bring the cookie dough together, then roll it out on the wooden counter with a thin French pin. A small round cookie cutter easily pierces the simple dough. In a matter of a few minutes I have three dozen small cookies in the oven baking in the rack over the tomato cakes.

Over the next thirty minutes I check the cakes often. I am tremendously distracted at this point in the day—many activities are going on in the kitchen and I am carrying on a conversation with Tyler the whole time as well. The schedule for the rest of the afternoon is too tight to allow for failure. If I were to burn these two cakes there certainly would be little time to remake them, and I used all of the butter allotted to me already.

I use the thinnest knife in the block to check, inserting it into the center of the cake to see if it is still moist at its core. The color on top is golden brown; it has just begun to pull from the sides of the cake pan and, most importantly, I can smell it. The olfactory indicator is the most important to me. It may have been that early French insistence on trusting my sense of smell, but I am now confident that when I can smell the baked goods in the oven, most likely they are fully cooked. I do, however, still double-check with the knife, however. Finally, after numerous checks, it comes out clean and I can pull the two cakes from the oven. I place them on wire cooling racks and find two large, flat, plastic cutting boards to be the final surface for the cakes.

I look for that sweet moment when the cake has cooled enough to unmold, yet is not so cool that it cannot be removed well. The sides of the cake that had just begun to shrink back from the pan will pull away completely. If the cake pan was well buttered on the sides it will not even be necessary to cut the edges to release it—it will pull easily and cleanly as it cools.

The butter cookies are thin and small and take just a few short minutes to bake to a golden, nutty color. I pull them from the oven and shelve the tray on the speed rack to cool through the afternoon.

The first cutting board is placed on top of the still-warm cake in its pan. One hand is placed on the bottom of the pan, the other on the board; a quick flip, and the cake is now on the cutting board, and the warm pan can easily be removed.

I remove the cake pan to reveal the top of the cake with its tomatoes. They have retained their shape during the baking, yet are tender and have melded with the cake. I pull off the waxed paper that is adhered by the syrup to the tomatoes. I spoon tomato jam that Dustin and I made earlier over the steaming fruit-and-syrup base of the cake. With the heat it quickly melts, filling in the cracks and crevices between the tomatoes. The warmth of the cake also heats up the jam, releasing the musky, sweet smell of the cooked cherry tomato jam. The cakes are put aside until they will be served in a few hours.

Luckily, Jorge is working today and can help out while the dinner is being prepared. He did the morning chores, milking the cows, feeding the chickens, feeding the pigs. When he finishes the chores he comes into the Cookhouse and begins lunch for the three of us. We have a pretty standard lunch at the farm when Jorge is working: tacos with beef or pork, beans, possibly some eggs and two salsas. Unbeknownst to me, he began soaking a cupful of shelled beans in water together with a dried chili when he first came in early this morning. The shelled beans are from last year's harvest, picked in late October before the rains came. In the garden now is a full bed of white cannellini beans with still weeks before they will be harvested, shelled and dried in the kitchen for next year's tacos.

Tyler and I are deep in conversation when Jorge quietly comes in behind us and begins to work. He turns on the small saucepan on the range and brings the beans to a slow simmer. He begins the two salsas—one green, one red. The red one is based on the dried chilies that are grown every summer in the greenhouse. The varieties change from year to year depending on which seedlings I get from Leda and which I have planted myself. Every year the greenhouse has a few bell peppers, a few small very hot chilis such as a Joe's long cayenne and a few larger chilis such as a Corno de Toro that have some heat. In the fall they are picked, strung together with a needle and thread and allowed to dry. Just less than twelve months later Jorge is standing on a chair to reach the *ristras* hanging from the beams in the Cookhouse, breaking off a handful that he will use for the red salsa. He is stealthy in his manner, finding an unused chef's knife and a bit of counter space to begin his work, saying little but certainly listening intently though casually to our gossipy conversation. He opens the dried chilies, removes the stems, the inner veins and the seeds and discards them. He puts the chilies aside and then heads to the shelf for a fresh onion, grabbing some garlic and the other ingredients he will need for the salsas. He finds the beef that he will use for his lunch tacos. When we slaughtered Boy, I saved a large flank steak for Jorge to use for today's lunch. The cut comes off of the belly. The forward part of the belly is the skirt, the rear of the belly is the flank. The flank is much thicker than the skirt and a bit easier to work with. As it is a heavily worked muscle, it can be quite tough if not cooked quickly and cut across the grain. For that reason, Jorge will grill the flank till just medium rare, let it rest and then cut it crosswise to minimize its toughness. Thankfully the grain on a flank steak is readily apparent—it is essentially all large grain running in one direction; impossible to miss.

Jorge tackles the red salsa. Over the years of growing vegetables here at the farm, few varieties have surprised me. Certainly I like 'Nantaise' carrots and Sun Gold tomatoes, but I can easily reorder those each year from the national seed companies and they can be found anywhere. The Ambition shallots of Leda's suggestion have amazed me and are now a part of the garden. In addition to Bill's Tomatoes, one of the very few varieties that I do in fact covet and save the seed are the tiny tomatillos that Jorge's wife brought me years ago. They are unique, different and special, and called milperos. I was familiar with the large supermarket variety of tomatillo: easily an inch and a half in diameter, with a light green exterior and a nearly yellow, juicy and acidic interior. They are perfectly fine as a tomatillo: ubiquitous and dull. They are not, however, interesting or special. Jorge explained to me when he first gave me the tiny seeds that those supermarket ones are for gringos—he wouldn't eat those if he could help it. I now completely agree.

The tomatillos are indeed tiny, at most a half inch in diameter, deep green with a much less yellow interior. And they are full of flavor, if not full of juice. They grow prolifically in this region and, I would expect, most of the nation. The only explanation for their rarity is that they are tremendously tedious to pick and clean. As with the larger varieties, they grow inside a husk, which must be removed before they can be cooked. The payoff is, however, worth it.

Jorge grabs a couple cups of the tiny, husked tomatillos that he picked last week in the vegetable garden. He reaches way up to the steel sauté pan stored too high for his shorter stature and pulls it down. The front burner of the ranger is turned up high and the empty steel pan is allowed to heat. In a couple of minutes the pan, although not red-hot, will certainly be adequately heated. Jorge will pour the small green marbles into the pan and watch as they immediately are seared black by the high heat. There is no oil in the pan, no liquid at all, and the small round fruits roll around, blistering rapidly. As the pan is quite large, each tomatillo rests on the black steel surface. With the flick of his experienced wrist, Jorge can move them around effortlessly to guarantee they will be evenly and completely cooked without burning. They are seared, certainly, but not burnt, not bitter in flavor. In a couple of short minutes, the task will be completed, the tall room filled with the smoke and scent of the fragrant cooked tomatillos. He removes the heavy pan from the flame, and rolls the steaming fruits into an awaiting bowl to cool.

With the steel pan still hot, he quickly sears a couple of cloves of fresh garlic, allowing the sides to blacken slightly. When he is happy with the look of the garlic, he slides it out of the pan and into the bowl with the tomatillos.

The chilies that he cleaned earlier will also get a brief kiss of the hot steel pan, not to burn or blacken, but just to bring out their flavor. In just a few seconds they are ready, and then they too will cool in the bowl.

Jorge now turns his attention to the beefsteak. With a sharp, thin, long-bladed knife he trims it of any silver skin and gristle that would spoil the tacos. On the far left of the range top is a broiler. It is a low, rectangular box set over the two left burners, the bottom made of strong, open mesh, the sides of thick steel and the top a lid of long steel rods a quarter of an inch apart running the full length of the box. Inside this low-rise box are lava rocks—chunks of porous rocks. It is difficult to discern if they are of a natural source or made in a lab. Either way, they heat up from the high flames of the range, radiating heat to the steel rods. It looks a bit like a metal shop project from a culinary-minded high school student, but it has served me well for years. Although a bit heavy, it is easily lifted onto the range when the need arises to broil a piece of flank steak for tacos. Soon after this lunch, Jorge will return it to its place under a low shelf in the kitchen, resting on the concrete floor and waiting for the next time broiled steak sounds delectable.

The broiler does take a few minutes to heat up, so he flips the front knobs to high and gas flames quickly ignite and begin to heat the center of the steel box, the lava rocks inside and the steel rods above. This will give Jorge a few minutes to grab a stack of tortillas from the cooler. They are smallish all-corn tacos, made in a large factory somewhere near Seattle. One of the few items to come across this table of which I have little idea or concern as to their origin. I may be beguiled by the Spanish language on the plastic sack they come in or the colors of the Mexican flag on the label, but I am calmed into trusting the integrity of these tortillas. I also have an inability to grow an adequate supply of corn, and don't have the time or inclination to grind the corn, make the masa and form the tortillas.

Once the broiler is sufficiently heated, the large slab of fresh beef is placed on the grill. It immediately sizzles, smokes and sticks to the steel. The overhead ventilation fan is turned on and adequately sucks the smoke out of the kitchen. The smell of cooking beef is readily apparent and welcome. It signals to Tyler and myself that lunch is imminent.

While the meat is cooking, Jorge takes the blender and purees all of the cooled chilies, tomatillos and garlic, together with some fresh onion and some water. In a few seconds a smoky, sweet sauce remains with the welcome acid of the tomatillos. He tastes and seasons the sauce and then quickly pours the red salsa into a small bowl.

The green salsa is next. It is a simpler sauce, with a fresher taste. He takes a small saucepan and adds more of the tomatillos milperos, some water, fresh onion and garlic, and brings it all to a boil. It is a small pan and the water quickly heats up. He turns his attention to the beef a few inches away on the grill, making sure it is cooking evenly, turning it as needed. When the tomatillos have burst, he pulls the pan off the heat and strains the tomatillo mixture in a small sieve, reserving the cooking liquid.

Jorge pours the cooked tomatillos into the blender, together with some fresh cilantro from the garden and a bit of the reserved liquid. He purees the ingredients, then adds a bit more liquid, then tastes it. He adds some salt and pepper, a bit more liquid, and purees again. In just a few moments, he is happy with his green salsa. It is fresh and bright and full of the flavor of the tomatillos and cilantro. He pours it into a second bowl and then adds a bit of fresh, diced onions.

He removes the small sauce pan from the back of the range where the beans have been slowly cooking while he prepared the other parts of the meal. He drains them slightly, checks the seasonings, salts them liberally and places them on the table.

In groups of four he places tortillas on the coolest part of the grill. The hottest sections, near the flames, he reserves for the flank steak, but the surrounding edges can accommodate the tortillas. He wants them to be warmed through, but neither dried out nor burnt. With a bit of attention he can accommodate all three goals. After the beef has been flipped to grill the other side and cooked to the desired doneness, it is removed to the cutting board surface of the kitchen counters. He allows it to rest for a couple minutes, allowing the juices to reenter the meat and him adequate time to warm the remaining tortillas needed to feed the three of us.

I have watched Jorge make this meal many times over the years; it is a standard: tortillas, grilled beefsteak, red salsa, green salsa, beans and sometimes some Mexican rice. What I did not understand for most of those years was that he did not grow up making this meal. In fact, he did not grow up making any food at home in Mexico. His family, and presumably most families in rural Mexico, had very traditional gender roles. He worked in the fields with his brothers and father and uncles, raising the corn and beans and peppers that they would need for their subsistence life in Michoacán. His mother and sisters would remain in the house cooking, cleaning and doing laundry, which, in this remote town of no electricity until the early 1980s, were all-day-long tasks.

Although he and his many compatriots in this country now work as cooks in restaurant kitchens from Seattle to New York City, he never cooked a meal in Mexico. It was not until he got married here and began to have his own family that he began to cook Mexican food. I felt a bit cheated when I learned this. I wanted to believe that when I was watching him here in my kitchen I could see back to his small town of La Ladera and observe how beefsteak tacos are traditionally prepared. Certainly his palate was developed there in that small nothing of a town, but he in no way grew up cooking in his family's kitchen alongside his mother and grandmother preparing salsas and moles and *birrias*. He was out in the fields, in the hills tending their cows, only returning to enjoy the lunch and dinner prepared by the women of the family.

I must say, though, that even if he learned these skills in his twenties, it is still a remarkable lunch. Quickly and methodically he wraps the warmed tortillas in a fresh clean towel and places the wrapped bundle on the table next to the salsas. He had set aside a small handful of chopped fresh onions from the salsa-making and puts them on a small saucer and takes them to the table as well. The beef he cuts—across the grain, decisively, precisely and thinly. Each piece is three inches across and less than a quarter-inch thick. The meat is juicy and still steaming, charred by the flames of the broiler yet red in the center. He salts the beef generously, scoops it up with the blade of his long chef's knife, places it on a small white platter and delivers it to the table. The table complete, Tyler and I complete our tasks and sit down, pushing aside some of the place settings to find room for our lunch. Jorge joins us slowly, taking care to make sure we have adequate cilantro and hot sauce from the cooler. He will join us and linger far longer than either of us at the table, savoring the lunch he has prepared with gusto. Tyler and I eat quickly and nervously, knowing that there is much to be done still before the guests begin to arrive in a few hours, while still enjoying the meal that Jorge has prepared.

THIRTEEN

Saturday Afternoon;
Dinner Preparation Is Finished

Jorge has cleared the plates, silverware and glasses as stealthily as he made lunch. Quietly and effortlessly he places the dishes from our lunch in the dishwasher, runs it and puts the clean plates away on the shelves.

The mood of the kitchen shifts perceptibly once Tyler and I get up from the table. Whereas the morning was light and conversant with many hours before the meal, now it is one o'clock and the guests will arrive in three and a half hours; each minute is now valuable and important to finishing in time. Realizing the time, I reach into the cooler, find the two small ramekins filled with rich, sweet Jersey butter, and place them on the table. They will spend the next four hours coming to room temperature. By the time the guests finish their pizza and take a seat, the butter will be soft and glistening and ready for them.

The soup has been slowly simmering on the back burner of the range since midmorning. The cubes of squash have completely broken down, the onions have softened to near-liquid and the moisture has been greatly reduced. Tyler pulls the weighty pot off of the heat and sets up the blender. Although the ingredients are certainly cooked, they are in no way pureed. One could not call this a rustic soup at this point. Ladle by ladle the soup is transferred to the awaiting blender. It is still steaming hot and clouds up the sides of the clear plastic blender immediately. When the blender is filled three-quarters full, and covered with the lid, Tyler begins to puree the squash soup. Within a few seconds the soup is transformed into a uniform, ocher puree. The soup is not yet finished, however. As each blenderful is pureed, it is poured into a large sieve set over a clean soup pot. With the outer surface of the large ladle, Tyler presses the just-pureed soup through the fine brass wires of the sieve, guaranteeing that the final soup will be not just smooth, but actually silky in texture. The extra few minutes of effort is well worth the time in the final analysis. There is no chance of any errant piece of squash or peppercorn or onion root spoiling the feeling on the tongue of sipping the warm, fragrant, golden soup.

A couple of years into the Cookhouse dinners, I threatened to remove the blender from the *batterie de cuisine*. My thinking was that a meal that was genuinely from this farm should have all of the ingredients clearly evident. I wanted to cook each item—the beefsteak, the tomato, the chicken liver—to capture their greatest flavors and textures and fragrance without destroying their integrity. I was interested in the simplest form of the ingredients, cooked to highlight their qualities. Transforming those essential farm-raised ingredients, manipulating their form, I felt was an act of treason; not respecting what had gone into their creation. A bit too much, I'm now aware. But at the time, I wanted to ban the blender from the kitchen. If we were to serve a squash soup, then the squash should be visible as a piece of squash. Perhaps it was a desire to return to a pre–World War II fantasy French kitchen. One where each vegetable was grown in the *potager*, the meats slaughtered in the village *abbatoir*, and the wine from the local vineyards picked up at the nearby *négociants*, all cooked by the resident *bonne femme* preparing the meal in gleaming *cuivres* on a large wood-fired *cuisinière*. Such a *bonne femme*, I assume, would only have a few knives to alter the vegetables and perhaps a mortar and pestle as well, but would not have had access to a blender or a food processor or other such method to mechanically transform her ingredients. It is a fantasy that I have dutifully attempted to re-create. The Cookhouse is a large French timber-framed structure, constructed by M. Frédéric Brillant. The vegetables are in fact all grown in a tidy garden inspired by the geometry of the gardens at Villandry. The pots and pans are in fact primarily from Dehillerin of Paris, and although made of copper, they are rarely gleaming. The idea of a soup or sauce, pureed to make the appearance of its primary ingredient impossible, seemed much too modern to me. My primary goal at this farm is to grow, to raise, to prepare primary ingredients of the highest quality, not to obliterate those ingredients.

Although the blender remains on the shelf here, I still stand by the larger goal of enhancing ingredients and not hiding them. On the menu this evening is a perfectly pureed soup that retains the color, the flavor and the smell of its primary ingredient, if not its shape and texture. There is a line that I would prefer not to cross and it is a line that I adjust at whim. A fine, silky liver terrine with not a chewy piece of pork liver in sight is acceptable; a Parmesan foam is simply going too far.

Residing now on my dining room table in the Log House is the weighty, five-volume, acrylic-slip-jacketed book entitled *Modernist Cuisine*. A Christmas gift, this exhaustive tome written by Nathan Myhrvold, Chris Young and Maxime Bilet is two-thousand-plus pages of detailed recipes, photographs and exhaustive studies on how to cook. I wanted to hate it.

I expected it to consist entirely of methods of using liquid nitrogen and dehydrators and centrifuges to create a meal that I would never recognize. Although there are certainly sections that do such magical stunts, a fair percentage of those fifty-plus pounds of text describe the proper way to roast a chicken, for example. Poring through page after page of superbly detailed recipes pushes the question of where that line is: When does cooking—the cooking of the *bonne femme* in the country kitchen—end and where does scientific manipulation in a laboratory begin? Difficult to answer, certainly, but it keeps me enthralled as I pore over the glossy pages of the book.

Back to the task at hand—Tyler has finished straining the

squash soup into the waiting clean soup pot, then sent the sieve, the former soup pot and the blender to the dishwasher for a quick soak and cleaning. Without a word, his face shows the relief that one item on the menu is essentially finished. It will need to be seasoned and garnished prior to service, but those are tasks that he can accomplish quickly during the meal. The soup is put in the refrigerator to chill until it is needed in three hours.

Next to be addressed is the beef roast in the oven. He opens the oven door and pulls the heavy orange Le Creuset covered pot onto the top of the range. The Bakelite knob has long since been broken off, so it is a bit of a challenge to remove the hot lid. As the weighty cast-iron oval lid is slid off of its base, the steam and the smell of the braising beef well up. Immediately Tyler has a sense of the progress of the main course. With a quick slip of a thin, sharp knife, the beef effortlessly yields, indicating its doneness. The wet, warm heat for hours has broken down the toughness of the roast. It is fork-tender and has been transformed from the tough cut that it was this morning to an easily enjoyed piece of beef later this afternoon.

With two main courses securely in good standing, Tyler's mood changes perceptively. From the slightest hint of panic and worry earlier today, now comes a lightheartedness and the desire to joke and prance a bit: he is confident that he can finish on time.

I check the trays of hard rolls rising on the speed rack at the end of the kitchen line. Throughout the early morning they have slowly warmed up to room temperature. Over the lunch hour they began to proof—they begin to rise. The yeast has slowly been expanding and growing, puffing out the rolls. At seven this morning they were cold, clammy and firm; now, at two in the afternoon, they are warm and light. I covered them with a towel to keep them from drying out too much. If they had dried too much on the surface and crusted over, the rising would have been hindered. It's good to see they have risen well and adequately. Also, the oven is empty now that the beef braise has been removed, and I can bake off my rolls. The towel is removed, a bit of flour is dusted over the tops of the rolls and they are placed in the oven at four-hundred degrees. With the two trays of bread now baking, I can go back to readying the dining room.

Tyler has begun to approach the vegetables. They require less time and their preparation was held off until the more time-consuming meats and starches were finished.

In large old plastic milk crates from the restaurant are stored the Yukon Gold potatoes that I dug from the garden. They dried in the sunny afternoons on the dirt after they were dug. Although they soaked up that sun, they still are very fresh; they smell of the earth, they smell like potatoes and soil and dirt. Weeks later potatoes feel inert, lacking in life or connection to the ground they were grown in. But these are fresh and lively. They will be a welcome addition to the beef braise.

Tyler picks through the bin, looking for twenty-plus spuds that are of the same size and shape—a couple of inches long and kind of fat and oblong. These aren't the large, rotund, bulbous russets from the supermarket. Those russets feel vulgar and grotesque compared to the serious, humble Yukon Golds. The skins of these beautiful tubers have a corresponding texture—they are in fact as golden as their name implies, and they are not uniform in texture. The skins are mottled and varied; they look like the gems that they are. When Tyler has found those that he likes, he washes them quickly but lightly. He wants to remove any remaining dirt, yet not remove the still-fragile thin, fresh skin.

He grabs a stockpot, a smaller one, fills it with cold, fresh water and drops the twenty Yukon Golds into the pot and adds a healthy amount of salt to season them while they are cooking. Just outside the front door of the Cookhouse are the two large sweet bay laurel trees. He clips a large branch of the fresh bay and brings it into the kitchen. Like the potatoes, these bay leaves in no way resemble the versions in the supermarket. They are bright, green leaves, full of life, and smell greatly of their grassy spirit. As Tyler can be a bit excessive even when I think it is unnecessary, he takes each leaf from the branch, washes it quickly and with a sharp, small paring knife makes a few slits in the leaf. The cuts are parallel to each other and perpendicular to the stem.

The goal of the leaf-cutting is to release the essential oils contained within the tender bay leaves. Most likely the potatoes will be adequately scented without such extra steps, but fine cooking is the accumulation of many small details.

The potatoes will sit in cool water loaded with bay on the back of the range until they are ready to be cooked. The goal is to have them finished cooking just before they go onto the plate with the beef.

With the potatoes safely ensconced in the cool water, he turns his attention to the remaining vegetables needed for the dinner. He and I head out to the kitchen garden. It has been warm, never too hot, but adequate for the ripening of most that was planted. It has been the kind of summer I am accustomed to here in the maritime Northwest.

We still need the kale for the poached egg course. In the first bed as we enter through the surrounding deer fence are a collection of kale varieties. There is Winterbor and red Russian kale and white Russian kale and the Lacinato kale that is on the menu. I prefer the more frilly Winterbor kale or the more tender flat leaf of the Russian kales, but the favorite son of the kale world for cooks is Lacinato, sometimes known as Dinosaur Kale or Tuscan kale. I think it is the term *Tuscan* that has made it so very popular among restaurant cooks. It brings up images of the Italian hillsides and rich, flavorful, traditional meals. Winterbor or Russian kale implies dreary Siberian meals of little flavor or style. The frilly, common varieties are also dragging around a legacy of last-century, dirty vegetarian restaurants and cooperative college houses. They pair well with bulgur and tamari salads, to be eaten out of reused plastic Nancy's yogurt containers. Lacinato kale has no such tainted background. There are times when I think that the chefs in this country are so terribly insecure that none could stand up and say that they use an unhip ingredient because they like it. Certainly iceberg lettuce has received a bit of a renaissance on menus as a nostalgic, ironic, tongue-in-cheek ingredient, but it is rare to see a respected restaurant serve anything but the hippest vegetable varieties.

And so I have given in to the preference of the cooks who come out to Cookhouse and I plant Lacinato kale. The plants are vibrant, stalky beasts. The central core is thick and strong, and from that core come foot-long leaves maybe three inches wide with a central vein running the length. The surface appears to be blistered—concave and convex bumps covering the deep green, nearly black leaves.

Tyler and I snap off the leaves at their base where they attach to the trunk. They do not snap as easily as the less-fashionable kales, leaving remnants of the leaves attached. When we are finished harvesting, the plants have the look of a poorly done haircut with ripped bits surrounding the rough crenellated stems. We return to the kitchen, where Tyler will wash the kale thoroughly and devein it by slicing lengthwise with a sharp paring knife just adjacent to the central vein.

There is little need for me to accompany the cook into the garden to harvest the vegetables. He is perfectly capable of recognizing the Dino kale or the herbs or vegetables he is interested in. Cooks do, however, tend to have a focused interest; they cut and pick that which they need for the meal at hand. My goals are more varied: I want great vegetables to grace the table while at the same time preserving the plants in the garden for future harvests. At times my goals and the cooks' are in opposition. Kale is generally harvested from the base, upward toward the newest sprouts at the top. The lower leaves are older and larger, the higher leaves are younger and smaller. If the uppermost leaves are picked, the plant will be given the signal to not grow taller, that it should only grow laterally. With both Tyler and myself harvesting side by side, we can accommodate both interests—great food for tonight and preserving the potential for great growth in the near future to assure quality food for the next meal.

Once the kale is released from its tough vein, it is sliced widthwise into two-inch pieces. These nearly square bits of waxy green are put into a large stainless-steel bowl, covered with a damp towel and removed to the reach-in cooler until needed during service.

While we were in the garden the rolls have finished baking. The Cookhouse is filled with the smell of freshly baking bread: yeasty and nutty. I quickly open the weighty oven door to check on their doneness. Each is ideal. The flour that was dusted on the top is nearly burnt—deep brown and dark. The sides of the rolls show the characteristic oven spring of a well-baked roll. The dough was flat and sagging when it was popped in the oven twenty minutes earlier. The high bottom heat gave the rolls an initial burst that caused the bottom edges of the rolls to rise up. And the outer crust is beautifully crisp and hard. I pull the two trays out and move them to the speed rack to cool. Over the next few minutes, the crusts will crack, resembling the segmented plates of a turtle's shell.

Tyler begins to go over the final menu for the evening in more detail and categorizes the herbs needed for the garnishes. Sage is needed for the squash soup, Italian flat-leaf parsley to chop finely for the beef braise, and oregano and thyme for the pizzas. Just north of the wood-fired oven, out the back door of the Cookhouse, are the herb beds. Similar to the large raised beds of the kitchen garden, the herb beds hold a motley collection of herbs. Ever-changing, herbs come and go depending on which froze out in the past winter and which have been removed from lack of use in the past summer. A few persevere year in and year out. The thyme, parsley, sage and oregano are certainly standards; the sorrels, although not really herbs will always have a place. Lemon balm has sadly taken over despite its lack of utility. The lovage is tremendously too large and tall to remove and so it gets a continued spot. Rose geraniums are often replanted each spring despite their tenderness in the face of the winter chills. The chives have thankfully spread handsomely from their early beginnings as a few seed-started alliums six years ago. A handful of those needed for tonight's dinner are picked and brought into the kitchen.

Tyler returns to the garden to fetch the rest of the vegetables. Although I most likely do not need to accompany him, I do, if only habitually. He is certainly capable of choosing a cabbage, but still I worry. The cabbages are located in a far bed of the kitchen garden, near the blueberries, past the asparagus and adjacent to the winter squash beds. These stout brassicas are in varieties of shapes and colors and apparent personalities.

There are Dutch flathead cabbages—an unlikely-shaped head, round yet not spherical, as if it had been grown under the weight of a large plank that kept it smooth and flat on the top. Next to the flattened ones are the cone-shaped cabbages. The extreme opposite of their Dutch neighbors, these are round in shape as well, but rise up to a high point instead of a flattened face. They appear to be much more regal, joyous and uplifting than the dour Dutch. The seeds came from a seed packet in my collection, the packet name and information long since faded and illegible. I planted them anyway, ignorant to the variety.

The third variety in the straight, regimented rows is Charmant, the largest and showiest of the cabbages. It is indeed round, and spherical as one would expect from a cabbage. The leaves are frilly and open and surround the tight, compact central sphere. It does in fact carry the French couture character that its name implies. The taste is sweet and tender as well.

The final cabbage, in the far end of the raised bed, is the Savoy. The first three are all odd shapes but are still essentially very similar—roundish green cabbages with smooth, flat

leaves. This fourth cabbage in the lineup, however, is different.
The Savoy is neither flat nor smooth. The leaves are lighter in
color, almost chartreuse, and are frilly and crinkly and much
more flexible and pliable than the more staid, rigid green cabbages of the rest of the bed.

The specimen selected for the salad tonight is one of the
Dutch flathead varieties. It is large, yet not grotesquely so.
Firm, yet not so old that it is tough; this one appears to be at
its peak. With the blade of a sharp knife I release it from its
grounding stem and hand it to Tyler. It is oddly heavy, unexpectedly for its size. Our eyes generally can size up the anticipated weight of an item quickly and accurately. Cabbages,
oddly, do not read as heavy as they in fact are. I am startled
every time.

With the walk back from the garden, past the large bay
sentries and into the Cookhouse, we now have all of the ingredients for this evening's meal in the kitchen. This growing and
accumulating of meats and vegetables and herbs and fruits
and dairy has spanned more than two years, and this cabbage
is the last ingredient to come through the clumsy French doors
into the kitchen.

FOURTEEN

The Guests Arrive; the Feast Begins

For thirty-plus years I have been *in service*. On most every week since I graduated from college, I would stand in a dining room and take care of diners. Some years I would be the actual waiter, in others a manager or eventually the owner overseeing the meal. In meals such as this one tonight, I have a hand in the preparation of the food, and in serving the meal. Even with three decades of experience, I am still nervous and anxious before service every time. Soon after we finish lunch and begin the final couple of hours before the guests arrive, I call out the time to Chef Tyler, letting him know how close we are to the time when the guests will arrive. Tyler is of a completely different personality than I am. He too has spent most of his adult life in restaurants. He is tremendously concerned with doing his best work, but he never appears to be as anxious as myself. He actually jokes about it with me, most likely to deflect from the possibility that he too is nervous.

With the bulk of the prep behind us and lunch finished, we go over the menu, settling on the details of the final draft. We had a good idea at seven this morning what the meal would be, but circumstances unknown at the time have altered the details. I will still wait a couple of hours to write my copy, in case of additional changes, but this is our last chance to make substantive alterations.

The menu discussion is a quick conversation and immediately afterward Tyler begins the rolling of the two doughs he made earlier and left to rest on the counter. The first he attends to is the pasta dough.

To roll both of these doughs to their desired thickness easily and consistently, we use a pasta roller, which is essentially a sheeter. Bakeries use sheeters to roll out a variety of doughs to a consistent thickness. The mechanism is two opposing metal rollers, which are either propelled by hand or by an electric motor to move the dough, with a way to mechanically vary the distance between the two rollers. As the distance between the rollers decreases, the dough becomes increasingly thinner. In a commercial bakery the rollers could be two feet across with a long counter on either side to accommodate an increasingly longer piece of dough as it becomes thinner and thinner.

For pasta making, this same concept is scaled down dramatically to where the rollers are eight inches across at most. A small household pasta sheeter might be just five inches in width. The pasta roller at the farm is an Italian model, restaurant-sized with a width of eight inches and it is hand-cranked.

The block of pasta dough made this morning weighs more than six pounds. It would be unwieldy to roll the entire volume at once and so it is cut into six pie-shaped pieces with the bench scraper. One piece is worked while the other five are rewrapped to keep them from drying out. One by one Tyler will roll the blocks of dough into ever thinner sheets of pasta. The width of the sheet will maintain at just under the maximum of eight inches and the length will slowly but dramatically increase with the thinness until the sheet is sixty inches long. When each sheet is adequately thin, it will be set aside to dry, and then Tyler will go on to the next block of dough. Only when all six sheets are finished and sufficiently dry will he return and cut them into the final noodle shape.

The goal of the rolling is threefold. We want the pasta to be very thin. They will increase in thickness when they are cooked, so the goal is to make them palatable, tender and refined. A thick noodle is most likely a gummy, doughy noodle, as opposed to a delicate pasta with a slight tooth to it. The rolling out of the dough also laminates the pasta, creating a strong, rigid noodle. By *laminates*, I mean that the dough has numerous layers, pressed together through the rolling process. The final goal is the creation of gluten in the dough. The kneading on the counter created most of the strength of the dough, but the rolling will contribute to it as well.

Once Tyler has firmly mounted the sheeter onto the counter with a large C-clamp, he divides the large block of dough into six equal parts. He takes out the first one and rewraps the remaining five with the plastic wrap to keep them from drying out. With a long French rolling pin he begins to create the shape and thickness that he needs. The rollers only open so wide, so it is necessary to thin out the pasta by hand with the rolling pin before it can be further reduced with the sheeter. The shape of the beginning dough is also important. Curiously, for years I would take a round ball of pasta dough, flatten it and begin to roll it through a pasta machine, endlessly frustrated in my futile efforts to create a long, rectangular-shaped final sheet of pasta. I would fold and push and cajole the pliable dough into my angular goal with little success. Only after watching far more experienced cooks did I realize that it was tremendously easier to shape the ball of dough into a rectangle at the very beginning and then to simply roll it out in the pasta machine.

Watching Tyler roll out the pasta dough is both calming and still mesmerizing to me. He is very good at it and has done it many times in his career. It is part of his practice. It is a physical act and yet it does take some thought. Not much, however, as he can keep a running conversation going the entire time and listen to classic rock, bouncing to the beat as he forms the dough.

Once he has created a small rectangle from a round of dough with his rolling pin, he feeds it into the rollers with his left hand, the right hand turning the large wooden-handled crank on the side of the pasta machine. He turns it clockwise, first just slow enough to engage the leading edge of the dough and then very quickly, the dough rapidly exiting from the other side. Once the dough is halfway through the rollers, he quickly and effortlessly switches hands, his right hand gently pulling the dough through, the left hand running the crank. When the dough has fully exited the rollers, Tyler quickly dusts the sheet a bit with flour he has left in a small pile on the wooden counter. And back through the pasta goes, his left hand rotating the crank, his right hand feeding the edge in and so on. Back and forth the dough travels in a lovely pace; not frantic or terse, but gentle and efficient. Every couple of trips of the pasta through the rollers, Tyler switches the knob one more notch—each time pulling the rollers ever so slightly closer together—making the dough even thinner.

After a few passes of the pasta through the machine, Tyler stops and refolds the dough. It is a long rectangle at this point, eight inches across and twenty inches in length. He folds one of the long ends of the dough one-third down the length. He takes the other end and folds it one-third of the way up the length. What Tyler now has on the board is a small rectangle of pasta— it is three sheets high and one-third as long as it was before the folding. He takes the rolling pin and flattens it just a bit to laminate the sheets together, then proceeds to feed it back through the rollers of the pasta machine. As it is thicker once again, he will have to open up the rollers a little and then proceed.

Throughout the process Tyler will fold the dough over three or four times, continuing to pass the dough back and forth through the rollers, dusting the dough as needed, all in a seemingly seamless ritual. The back-and-forth occasionally will be interrupted by the folding, but without much apparent thought. The chatter and the mouthing the words to the Led Zeppelin songs seem to take more thought that the actions of his hands. When the dough has reached the desired thinness, Tyler gently picks up the long, four-foot-plus piece of thin yet strangely strong dough, walks to the back porch and gently lays it out flat on the back table. When he returns he removes the plastic wrap from another portion of dough on the counter. The next portion follows the routine of the first and so on until no more dough remains on the counter and on the back porch are long lengths of thin, smooth dough.

The eggs gave the dough moisture. When the dough was resting the flour fully hydrated, distributing the moisture throughout. When the dough is rolled out thinly it will dry quickly depending on the weather. Today is ideal—warm, yet not hot, and neither humid nor terribly dry. In a few minutes the sheets will have lost enough moisture to be cut. If they had been cut immediately after rolling, the individual pieces of pasta would have stuck to one another.

The test for dryness is entirely tactile. He repeatedly feels the sheets of pasta between his thumb and forefinger, rubbing it a bit, getting a sense of how flexible and dry the pasta is. It is a warm and sunny afternoon and the sheets dry quickly. When each sheet in turn passes the tactile test, Tyler brings it back into the kitchen and lays it out on the wooden counter. The ends are already fairly square, but with a long-bladed chef's knife he trims the sheet on each end to square it up. Now the pasta is a perfect rectangle, about four feet long and eight inches wide, dusted lightly with flour and just dry enough to neither stick nor to crack. At this point the long sheet needs to be cut into individual lengths. Each length will be "as long as a shoe box." I am not sure just how long a shoe box is, but I would guess twelve inches, more or less. The first shoe box length is cut from the long four-foot sheet of fresh pasta. The remaining three feet of pasta is slid over on top of first length and lined up on its far edge. The second cut can then be made in the long sheet at the same length as the first. Then the remaining long sheet can be slid on top of the first two sheets, which are stacked on top of each other, and a third shoe-box-length cut, and so on until all that remains is the final remnant of the long pasta sheet. If Tyler has planned this well, and he usually has, that last piece will be identical to the others.

This symphony of actions—the back-and-forth passing of the dough through the pasta machine, taking the pasta sheets outside, checking them and bringing them back to be cut—continues until the large round of fresh dough on the counter is gone and in its place is a stack of thin, just-dry pasta. Perhaps a half hour has passed, and all the while Tyler has carried on a conversation, sung to the radio and appeared to barely look down at what his hands have been doing.

Each noodle is three-quarters of an inch wide for the intended pappardelle-style noodle. The knife is guided by the knuckles of Tyler's opposing hand. After each cut his hand moves the allotted distance down the pasta and the next noodle is cut. When the final cut is made, the knife is slid under the length of noodles and effortlessly lifts up the row of cut noodles. As the knife is raised, the noodles gently fall out of their fold, balanced on the dull edge of the chef's knife. Tyler slides them off of the knife by tilting it and he now has a perfectly organized pile of just-cut pappardelle. With a quick turn of his hand he creates a gentle nest of pasta and places it onto a large perforated sheet tray until he will cook them for the meal. He moves on until the sheet tray is filled with a beautiful grid of flour-dusted nests, each one made of golden noodles of identical length and width.

I describe this in such detail because it is remarkable and also because it is such an alluring skill. When you watch someone who has made pasta for many years, it appears effortless. There is seemingly little connection between his hands and his brain. His hands appear to have a memory of how to cut the pasta just so and to hold the dough just right as it is pulled through the rollers of the pasta machine. It is only when Tyler has left and I attempt to make my own pasta that I realize there is great effort involved. My pasta is still quite tasty, but it is a little less even and takes twice as long to produce. Until Ben started working here full time, I milked cows nearly every day and can do the mechanical act effortlessly. It is only when I try to teach someone else how to do it that I realize that it isn't effortless; that it is the constant repetition that makes it so. Tyler's pasta-making is the same.

Once the pasta is completed, Tyler grabs four of the hard rolls from the speed rack. He roughly chops each of them and places the chunks onto a small sheet pan and throws them into the oven. He realizes he needs bread crumbs for the pasta dish and begins to dry out some bread in preparation. It's a quick task and then he returns to roll out the crackers. The process is similar—the dough is divided into manageable portions, each in turn is rolled out with the pasta machine till it is at its thinnest level. There is no need to build up the gluten, however. The goal is the opposite, in fact—the dough is rolled out quickly without an attempt build up strength in it. The cracker dough is tender and weak, barely able to hold together once it is as thin as possible. When a full sheet is completed, it is laid flat on the board and quickly cut with a pizza roller into cracker shapes of an inch across and six inches in length. With the help of a bench scraper they are gently lifted off the counter and laid out on the perforated baking sheet. Before a tray full of crackers is baked they are lightly salted and then a generous dose of cracked black pepper is added. They are baked immediately with no need for the dough to dry or rest. With the small amount of baking powder in the dough they will puff slightly in the hot oven. The thin crackers will bake quickly and the telltale sign of their completition is the smell of browning flour. The nuttiness will fill the kitchen, indicating the lightly toasted crackers are done. A minute more, and the waferlike crackers would burn and the nuttiness would turn to an undesirable burnt bitterness.

The crackers are set aside to cool, filling the kitchen with the pure, sweet, nutty smell of toasted crackers.

Tyler turns to preparing his *mise en place*. This bit of classical French culinary terminology continues even in the most modern and non-French of kitchens. *La mise* is the past participle of the French verb *mettre*, meaning "to put." The second half of the phrase, *en place*, is as it sounds—"in its place." Even though this is a leftover of the Escoffier era, it still remains, albeit in a grossly abridged and bastardized form. If you walk through a restaurant kitchen anywhere in America today just before service, you will most likely hear chatter about the "meeez."

What this leftover of the French dominance in cuisine refers to is to have everything set up and ready for service. Specifically, all of the ingredients needed to stock the *garde manger* and other stations of a standard restaurant kitchen. In the case of Tyler preparing his *mise* this afternoon, he will prepare a series of white ramekins, each filled with the chopped herbs and chilies and garlic and other ingredients necessary for him to quickly complete this evening's dinner.

He reaches for a couple of the dried chilies that hang in a *ristra* above his head from one of the beams of the Cookhouse. He removes each dried green stem, splits the brittle chilies lengthwise and allows the dried seeds to fall out, then proceeds to finely dice the faded red chilies. With the side of his knife, he scoops of the small pile of spicy bits and slides them into a small ramekin. Reminded of the rolls drying in the oven, he grabs a towel and pulls them out, leaving them to cool on the counter. Soon he will chop them finely for the pasta. Next up, he will cut a sprig of oregano from the herb garden together with a small bunch of chives. On his short walk back into the Cookhouse he will pass by the small-leaved thyme cascading over the sides of the garden beds and cut a sprig of it as well. He strips the leaves from the stems of the thyme and oregano and gently chops the aromatic herbs, filling two more ramekins with their respective herbs. The chives as well will be finely chopped and fill a fourth small soufflé dish. A few cloves of the fresh garlic are peeled and finely diced, a large head of a robust Ambition shallot as well. In the end six ramekins are lined up on the edge of his counter. He turns to the onions and picks out two of the best fresh Copra onions, dices them in nearly identical pieces and places them in a large plastic container by the side of the range. As a last bit of preparation before the guests arrive, he wipes down the round hardwood butcher block and the rest of the counters, scrubbing them clean. He drops his soiled bar towels into the laundry in the bathroom and proceeds to grab a new set from the dryer. One he will fold methodically, creating a eight-inch-long rectangle a couple of inches deep. It will be placed next to his chopping block parallel to the long edge of the counter. On it each of the knives he will use during service are placed. He picks up each, wipes it clean with a fresh towel and places it deliberately on the folded cloth, the tip resting on the fresh towel, the handle on the counter. As he finishes up this fanatical ritual, the first guests start to arrive.

The cars come down the long driveway, the gravel making enough noise to alert Daisy to visitors. Byron, fast asleep under the dining table, awakes and begins his boisterous barking. He has no idea what he is barking about, but he has been awakened by Daisy's much more observant nature and proceeds to join in, however tardy and unknowing.

In a few moments the guests have parked their cars and have headed down the sidewalk to the Cookhouse. The concrete walk is parallel to the building fifteen feet from the long wall of windows. Both Tyler and I immediately look up to see a small parade of welcome guests pass by before turning to walk between the two oversized bay leaf trees and to the French doors. In those few moments, while the casual, chatty guests amble down the short walk, Tyler manages to change the music from his ubiquitous classic rock to a more apt musical selection for the evening. I give a few last moments of attention to the table, adjusting a few wine glasses and silver unnecessarily. As the guests reach the doors, Tyler and I glance over at each other, aware that our private day that began nine hours earlier has ended. From now till the end of the evening the room will have visitors in it, and even though we both know everyone attending, we approach this as a job and not as a friendly dinner party.

My voice and attitude change, the music has slowed down and Led Zeppelin will not be played for days, if not months, in this room. Tyler will put on a different air—friendly and flirtatious but in a very public way. I will be gracious and kind, but I easily fall back into the role of service that I was taught thirty years earlier. It is a way of communicating and presenting myself that I find comforting but which I abhor at times. These twenty guests will only see a public me, although they believe it a true representation. They view this farmer, this host, as a contented, confident man, loving this rural life alone on this farm. This has some truth to it, certainly, but I present a vision that they want to see.

On my last birthday, I made dinner for just a few of my closest friends. As I stood up at the head of the table, I began a short speech about the meal and the wines to be served. Two of those who know me best immediately screamed out to me to shut up and sit down. They then proceeded to inform me that they had no interest in that "Cookhouse voice," and they were there to see me, the authentic me. Tonight this table will be content with the professional me, unaware that there is any other.

The Cookhouse is beautifully designed for this opening act of the evening. The guests enter through the front double doors, come straight to me in the middle of the room for a glass of wine and then pass through to the back double doors, out of the Cookhouse, to the wood-fired oven, the herb beds and the creamery.

As the guests enjoy their wine, Tyler has been preparing to make the pizzas. The wood oven is full of fire, hot and ready to bake the thin pies. The doughs were portioned earlier in the day and have proofed beautifully; they have easily doubled in size.

On the counter is the aluminum tray with the proofed rounds of dough, a small bag of semolina flour, a rolling pin, the small copper pot of tomato sauce and the *mise en place*.

To ready the oven, Tyler pushes the fire back to one of the

far corners of the masonry chamber. The fire has burned in the front center since I lit it early this morning. The ceiling of the barrel-vaulted oven has changed from the black, charred color to a dull white, indicating the high heat needed to bake the thin pies. The pizzas will be baked in the center of the oven. To maintain the heat needed, the fire will be kept lit throughout the baking.

The deck of the oven is swept clean of the ash that has built up through the day. A long-handled brush with metal bristles easily pulls the fine ash forward into the ash drop located at the front of the oven. When the bulk of the debris has been removed, Tyler wraps a well-moistened bar towel loosely around those same spiky metal bristles and drags the wet cloth around the brick deck of the hot oven. The towel will be ruined for any other task by the heat and the ash that it will pick up, yet the bricks will be clean and ready for the incoming pies.

Back in the kitchen, just a few steps from the wood-fired oven, the pizzas will be rolled and prepared. The pizza dough that I prepared last evening and pulled from the cooler this morning has now fully proofed. It is large and puffy and filled with gas from the day-long growth of the yeast. Tyler punches each of the eight rounds of dough down; the air held within rapidly leaks out and what remains are flat five-inch disks of deflated dough.

Tyler begins to roll the doughs into their desired form. It is a mechanical act and not unlike that of rolling out the pasta dough. He neither thinks about it nor watches what he is doing. I want to describe it as an act of muscle memory. I tend to snicker when I hear such terms during yoga class, but it makes sense here. His hands know how to transform the thick, puffy mixture of flour and water into a thin, consistent disk ready for the hot brick oven. It is a deft movement: one hand pushes the dough out from the center, extending the radius of the round form, the other hand rotates the disk on the floured counter. In tandem, these two motions slowly enlarge the lumpy five-inch disk into a flat eight-inch one. This quick action could suffice, but Tyler is too much of a showman to let an opportunity to impress pass. His first job a decade and a half ago was at a small-town pizzeria—Sidney's Pizza Café. I don't know what this spot was like, but I have an idea. Since it was located in Billings, Montana, I would anticipate that the food was rather tasty, the staff terribly earnest and the menu as far from the trends and fads of the nation's gastronomic centers of New York and San Francisco as Billings is geographically.

What Tyler did gain from his tenure at the provincial pizza café was the ability to throw pizzas. As an energetic sixteen-year-old, amused entirely by video games and pot smoking, he must have found the challenge of perfecting this physical task rewarding. I envision him spending every available moment during the down times throwing pizza dough in the air—both to master the task and also to impress the young high school students who frequented the bustling restaurant. He has changed little in those seventeen years. Still obsessed with mastering the task at hand and also thrilled to impress the ladies—in this case, those food-obsessed folks who come to the farm for dinner.

What is so impressive is his ability both to toss the thin, flimsy pie dough into the air, giving it a bit of a spin and then catching it in his awaiting hands, and also to keep his eyes on those in front of him, laughing and telling stories all the while. It is multitasking of a level more advanced than simply texting while waiting in line at the bank, or checking Facebook while writing a manuscript.

With a confident smile and a flirting manner, Tyler continues to throw the dough into the air, pushes it out a bit more, turns it a little and throws it again, catching it each time with aplomb until the dough is consistent in its shape and thickness and size.

Waiting just in front of the doughs and flour on the counter is a medium-sized copper pot with the tomato sauce, and next to that a white ceramic ramekin with chopped chilies and a second one filled with finely chopped fresh herbs: the *mise en place*. A bit of sauce is ladled out of the copper pot and with the back of the ladle it is smeared evenly over the dough; a spiral motion coats the entire circular shape easily and quickly. Then a bit of chilies are picked up with the thumb and index finger and distributed out onto the awaiting sauce; the fresh herbs as well.

The pie, ready for the oven now, lies on the floured counter. To transport this flimsy, unbaked jewel to the heat of the oven a peel is needed. We use a modern aluminum peel, common in any pizzeria in the nation. At first a beautiful beech peel was attempted. It was old and from Eastern Europe and terribly stylish. It also was hand-carved wood and hence was thick and unwieldy. I am sure the Europeans of the time managed just fine, but ours has been relegated to the dustbin and replaced with a highly functional aluminum model with little or no stylish cachet.

The job of the peel is to pick up the pizza and then to drop it well into the hot chamber of the brick oven. And to return to pick up the crispy, baked pie from the floor of the oven and pull it out and into the kitchen. The design of this tool is simple: a long wooden handle connected to a flat, square or rectangular thin plate. The handle is long enough to reach the far corners of the oven.

Tyler dusts the blade of the peel with semolina flour. The semolina is coarse and grainy and gives an additional texture to the final pizza. Some of the flour used to load and unload the pizzas into the oven will remain on the underside of the pizza. The coarseness of the semolina also allows the flexible, uncooked dough to easily slide off of the peel and onto the hot bricks of the oven.

Once the aluminum peel is dusted with the semolina, he carefully slides the thin blade under the delicate pizza on the wooden counter. With one hand he lifts up one edge of the round pie, with the other hand he guides the peel under the dough. With a bit of luck the dough slides up the slick metal blade; in another's hands it would be a smashed wad of sauce and dough and flour, unwilling to ride up the blade, defiantly remaining on the counter. Even with his years of experience, the shape of the formerly round pizza has changed, a bit more oval, a bit stretched out here and there where he helped it along.

He turns and heads out through through the double doors of the Cookhouse to the oven a dozen feet away. The fire is burning in the back corner, the ceiling of the brick-lined chamber is white and the oven deck is swept and cleaned. And hot. He reaches the peel into the chamber, places the pizza over the back center hot spot and jerks back the long wooden handle. The peel exits the oven, the pizza slides on the gritty semolina and falls onto the bricks and begins its nearly instant cooking.

The temperature is in a workable range: six hundred to seven hundred degrees. The dough is not in a pan or tray but is sitting directly on the bricks. Almost immediately it begins to puff up: the air bubbles from the yeast expanding in the heat. The formerly delicate dough stiffens and browns at the base. The tomato sauce begins to heat and bubble, surrounded by a robust inner tube of puffy dough. In another minute the bubbling sauce and the puffy crust will change from brown to blackened. As is the style of the day, a perfect pizza is thin, crisp and blistered. Tyler is looking to have at least one large bubble in the pizza that rises up above the level of the rest of the pizza and blackens from the increased closeness to the heat and the thinness of the crust.

It is a stylistic preference and one of the times. I still hold dear to a chewy, doughy pizza pie from any one of many small pizza shops in New York, coated in olive oil, sweet tomato sauce and slices of pepperoni and questionable cheese. The thin Neapolitan pizzas that come out from this wood-fired oven bear little resemblance to that icon of Gotham nourishment. The sauce is just a smear on the crackerlike crust. Only the edge has a bit of chewiness to it. These styles and trends are dynamic, ever-changing. I can foresee myself in my seventies, still at this farm, baking pizzas with chewy, glutenous crusts complete with toppings, perhaps even pineapple and Canadian bacon, my favorite during the 1970s.

Today, however, thin rules and Tyler picks up the quickly cooking pizza from the oven with the peel. The danger now is not in smashing the uncooked dough into a wad of raw sauce and dough, but rather in not being able to pick up the firm disk. A nervous hand will simply push the pizza deeper into the oven chamber. The oven has little room to push the pizza around and at the rear remains the burning fire. Certainly I have seen well-intentioned cooks push a finished pizza right into a hot fire, unable to capture the pizza with the peel. The trick is to jerk the handle toward the pie in the same way that it was jerked back to drop the pizza on the deck. Confidence is the key, and Tyler has it in spades.

He picks up the first pizza, turns and strides to the kitchen and easily slides the finished pizza onto the maple chopping block in the center of the room. He picks up a pinch of fresh, chopped herbs and sprinkles them over the steaming pizza. He grabs a long-bladed knife from the rack on the side of the chopping block and rapidly cuts the pizza into eight slices. It's a practiced action—the blade rocks back and forth, cutting across the circle, then turning and cutting again, and then again and again. With luck, the result is eight equally sized slices, ready for the guests milling around nearby. Before eight sets of hands have reached in to grab a steaming slice, Tyler has returned to the counter, picked up another raw disk of dough and begun the process all over again. In a few moments he will be headed out of the kitchen with another pizza for the oven.

The pizzas are ideally designed for this service. They are superior when eaten immediately. When hot they are still tender, the crusts flexible, the sauce filled with the flavor of tomatoes and chilies and the herbs blooming with their fragrance released by the heat. The bits of semolina that cling to the bottom of the crust are crispy and gritty. The large bubble in the center of the pizza is thin and cracks and is full of the charred, blackened taste from the high heat of the fire. In a few minutes the steam will have fully escaped, the crust fully crispy, and the tomato sauce will have set into the crust, the herbs flat and dull. Still a tasty slice, but nothing like the experience of the moment when the pizza is sliced and fresh from the oven.

The guests continue to peck at the pizzas, coming in to grab a slice, retreating to savor it, then returning to grab a second. Simply the fact that only eight slices come from the oven at a time makes it a dynamic situation. If sixty slices could be set out on the butcher block all at the same time, folks would enjoy their pizza, no question, but the vibrant nature of the pizzas coming out one at a time would be lost. Everyone gets fed, but the tension of eight slices at a time for twenty folks adds to the excitement. Twenty respectable friends, casually standing in the Cookhouse, wine glasses in hand, chatting with others yet keeping an eye on the back doors, waiting for Tyler to return with another pie, makes this course more exciting. Scoring a fresh, hot slice makes one savor the experience that much more. Missing out on the first or second pizza gives the diner a resolve to move in a little closer for the next round, listen a little more casually to the story from their friend, to feign casualness when reaching for a slice of that third pizza. We all like to win; to eat what we kill, even if we are well dressed and have a glass of rosé perched in one hand.

When the pizzas have run their course, the folks ebb and flow from the three sets of double French doors of the Cookhouse, checking out the oven, watching the cow-milking in the parlor and popping into the greenhouse to see how the tomatoes and chilies are faring. A few venture farther, walking to the gardens and going up and down the rows, looking over each of the raised beds, noting the Brussels sprouts or the cabbages or the asparagus that is fully unrecognizable from its spring-time state.

I live here year-round, work here most of every day and it is of my creation. Still, I am amazed and bewildered by the actions of the crows or deer and each year find new varieties to plant or can be overcome with joy when I bite into a fully ripe Charentais melon as if I have never had one before.

I forget some of the charms of this farm until six or seven cars full of friends descend on it for a Saturday afternoon and evening and wander among the vegetables and fruit trees and pastures, exclaiming about a cherry tomato ripe on the plant or a baby cow in the stall or the diminutive Seckel pears on the trees. I am reminded that they are exceptional and exciting and beautiful.

Slowly the folks reassemble in the Cookhouse. They come back through the doors; the odd one or two have to be found still out in the barn or sitting at the raised beds in the garden. When the full lot have returned and taken a seat at the fir table, the meal can commence. Half slide down the long, smooth bench that lines the wall under the windows, the others grab one of the chairs that line the other side of the table. Those on the bench can watch the kitchen easily, those in the chairs can see across the grass and into the garden.

Tyler has cleaned the butcher block of the last errant pieces of pizza, whipped it clean and put away the remaining ingredients from his pizza making. The counter is now clean and scrubbed, the flour that dusted the counter for the rolling of the pizza doughs is scraped off and in its place are the trays of cooked rolls, a small ramekin of fresh sage leaves, and on the range is the pot of squash soup, along with a small copper pot with melted butter.

Once all twenty have settled into their places and filled their glasses with wine, I step up to the table and tell them about dinner. I have done this at least two hundred and fifty times, and yet I am still apprehensive. I have something to say about the food and why this dinner is different, how everything they will eat tonight comes from this farm. Everything except flour, sugar, salt, pepper, coffee beans and wine. It is a short list and I wish it were shorter, but without question it is an admirable accomplishment. I have printed out a menu for them each, so I can speed through the menu fairly quickly. Throughout the evening they will refer back to that small card and refresh their memories. A few will generally want to know the name of the squash that is used for the soup, and which squash is used for the pickled pumpkin slices, but most will simply want to enjoy the meal.

While I have been speaking, Tyler has put the two trays of cooked rolls into the hot gas oven of the range. The butter in the copper pot is slowly browning over a low flame. The soup has slowly been heating without ever boiling. Tyler loves theatrics and after cooking here for many meals has found one of his favorite tricks. When I go over the menu, I mention that the soup is garnished with brown butter and sage. At that moment—and I am always impressed by his timing—he drops the oily chopped sage into the hot brown butter and it immediately sizzles, easily heard by all at the table ten feet from the stove. The diners who were at least partially rapt by my talk turn in unison to Tyler, who puts on a wide, toothy grin, loving the attention.

Once I finish, the meal commences. I am picky about a few things and the rolls are at the top of my list. They are not a particularly unique bread. Certainly the dough was made yesterday and allowed to proof overnight and gain a great yeasty flavor, but to me their unique distinction is the way they are served.

By reheating them completely in a hot oven a few hours after they were baked, the rolls are transformed. The soft crust is completely crispy, cracking off in shards when the diners break them open to butter them. The moisture that still remained inside is now steam, escaping and full of the essence of the wheat rolls. On the table are ramekins of the fresh Jersey butter, and all will pass the golden butter and smear it on the interior of the rolls. It will melt immediately, further flavoring the simple and now not so very dull rolls.

The soup is dished out into twenty shallow white ceramic bowls and each is given a spoonful of the brown-butter-and-sage garnish. The colors and smells are tremendous. The soup is silky and smooth and deep orange in color. It smells sweet and rich as it is passed down the table by the guests. In the center of that sweet-smelling soup is the bit of green and brown oil. It is acrid and nutty and contrasts beautifully with the soup.

Each of the friends picks up an oversized German silver spoon made before the Weimar Republic and begins to sip this silken course. I have a penchant for this early silver. Both the French and the Germans preferred this scale of utensil. They are greatly oversized and appear to be serving spoons to our contemporary American eyes. The Germans, sadly, have followed the lead of our customs and reduced their cutlery, but the French have held on to their culture of weighty spoons and forks. The French also continue to stamp their hallmarks on what we would call the front of the forks and spoons and when setting the table flip the utensils over, the hallmarks facing the table, the tines facing down, the bowls of the spoons as well. The Germans' utensils, including this service used tonight, are stamped with their hallmarks on what we would call the back, the tines facing up, the spoon bowls too.

This service is not sterling per se, but rather eight-hundred-grade. *Sterling* refers to British sterling and to the percentage of silver in the alloy. Sterling—British sterling—is 975 parts pure silver and the remaining 25 parts a non-silver addition. American sterling is 950 parts pure silver and 50 parts other. The Germans, however, use 800 parts of pure silver and 200 parts filler.

I purchased this service years ago at an auction in downtown Seattle. It had been sold earlier in the year, with the auctioneer verbally stating that it was sterling. The winner of the bid then took it to her jeweler, who declared that it was not sterling. She returned it, claiming fraud, and they refunded her purchase. I was thankful and easily arranged to purchase the beautiful, weighty set of forks and spoons, even though the rest of the auction room thought it a disgraced service.

I would contend that British sterling is too pure and perhaps too soft for daily use. The Germans—and Austrians as well—were more practical and cut their silver with harder metals to guarantee the rigidity of their tableware. Perhaps it is my love of these pieces that clouds my judgment. And my German heritage.

Those eating here for the first time—and there are a couple here tonight—pick up the grand spoon set to the right of their plate and marvel at its deep bowl and long, deeply engraved handle. Early this morning I polished them, creating a luster unmatched in any spoon not made primarily of silver. It is shiny, but not flat. There is a tremendous depth to the surface, full of colors and hues unmatched in any simple spoon stamped out of stainless steel. The large concave shape of the deep bowl only contributes to the illusion of depth. Few can resist peering into the mirrorlike spoon before lowering it into the golden, steaming soup for their first taste.

I brought the hard Francesca's Cheese into the kitchen early in the day so that it would have a few hours to temper—to come to the warmer temperature of the kitchen from its comparatively chilly fifty-five-degree domicile of the past many months. After a bit of a pause and with the broad edge of an oversized chef's knife across the top I split the cheese in half, immediately revealing many of this cheese's secrets. As I am cutting through the cheese I can feel that it is fully aged. There is a resistance in the knife as it moves through. If the cheese is inadequately aged the knife will slip too easily through the still-moist interior of the cheese. Today I can feel the resistance—the cheese is dry and firm, not moist and easily cut.

Also, I can smell the cheese better than I could simply from the exterior. It is sweet and pungent. Not pungent in an over-ripe, rotting, ammoniated sort of way, but rather full of flavor; odiferous. It is a good smell. The interior of this Francesca's is deep, bright yellow as expected, and has tiny eyes across the interior—referred to as the paste. Another quick cut, and I now have reduced one of the half wheels to a couple of cheese wedges. I have said that I am cutting through the cheese, but in fact I am splitting the cheese into these requisite pieces. The cheese has aged for a year and a half and has lost most of its moisture. I would expect that it has been reduced to 35 per-cent moisture. Over the past months that moisture has left the cheese, concentrating its flavor, reducing its weight, shrinking its overall dimensions and changing the texture from semi-hard to hard and then to extra-hard. This final texture in the life of this cheese is not simply that it is extra-hard but rather that it flakes rather than cuts.

With the tip of the chef's knife I chip off pieces of Fran-cesca's: little nuggets of cheese, each as big as a quarter or so, some as small as a dime. When I taste this cheese I smile with pleasure. The flavor is rich and a bit caramelly; sweet. It is salty, but not too salty. And it contains crystals.

Crystals are the holy grail of hard cheese making. Falsely thought of as salt crystals, they are in fact not made of salt but rather of concentrations of the amino acid tyrosine. After many months of aging, the amino acid is produced by the breakdown of the proteins in the cheese. Falsely or not, they feel like salt crystals on the tongue and give a wonderful bit of textural excitement to an otherwise uniform cheese. It is only after a full extent of aging that the crystals become apparent. I enjoy tasting early samples of Francesca's Cheese and feeling the seeds of those later latent crystals. The sample today has the appropriate amount of crunch.

Little by little I chip flakes off the wedge of cheese. When I have enough I scoop them up and put them on two six-inch plates. They are tidy plates, with a beautiful wide forest-green band with a thin gold band at the rim, the center of the plate bright white when the plate was produced a century ago and now deepened to ivory. In the center of each of the plates is a small mound of golden flakes of the year-and-a-half-aged cheese. The luxury of the deep green glaze on the porcelain contrasts beautifully with the rustic, errant shapes of the flavorful cheese. I cannot help but smile as I set the plates aside; to me this is the perfect course—simple, flavorful, complete and evocative of a place and time.

The plates of Francesca's Cheese are just one in a series that makes up the antipasti course. In all there will be six items. Each will represent a different sensation—one is salty, another sweet, a third is crispy, the fourth is sour, one is earthy and the last is creamy and rich. The goal is to enliven the taste buds; to prepare them for the meal that is to begin. I think these six items fulfill that goal.

The sweet item is the membrillo, the quince paste that I made with the fruit from the quince picked off the tree just outside the Cookhouse windows. On Wednesday the thick, deeply ruby-colored quince paste was poured into a low sheet tray lined with plastic to cool and set. I set the weighty sheet tray on the rack at the end of the kitchen and walked away. I wanted to check it and pick at it and make sure it was setting properly, but I knew enough to let it rest. And there were other tasks to fill the week. In reality I forgot to obsess over the quince paste rather than was mature enough to just let it be.

Now is the time to check it out. Tyler pulls the large tray from the rack and flips it with a bit of effort onto the stainless steel counter that he has lined with plastic wrap. The heavy, jelled sweet falls onto the plastic and he can lift off the aluminum sheet pan. The quince paste has held up well and jelled adequately. There is no oozing or running onto the counter; just a loud thud as it hits the counter. He peels off the original layer of plastic wrap and reveals the smooth surface of the sweet, gritty jelly. We of course both immediately trim off a bit of an edge with our own knives and taste it: sweet, rose-scented and with the gritty texture that keeps it from feeling like you are sneaking a spoonful of jam out of the Smucker's jam jar in the refrigerator. The grittiness makes it feel serious and savory and grown-up. The quince paste immediately passes inspection and Tyler continues cutting to plate it up for the antipasti course. The quince paste has the ability to hold its shape beautifully and therefore lends itself to intricate cuts of Chef's thin, long, sharp Shun knife. He cuts identical lozenge shapes and delicately arranges them on two bright white contemporary rectangular serving plates. The contrast is striking—the ruby jewels with the sharp facets stand out against the glossy white plate.

While Tyler is cutting the quince paste, I pull the trays of crackers from the cooling rack and arrange them in muslin-lined French *banneton* baskets. These baskets are beautiful objects, designed to proof bread, but now their primary use on the farm is to hold crackers. They are round, eight inches in diameter and four inches high, made of reeds woven to create a flat base and high sloping sides. The interior is lined with muslin fabric, crudely sewn into the basket on the rim.

The baskets had been used in France for years to proof wet doughs before the bread was to be baked. After the bread dough was mixed and kneaded, it was formed into the intended shape—in this case it would be a *boule*, or ball shape—and then dropped into the *banneton*. The muslin lining would have been dredged with flour to keep the dough from sticking to the fabric. After a long, slow rise, the bread dough would fill the *banneton*. It would then be quickly flipped onto a peel dusted with cornmeal and the risen but not yet baked *boule* would land on the flat wooden surface of the peel. From the peel the *boule* would be dropped onto the hot fire bricks of the wood-fired oven. Although I do use the French baskets from time to time for their intended use, they also make fine cracker baskets, the muslin still dredged with flour from past bread doughs.

The still very fresh and crisp crackers fill the two baskets, their sharp, pointed ends splayed out. They will absorb the moisture in the air by morning, but now, just a couple of hours out of the hot oven, they are tight and full of the nutty flavor of the flour.

The next flavor to be considered is sour. Filling this role is the pickled pumpkin. From the large reach-in refrigerator on the side wall of the Cookhouse I pull out a large square plastic container filled with the pickles. Through the semi-opaque plastic I can see the stacks of bright orange slices of the Long Island Cheese. When I open the rigid square plastic lid, the harshness of the vinegar and the sweetness of the pumpkin are immediately apparent. My nose feels the sting of the acid before it smells the scent of the pumpkin pickles. Floating with the tidy slices are a few black peppercorns and long slices of white onions.

With a slotted spoon I ladle a few of the rectangular bright orange slices into two low, oblong porcelain dishes. After a few such scoops, each dish is filled with the crunchy, sour, peppercorn-flecked pickles. The brine is both salty and sweet but without question acidic. The hot vinegar cooked the firm pumpkin slightly so that the pieces have a give to them while retaining their structure and the bright orange color reminiscent of cheap dime-store Halloween candy remains.

For the rich earthy taste in the antipasti course, the chanterelle mushrooms that Michiko and I foraged take the stage. For dinner service tonight, Tyler pulls them from the cooler, trims the bases slightly to remove the less presentable bottoms of the mushrooms and thinly slices the fungi. With its sharp edge the thin knife blade effortlessly cleaves through the tender mushrooms. In a few moments he has a cutting board with a small pile of earthy slices. In a small stainless-steel mixing bowl he adds a bit of red wine vinegar, a bit of warmed honey and a healthy bit of salt, mixes the ingredients gently but completely and slides the tender mushrooms into the bowl. A quick toss coats the taupe-colored slices in a thin covering of the vinaigrette. He gently picks up half the contents and places them in a graceful mound on first one plate and then the second. The mushrooms are further seasoned with a cranking of the pepper grinder and they are good to go. These two plates are about the scent and the flavor and the colors of the forest. The small amount of vinaigrette is only to bring out those subtle flavors, not to overwhelm the delicate fungus flavor. The texture is crisp, yet not like a potato chip or a pickle or a cracker. Maybe *firm* is a more apt description. It is an ephemeral texture; in another day or two on the moist forest floor the chanterelles would have melted back into the ground, soggy and wet and limp. We are lucky enough to savor this place and time and flavor; it is fleeting.

The last plate of the antipasti course is the rich, creamy ricotta dish. Now, as the meal begins, it is ready for the string to be cut, the muslin opened and the ricotta seasoned and sent out to the guests. It is a sublime product: smooth, creamy and subtle without being bland. A bit of salt brings out the milky flavors. The feel of this velveteen ricotta on the tongue is uplifting. It makes me happy to taste a spoonful. What is more remarkable is the simplicity of its preparation: it is not smooth and without grain or grit due to a mechanical process, but rather because of its long, passive draining through the night. I neither forced it through a fine-meshed sieve nor whipped it with a sharp blade of a food processor; I simply left it on the counter to drain overnight.

Tyler adds a bit of salt to bring out the sweetness and flavor, finishes it with a couple tablespoons of finely chopped herbs from the garden and it is done. He could put it in a small ceramic ramekin and it would be entirely enjoyed. I prefer a more detailed presentation and he acquiesces. He takes two of

the large silver spoons and a small glass of cool water together
with the bowl of ricotta and two small serving plates. And then
he begins the process of making twenty fine quenelles.

When I started in restaurants thirty years ago, the era of
haute French cuisine was still in place. I worked at one of the
fanciest French restaurants of the day and the menu included
quenelles de brochet—loosely translated as "footballs of pike."
Although I am waiting for a return of such items on the trendi-
est restaurant menus, it is unlikely that there is anyone serving *quenelles de brochet* outside of France today. The dish is
pureed fish, bound with egg, formed into small ovoid shapes,
poached and then generally served in a cream sauce and finished under the salamander for a bit of color.

Although no chef in this country today would be caught serving such a dated dish, the shapes do remain on contemporary
menus. In this case, made of fresh whey ricotta. To produce
such ovoid, football-esque forms, two moistened spoons are
used.

With the first spoon, Tyler picks up a small amount of the
spreadable ricotta; he transfers the ricotta to the second,
moistened spoon and in the process smoothes out one face of
the cheese. A quick dip of the first spoon in the nearby glass
of water, and he proceeds to transfer the ricotta back to that
spoon, smoothing out the next face, and so on until he holds a
beautiful blimp of smooth, sublime ricotta with no rough edges
and places it gently on the plate. It is fussy and old school,
but it makes me smile and the rapid, dexterous movement
of the polished spoons and the cheese passing back and forth
is hypnotic and catches the attention of the guests a few feet
away. And as with the rolling of the pasta, one's first impression is that it is simple and easy to replicate. Until you pick up
a couple of similar spoons and end up with a mess of smeared
wet ricotta as the result. In that case a simple bowl of ricotta
in a ceramic ramekin presents itself as a beautiful, and much
easier, alternative.

Once the set of antipasti are all readied on the wooden counter, I deliver them to the table one by one. Each side is given one of the two identical plates or dishes or baskets to select a bit from each and then pass it down the row to their neighbor. In a couple of minutes each of the large white service plates has a bit of the six items on it. It is a beautiful palate each guest has created. The shapes are varied, the colors as well. The tastes and textures are equally varied: sweet, sour, crunchy, smooth, rich and plain. It is my favorite part of this meal. It is participatory: the diners can mix and match and take the meal into their own hands. They can eat the sweet sticky quince paste with the fatty, creamy cheese or on its own. Or with the crackers. Or quickly followed by the crisp, sour pickled pumpkin. Or any other combination.

While the diners are busy tasting and eating and returning to their favorites of this course, Tyler has moved on to the two vegetable courses that are to follow: the slaw and the eggs and kale.

The slaw will be served first, followed by the poached eggs. The slaw is one of the easiest dishes of the evening, but one well needed in this rich and rather fatty feast. It is crisp and simple and vegetable-based, with the added benefit of acid: the vinegar giving the needed contrast to the earlier course of cheese and butter and ricotta and soup and the courses to come of braised beef, butter-soaked pasta and poached eggs. I think of this meal as playing with the guests like marionettes: pulling them forward with the richness of some dishes and then letting them drop back with the crispness and acid of dishes like the slaw. Their palates are filled with the body of the soup and the cheese, then relaxed with the acid dressing and pickled red currants of the slaw. Too much of one would be exhausting and too much of the other would be bland and flat. I prefer the back-and-forth; manipulation, if you will, of the folks around the long table.

Tyler uses the same tool as I did to make the pickled pumpkin: the mandoline. Its sharp blade, set a slim one-eighth inch from its base, slices the cabbage thinly and consistently. In a few moments the mandoline, set across the top of a large stainless-steel bowl, quickly cuts the half cabbage, transforming it from the weighty, solid block of green matter to a fluffy, light chiffonade of easily eaten salad. The change is dramatic and proves a basic tenet of cooking: the size of the item is paramount to the way it is enjoyed. The original cabbage was certainly edible, no question, but it had no tenderness, no ease of consumption. Cutting into it would have been laborious if it had been served whole as it came from the garden. In fact, Tyler used the largest knife here—an eighteen-inch German scimitar—to cut across the robust and firm vegetable. His method appears no different than when I made the first cut into the eighteen-month-aged eight-pound hard cheese: a rocking motion as the blade of the bulky knife hits one edge and then the other of the cheese or the cabbage. This is not the description of a light, tender vegetable to be easily eaten; it sounds of work and exertion.

I learned the basic idea of scale from one of the cooks who graced the Cookhouse years ago. The item in question was a pork heart, a notoriously tough bit of meat. The heart is the muscle that most likely has the most activity in an animal, beating each and every second throughout the life of the animal whether asleep or awake. The options for cooking a heart are limited. The most likely way to make it edible would be to braise it for hours, breaking down every bit of muscle and connecting tissue. The problem with that would be that a heart has little or no fat and would be quite tasteless after hours of cooking. The solution that Justin proposed was to cook the heart quickly yet completely, boiling it in a seasoned stock until just cooked. When he removed it and cooled it, it was indeed tough as could be. He placed it on the large meat slicer and sliced it paper-thin, creating a tremendous volume of delicate slices from the formerly tough, compact organ. Each of the delicate, seasoned slices of heart were delightful, seemingly transformed with the simple act of a good cut.

The same basic idea is used on the cabbage. The result is a delicate salad ingredient ready to be seasoned. Tyler takes a small bowl and drizzles into it a few teaspoons of honey collected a couple weeks earlier from the hives next to the garden. It is light and fruity and clean. The summer was long and bountiful and the bees easily fed. The honey reflects this season. Absent are any deep, sticky elements the honey would contain if it was collected later in the season.

Over a low flame on the range he carefully warms the honey to make it more liquid. Off of the heat he adds a few tablespoons full of apple cider vinegar. The pungent, ocher-colored acid is stored in the largest oak barrel on the floor next to the kitchen counter. Made from the apples that grow in the orchard in full view of the Cookhouse windows, this vinegar is very much of this farm.

This simple combination of sweet and sour defines the role of a vinaigrette in the salads made at the farm. When I first started the Cookhouse, preparing and serving dinners made only from the produce, meats and products of the farm, I worried about oils. I fantasized about the two walnut trees planted adjacent to the kitchen producing adequate volumes of walnuts that I could press for a French-style walnut oil. Although I planted the two trees early on when I moved to Vashon, they still produce an inadequate supply of the small nuts to contribute greatly to an oil supply. The squirrels additionally challenge my ability to fully harvest the bounty of the two well-formed trees. Instead of despairing and resorting to buying olive oil or some other oil, the earliest cooks came up with dressing salads with a simple vinaigrette of honey and vinegar. Both ingredients are superb, from this farm and in great supply. And the resulting salads do not lack for anything in taste. I find them superior, in fact, although I am greatly biased. This is not an outcome of some sort of hatred for fats and oils. On the contrary, any meal here, from the simple breakfast muffin to the complete feast, contains more than a modicum of fat. Both lard and butter are equally represented in great volumes, followed by heavy cream and cheeses appearing on the table as well. An early attempt at producing a dressing utilized melted lard as the oil of choice. Although those eating the salad while the lard was warm enjoyed the full, porky flavor, when I noticed the remainder of the salad on the platter a few minutes later included the thick, opaque sauce congealed onto the ceramic plate, I was horrified and never again was a salad dressed with lard.

Once the honey and apple cider vinegar are well incorporated, they can be drizzled over the cabbage and freely mixed in. A simple seasoning of salt and pepper brings out the subtle flavors of the honey, vinegar and cabbage easily. Tyler composes the salad with the addition of the pickled red currants, sprinkling them among the slices of cabbage. Two platters are filled with the simple salad: crunchy, sour, a bit sweet, with small nuggets of acid flavor and color. Few recognize the small red pickled currants, yet all enjoy them. Whereas the acidic nature of the vinaigrette is distributed throughout the salad, the small red berries are their own burst of sourness, unexpected and yet welcomed.

The next item on the menu is the poached eggs on Lacinato kale with a béarnaise sauce. This dish is a bit of a riff on the classic eggs Florentine, where poached eggs are nestled on a bed of cooked spinach and topped with a béarnaise sauce. Although I do enjoy such a combination, my inability to grow spinach well and consistently has kept me from ever serving such a combination.

Spinach is one of the most difficult plants to grow well, in my opinion. It has a natural tendency to bolt, or go to seed. Perhaps it is the climate here in the Pacific Northwest, or perhaps it is my inability to plant at the right time, but the window of

opportunity for spinach is greatly reduced by its bolting preference. Oddly, it is quite inexpensive in the grocery stores.

Spinach is sensitive to the length of daylight in the same
manner as onions. Both respond to the length of daylight
versus darkness by viewing the longer days and shorter nights
as a tell that their life is coming to an end and that it is time
to send out seed to guarantee their continued lineage. I am all
for the preservation of spinach through the ages, but I would
prefer that it could continue to grow nice, tender, edible leaves
rather than squander its energy on a thick central stock, flowers and eventually seeds.

The answer is to only plant spinach in the cool season of
late winter. With no expectation of coming doom, the spinach
plant will happily continue on growing deep green leaves full
of flavor. But I find that the answer, at least in terms of an eggs
Florentine dish, is to replace the temperamental spinach with
the far less demanding Lacinato kale.

Tyler had already harvested, cleaned and sliced the kale earlier today. What remains is to poach the eggs and prepare the
béarnaise sauce. The eggs will be prepared at the last minute,
but the sauce will be prepared first.

Béarnaise is without question my favorite sauce. It has
gone out of favor stylistically, but I still stand behind it. My
last job before I ventured off on my own and opened my first
café was at a private club on the seventy-sixth floor of an office
building in downtown Seattle. It is hard to imagine any longer
path than working at that completely forced environment to
my present-day location deep on the ground, growing food,
raising animals and making cheese from the milk of my cows.
What was great about my brief stint in the sky was it still had
béarnaise sauce served in gooseneck sauce boats on the side of
the large grilled steaks. I can fault that dining room for many
things, but I loved the thick, smoky steaks, cooked medium
rare, and the rich, fatty, tart butter sauce that accompanied

them. I and the other waiters would hide in the service bar, chewing on the bones of porterhouse steaks, dipping the meat in the remaining sauce, left over from the delicate nibbling of the city's elite.

I love to serve this rich, old school sauce. If nothing else, to keep it alive and in the minds of the current generation of foodies. And I enjoy it.

Béarnaise and its cousin hollandaise are simply emulsified butter sauces. Béarnaise is a hollandaise sauce with the addition of chopped tarragon. As the fall weather has been mild here, the tarragon plant is still full of vibrant green leaves. If a freeze had come early, the menu would have quickly been changed to poached eggs with hollandaise.

I must confess that for years, until very recently, I believed the sauce in question to be called *sauce Bernaise*, translated as "sauce in the style of Bern." In truth, I was distinctly mistaken. The name is *sauce Béarnaise,* and refers to the southern French province of Béarn. I had always imagined Bernese mountain dogs and steaks with Bernaise sauce as somehow being connected. I stand corrected.

This sauce is ideally suited for the farm. The list of ingredients is short and all of them are of great quality here. The ingredients are clarified butter, egg yolks, shallots, vinegar and fresh tarragon. Without question the butter and pastured eggs are of superior quality, but as of this year, the shallots are as well.

In years past I would break up clusters of diminutive shallots and plant them early in the spring, only to be barely rewarded in the fall with a large quantity of equally diminutive shallots. The shallots would certainly divide and reproduce dutifully, but would never achieve the robust form that I had hoped. I was raising an army of marbles, each too difficult to peel and finely dice.

There is a current trend in food to obsess over the heirloom nature of a plant or animal or process. The best tomatoes are termed heirlooms, the best hogs are considered of heritage

breeds. Little thought goes into this aggrandizing of varieties beyond the sense of "things were better in the past." This
distrust of current selections I find tedious and odd. Certainly
some fruits and vegetables and animal breeds from the past
are quite tasty, but I think we take the moniker of heirloom to
mean superior with little or no critical thought.

To me this reflects the fatness of this nation; the ability to
grow vegetable gardens in our backyards, not to keep us from
starving, but rather to add to our otherwise luxurious lives.
Our goals are a perfect Caprese salad, not nourishment or
volume. If the tomato for the salad in question was the same
variety as that chosen by Thomas Jefferson, then indeed it is
deemed worthy to be planted in our small Monticellos.

Jefferson may very well have had the finest fruits and vegetables in his expansive gardens, but they must be seen as the
finest of the eighteenth century. Thankfully, we live well into
the twenty-first century. And the scientists and backyard growers of the past two hundred years must certainly have contributed something to the pantheon of varieties.

One such welcome addition is the Ambition shallot. What
makes this allium special is that it is grown from seed. Prior
to its introduction in 1992 by a Dutch seed company, shallots
were grown by division, as I had always done. Far better growers than I most likely can indeed grow large shallots with the
heirloom method, but I enjoy the introduction of seed-grown
shallots as a great improvement in shallot technology.

Tyler's first task is to peel the reddish-hued skins and then
to finely dice the firm alliums. He takes great pleasure in the
challenge of producing hundreds of identical cubes, each one a
single centimeter across, with a small, thin-bladed knife from
his quiver. Those tidy cubes are scooped up and added to an
equally diminutive copper saucepan with a finger of vinegar.
With a bit of a flame, he reduces the shallot-and-vinegar mixture by half, the acrid steam filled with the subtle onion flavor.

On another burner of the range he melts a small block of the butter, not bringing it to a boil, but fully liquefying the golden liquid. When it is warm enough that the milk solids fall to the bottom of the pan, he pours off the top, leaving the cloudy white milk solids remaining behind. The clarified liquid—the ghee—is nearly transparent, yet filled with color and flavor.

The eggs also need a bit of attention, separating the yolks and the whites. The whites and the shells will go to the pigs; the yolks will remain as the base of the béarnaise.

The essence of the emulsified sauce is the practice of suspending a liquid in a fat. There are short-term emulsified sauces and long-term. A vinaigrette is an example of the former—the oil and the vinegar are in suspension only for a short amount of time after they are physically incorporated using a whisk or fork. A hollandaise or béarnaise sauce is an example of the latter—partially cooked egg yolks hold the suspension of melted butter and vinegar together.

Tyler readies the three distinct ingredients: the melted butter, the yolks and the vinegar/shallot mixture. Into a small stainless-steel bowl the vinegar mixture is poured. The bowl is then placed over a pot of steaming water. The yolks are added and whisked into the vinegar mixture. With one hand he whisks, and with the other he slowly pours in the clarified butter. At first it will resemble a thin, rich liquid, and as the bowl begins to heat up from the steam beneath, the yolks will cook slightly and absorb the butter. As this process begins, the sauce will also begin to absorb air from the whisking action. The sauce will gradually thicken and increase in volume. Too much heat, and the eggs will overcook; too little heat, and the sauce will resemble a vinaigrette, the three principal ingredients not in solution but simply stirred together.

Once Tyler has finished the béarnaise sauce, wrapped the bowl with a heat-holding towel and left it on the shelf above the range, he turns to the poaching of the eggs and the sautéing of the kale. The wilting of the greens is quite straightforward.

They are already cleaned and cut and ready. A simple heating in the sauté pan with a bit of lard is all that is necessary. Some water is added at the onset to encourage steam until the leaves begin to wilt and release their moisture. The Lacinato will wilt, shrink and become tender, and will gain a deep green color. Gone is the rigid, crunchy nature of the fresh leaves. The flavor is enhanced: more earthy and sweet.

And then the attention turns to the poached eggs. I love poached eggs. I eat them most every morning for breakfast. Partially because I enjoy the texture and flavor, but also because it is a source of protein that is readily available at the farm year-round and requires little preparation time. It's true there is a large chest freezer filled with the most tasty pork loins and whole stewing hens and beef leg roasts and the like. But pulling a piece of meat, defrosting it and cooking it up is far more time-consuming and takes more forethought than simply grabbing a couple of eggs from the chicken coop, heating up some water and poaching the tasty eggs.

I have tried a few methods and learned a bit about this simple technique. And I have consulted Harold McGee as well. Although I have retired most of my reference books in favor of the virtual reference of the Google search, one reference book remains on my shelf: McGee's *On Food and Cooking*. I even went so far as to purchase the newest edition to supplant my old, battered copy. Surprisingly, and sadly, McGee—can I call you Harold?—only devotes part of one page to this important part of my morning routine. He does address a few issues, however.

The common trick of egg poaching is to add a bit of vinegar to the water on the thought that it lowers the pH and increases the cooking speed of the egg whites. The idea goes that if the whites cook faster, then they will not break apart as easily during the cooking. Although I have heard this for years and generally did partake in the practice, Harold dispels it as ineffective and also notes that it "produces shreds and an irregular film over the egg surface." I missed both of these flaws, but I trust he is correct.

The other method that is addressed here is the tall-pot method. A few years back, a big Seattle chef came out to cook a dinner here and explained the practice. Instead of the customary shallow pan of water, he utilized a tall stockpot. He insisted that the eggs will drop to the bottom initially and bob to the surface when fully cooked. Harold gives a recipe for the addition of salt and vinegar to the water to achieve the levitating effect of the soft poached eggs. I must confess that I have tried it to little success and the time allotted to boiling a deep pot of water confounds me. I shall stick with the customary method.

A wide and shallow pan is filled with an adequate volume of water, perhaps three inches. The flame is lit and the water heated to almost boiling. While the temperature rises, the eggs you want—plus a couple of extras just in case—are cracked and dropped into individual ramekins. Tyler insists on this, although I question its efficacy. To me, the goal is to release the raw eggs quickly into the water. It works well; most likely the additional small wares to wash is what annoys me.

The water needs to be nearly boiling, yet not a full boil. If the water is fully engaged, the bubbles will physically break up the whites. However, the high heat is needed to quickly set the whites so that they don't just spread out throughout the tepid water. The happy medium is not quite boiling. When I am making my morning poachers, I can bring the pot to a boil, turn the heat down and add the eggs when the water is just simmering. The added complication now is that the addition of two dozen room-temperature eggs in a short amount of time will drop the temperature below that ideal simmer. Because of this, Tyler will stagger the addition of each egg, keeping the heat adjusted and the water temperature as consistent as possible.

We have learned from the advent of *sous-vide* cookery that

high-temperature cooking is not always necessary. Once the whites are set and the final form of the eggs completed, the yolks can be finished very slowly. No longer is a two-hundred-degree temperature needed. The higher temperature will certainly cook the eggs faster, yet additionally will increase the tendency to overcook the yolks. At one hundred and fifty degrees the converse is true. The time allotted to the process will increase, yet the chance of overcooking the delicate yolks is greatly reduced.

Tyler has the three parts to this dish ready to assemble. The béarnaise was been made and is ready and warm. The Lacinato kale is in the sauté pan and now tender and wilted yet not overcooked. And the eggs are slowly coming close to being ready; the whites are firm and fully opaque, the yolks are completely runny at the center and firm on the very edge.

He takes two platters from the shelf and covers each with a bed of the deep green vegetable. On top of the Lacinato each egg is delicately placed. At this point, when the eggs come out of the water, they appear to be oysters. Each side is distinctly different. The bottom is flat and smooth, the top has a high rim and a sunken center; and off to one side is the large yolk, cloaked in white. The flat, smooth bottom holds none of the poaching liquid; the deep variegated top always cups some of the warm poaching water. It reminds me of a fresh oyster, about to be slurped from the half shell. It has that oval shape, glistening, tender and hiding a great secret at its center. The feel of the warm, golden yolk as it is eaten feels not unlike the texture of a fresh oyster as it is swallowed. Although a slotted spoon can hold these chicken bivalves, the palm of one's hand is best to quickly flip the warm egg, draining off the water before setting the poached egg down onto the green base of kale, crenellated side up, smooth side down. Luckily four extra eggs were included. A couple break apart as they are added to the simmering liquid and a couple will be held aside for Tyler to enjoy at the counter.

While Tyler finishes moving the eggs onto the platter, I begin to coat each with the béarnaise sauce. It has thickened slightly since it was finished and needs a few drops of warm water to restore its luster and ability to gently and completely coat the eggs. If the sauce is of a proper consistency it will enrobe the ivory-colored eggs, slowly enveloping all of the nooks and crannies. If it is too thin, it will simply run off to the sides of the eggs, a small pool of golden sauce surrounding each. Too thick, and what appears to be a lump of butter will sit proudly on top of the lonely, naked eggs. Tyler has hit his mark and the eggs are enrobed in golden, rich sauce. The colors are vibrant and true: the deep green of the still-moist kale, the deep golden hue of the butter-enriched sauce and small amounts of the bright whites of the pastured eggs shine through. The tiny bits of fresh tarragon in the sauce break the monotony of the coloration and give the sauce an additional bit of zest.

The guests scoop a full egg together with a modicum of kale onto their plates. The eggs have been cooked enough that they do not immediately fall apart either in the transfer to the platter from the pan or from the platter to the final plates. And then the heavy silver forks begin to cut into the eggs. Each tender yolk around the table breaks open and out spills a soupçon of deep golden liquid yolk. It spills onto the kale and onto the bright white plate beneath. It is a rich dish, certainly, but one that is well enjoyed around the appreciative table. The kale is relatively bland and can take the fatty goodness of both the poached yolks and the nearly raw yolks in the béarnaise. The presence of the finely diced shallots, the French tarragon and the vinegar add a relief to the fattiness of the dish. The vinegar cuts through that richness and makes it palatable and pleasurable. In a moment the green, the white and the golden colors are gone, wiped clean by the diners, a bit of bread aiding the final bites. A couple of eager ones at the table pass the sauce boat with the extra béarnaise that I brought to the table and attempt to consume that as well. With luck there will be a bit remaining for me to dip bits of bread and crackers into. Those days of hiding in the service bar, eating from a silver sauce boat, are thirty years past, but I relish the practice nonetheless.

FIFTEEN

The Second Half of Dinner

On the back burner of the range sits the large aluminum stockpot filled with nearly boiling water. Tyler filled it just after lunch and turned it on when guests first arrived a couple of hours ago. It certainly didn't take two hours to heat the four gallons of water, but it is great insurance to have it ready. Many errors in preparing a large dinner can be quickly remedied, but trying to quickly bring four gallons of cold water to a boil is nearly impossible to hurry up. I know this from experience.

The pasta water is heavily salted—the water will give flavor to the unseasoned noodles. The finished dish will be seasoned as well, but the salted water will make the noodles themselves full-flavored.

Tyler pulls a large rondeau from the shelf and places it on a front burner of the range. It is a deep pot—eight inches high—and nearly double that in width. Thick on the bottom, it can withstand the high heat of the initial sauté and also hold a great volume of pasta when the dish is finished. He turns the flame on high and adds a healthy spoonful of butter and lard. Both will add flavor and color and that ever-desired quality: mouth feel, to the final dish. They quickly melt as the large pot heats up. Once the fat has heated and the foam of the butter subsided, the aroma of butter and lard fills the kitchen. First to be added are the chopped chicken gizzards. Their dark mahogany color deepens when they are cooked in the rich fat. Their earthy smells are released by the heat as they pop and sputter. He moves the gizzards around in the rondeau by grabbing one of the thick handles bolted to the side of the heavy pot and shaking the pot back and forth across the top of the range. With each rough yank the gizzards move across the base of the pot, shaking up the butter and lard and flavorful bits. If the gizzards get stuck to the bottom of the pot, he grabs a long-handled wooden spoon and scrapes the goodness. He wants the deep chestnut-brown bits that are stuck to the bottom of the pan. The flavor resides in these caramelized crusty bits. The goal of this style of cooking—*dirty* cooking, if you will—is to create these residues on the bottom of the pan and release them through physically scraping the pan and also by deglazing with a small amount of liquid. This builds up a great amount of rich flavor in the final sauce. It is a slower, more *dirty* manner of cooking than the standard sauté, deglaze and finish of a customary sauce. It isn't always pretty and tidy.

To add moisture, Tyler adds the roughly chopped chicken livers to the pot of gizzards. The livers will cook quickly and release their liquid into the mix. The liquid pops and sputters as it hits the hot oil and gizzards. The resulting steam is filled with the sweet smells of the chicken parts. Chef continues to shake the pot back and forth on the range, mixing the gizzards and livers. The livers cook through and their liquid quickly pulls up and deglazes the caramelized bits on the bottom of the pot. Once the gizzard-and-liver mixture has cooked for a few minutes it dries out and begins to stick to the bottom of the heavy pot once again. Tyler continues to scrape up the bits, then allows it all to stick again, continuing to build up flavor in the rich pot of chicken bits.

Soon Tyler adds the chopped cippolini onions and finely diced garlic. They too fill the kitchen with their aroma—sweet and pungent. He turns the heat down now to avoid burning the tender onions, which are prone to burning; the risk of bitterness is high from the thin edges of the diced onions in the hot oil. He also salts the onions to get them to release their liquid as well. The heat begins to break down the onions, adding more moisture to the pot, deglazing the stuck bits. Then it is cooked down and scraped again. Little by little Tyler builds up the flavors. As the pot needs more moisture he grabs the small copper saucepan that has been silently simmering on the back of the range since morning. It is filled with the trim and beef scraps from the cleaning of the beef roast earlier in the day. Throughout the day Tyler kept his eye on the small pot, adding more water as needed to keep it fed, slowly cooking it down, then adding a bit more water, in the same manner as he is now building up the foundation in the rondeau. Slowly a rich, deep, *dirty* pot of chicken goodness remains. It isn't a three-hour process but rather thirty minutes. He adjusts the heat up and down constantly in the process. By the time it is ready, the gizzards and livers look nearly indistinguishable—both small bits of chewy meat—and the onions have all but disappeared, the flavors remaining. The last addition of liquid from the small pot is used to deglaze the final bits, and the temperature is turned way down to keep it warm.

When the mixture is as he wants it, he raises the flame under the large, covered stockpot of salted water and brings it to a boil quickly. When it is rapidly boiling he picks up the individual nests of papardelle that he'd rolled out hours earlier and drops them into the water. They fall to the bottom and the boil ceases for a few moments. He replaces the lid to get the temperature back up to a full boil. When it is back up to temperature, he removes the lid and gently stirs the noodles with the long tongs that always hang from the front handle of the oven. While waiting for the noodles to cook, he moves his attention back to the rondeau. He adds a large knuckle-sized lump of sweet Jersey butter to the mixture. The butter will make the sauce richer and fuller and help it to coat the noodles. He takes a spoonful of the sauce and tastes it for seasoning. The smile on his face tells all. He is happy and begins to add salt and pepper generously to bring out the full flavors of the gizzards and chicken livers. The noodles are nearly ready when he is finished. As they cook, the noodles slowly begin to rise to the top of the steaming, boiling water. With those same tongs, Tyler grabs a piece of noodle, pulls it from the water and brings it to the counter so he can taste it for doneness. When he is content with his noodles, he turns off the flame and begins to drain the pot. He picks up the weighty pot filled with boiling water and pours in into a large, waiting sieve held over the prep sink. The steam rises as the noodles fall gently into the aluminum mesh sieve, the boiling starchy water draining away. He holds back a bit of the pasta water in the tall pot to moisten the final dish if needed, setting the pot down on the side counter.

The noodles are dropped into the awaiting rondeau, nearly filling the voluminous pan. Gently, confidently, he begins to stir and fold and cajole the pappardelle in the pan, thoroughly coating the warm, golden noodles with the crusty, *dirty*, tasty bits of the sauce. Next to the range sits a small plastic container filled with the dry, crusty bits of bread crumbs that he made earlier in the day; he begins to add half of the container to the mix, folding them into the noodles as well. When the sauce and noodles and bread crumbs are equally distributed, Tyler picks up the weighty pot by both of its sturdy handles and moves it to the serving counter where the large serving platters are waiting.

With the spring-equipped tongs he picks up large amounts of pasta, carrying them to the long white oval serving plates, twirling them slightly as he gently places them down. I learned early on that good cooks plate dishes by picking up the food from a sauté pan or a rondeau and placing it on the plate; sloppy, mediocre cooks upend the pan and slide the pasta on the plate. Tyler is the former, never the latter.

When the noodles are all on the plate, some sauce remains in the pan. He picks up a large spoon and ladles the remaining bits of goodness onto the noodles. Nearby is the remaining half container of bread crumbs, and those too will be added to the noodles. The first half have absorbed some liquid; the second half will be crisp and fresh but have less of the flavorfulness of the sauce.

While Tyler is draining the pasta and preparing the finished dish, I am readying the grated hard cheese for the pasta. With a razor-sharp micro-planer I grate the remaining wedge cut from the wheel of Francesca's Cheese. When I pick up the simple tool that is a micro-planer I realize how much I love the modern world. This inexpensive, extraordinarily facile item has given us the ability to transform a cheese such as this into a beautiful new form. I do not in any way miss the clunky, crude box graters of my youth. The rudimentary shards that were produced by those knuckle-cutting graters pale in comparison to what we have today. I have no intention of looking back and digging the old box grater out of the attic. The planer easily cuts through the hard, aged cheese, transforming the wedge into a pile of light, airy pale cheese. The transformation in volume and taste and feel is remarkable. Instantly the crunchy, chewy nuggets of cheese become delicate slivers with barely any weight; they melt when placed on the tongue, yet are still filled with the acid and salt and sharp flavor of the original wheel. Back and forth I rapidly move the simple modern tool, working through the wedge in a couple of minutes. In its wake lies a voluminous mound of cheese. I pick up half and place it in a oval-shaped porcelain dish, grab the remainder and find an identical dish. By this time Tyler has finished plating the potful of pasta and sauce, mounding it nicely on two grand, oversized platters. Once he has cleaned the bright white rims of the plates, I hover over the steaming noodles and grate more of Francesca's Cheese directly onto the dish. Not so much as to obscure the glistening noodles, but rather just to add another texture.

The movement of the heavy pot full of noodles to the serving counter was not lost on the twenty friends at the long table a few feet away. Their active conversations covered up the sounds of the livers and gizzards popping and sputtering in the pan, and they had long since been lulled by the ever-present smell of great food since they arrived hours earlier. But with long strands of beautiful draping noodles evident, one by one the guests stop talking and turn to watch Tyler pile the platters high. Their anticipation is palpable; even though they have eaten enough for a normal evening meal, they are looking forward to this course with gusto. Thankfully it only takes him a couple of minutes to load the platters and I place one at each end of the table. Those sitting nearest are quickly rewarded; those sitting in the center anxiously wait as their compatriots generously serve themselves. I can see the look of worry on those who sit farthest away, fearful that the pasta will run out before the platter gets to their part of the table. There is no chance of such a debacle; the platters are high with pappardelle, but the concerns are understandable nevertheless.

The two oversized platters have the unique ability of holding more noodles than they appear to at first glance. I worry each time that the first three guests will consume the entire platter meant for their entire row of ten folks. In fact there is a nearly unending supply of noodles and sauce and cheese and the platter easily reaches the end of the row with some remaining. The platters play a slow and simple game of pinball, bouncing back and forth up and down the table, occasionally being passed across the table as well, each time a few more noodles grabbed by a still-hungry guest. Until only a spare bit of chicken gizzard sadly remains on the side of one plate, the other plates clean. The two ovoid side dishes that were mounded high with the airy, downy cheese—they too are now clean of any food; only the small silver spoons are absently left in the bottom of each dish.

It is apparent at this point in the repast that the guests are satiated. They should stop eating, truly they should, and I believe they think they are done—and yet I am fully aware from past experience that they will continue. There is still the roast course and then dessert as well, and all will partake.

Certainly not with quite the same gusto with which they attacked the pasta, but they will without question make a hearty attempt on the last two courses. At this point in the evening the feast has had a physical effect on them. They are slower, and a bit more pensive, you might say. They are looking outward, absently into the air, pondering the meal. The rapid-fire conversation of thirty minutes earlier has ceased. Now it is a docile chatter I hear, and mostly centered on their present shared experience. The long stories of their children, where they went to college and the joys of their past vacations have switched to identical statements of disbelief in how much they enjoyed those noodles just moments ago and also how they could ever have eaten such a volume of them. Utter disbelief.

I have witnessed this for years and yet still enjoy it. I like that they are sharing an experience, and especially a pleasant one. I know they will be ready for the beef in a few minutes, and so I help Tyler get it ready.

While the noodles were cooking and after the sauce had been finished, Tyler popped the large flame-colored covered Le Creuset pot back into the hot oven and then flipped on the gas under the small stockpot filled with the boiling potatoes and fresh bay sitting ready at the back of the range. The beef is back in the oven simply to warm it. The five-hundred-degree oven has quickly warmed the beef and the sauce surrounding it in the nearly thirty minutes since it was returned to the oven. When the guests have finished the platters of noodles and I have cleared the platters from the table, he pulls the pot from the oven and with a bit of a thud sets it on the counter. The lid is removed, revealing the steam rising from the interior and the smell of the beautiful beef roasts. With sturdy stainless-steel tongs, he lifts the tied roasts from their surrounding sauce and places them on the round maple cutting block to rest while the sauce is prepared.

The sauce, if you can call it that at this stage, is ghastly.

There is nothing beautiful or striking about it. It is without question broken—the solids and the liquids have separated. It looks like it is burnt around the edges where it cooked against the sides of the hot, glazed cast-iron pot. If I hadn't seen it finished in the past I would have little hope for a striking outcome.

But this is in no way hopeless and in fact is certain to be delightful. With a bit of apprehension, Chef lifts the still-hot pot half filled with steaming sauce up, upends it and begins to pour the contents into a blender waiting on the side counter. It is a large commercial blender and can easily contain the entire contents of the crusty pot. With a rubber spatula in one hand and the still-heavy pot balanced on the lip of the blender with the other, he scrapes all the bits of gustatory goodness into the blender. When milk was originally put into the pot the level of the sauce was nearly at the top of the bulky beef roasts. Over the course of the three-hour slow cooking, a large percentage of the moisture steamed out of the not-perfectly-sealed pot. Little by little over the three hours the level of the sauce dropped until its final level a few minutes earlier. As the level descended, the milky, sweet sauce coated the interior of the hot iron pot, caramelizing the sugars in the milk. It never burned, but it certainly created a rich, caramelly base that Tyler now scrapes into the blender.

Because the sauce is also based in milk, it has curdled. There is truly nothing striking about it. Clumps of milk solids are floating, the thin liquid that is the base of milk can be seen, the thin, clear meat juices that came from the cooking beef also are part of this yet-to-be sauce. Miraculously and effortlessly, that all changes with the push of a button. The rubber lid is firmly attached, the speed set on high and the on switch is pushed. An immediate whirl begins inside the blender, in this case a beneficial tempest in a teapot. The noise is less than pleasant but the results are well worth the necessary auditory annoyance. The overfed guests are temporarily awakened from their partial slumber by the high whirring sound, but then immediately return to their slow conversations.

The transformation is amazing. The blender is clear and it can easily be seen that the different colors of the original sauce—the bleak pale white of the milk, the thin brown of the beef juices and the slightly golden clumps of curdled milk—have now combined to a terribly pleasant rich coffee-hued sauce. The curdled milk has also given the thin juices body. No matter the flavor and seasoning, a thin sauce is entirely that: thin. The robust mouth feel of a thickened sauce is necessary for an enjoyable sauce, and this one has that. It is not a sauce that uses starches such as flour to provide that body, but rather the deeply reduced sugars of the milk and the body of the milk curds.

Tyler leaves the sauce in the blender with the rubber lid on to keep it warm, checks on the pot of potatoes on the back burner, tests them quickly for doneness with a thin knife and then returns to the roasts sitting on the round cutting board. This morning he tied them with string to create and maintain a cylindrical shape, and his first task is to locate those strings and remove them. Tyler used a continuous method of tying off the roasts. Once the first cut is made, most of the remaining string unravels with little effort. If there was a series of individual knotted loops around each roast, then there is always the chance that one could be forgotten, the thin cotton string obscured by the hours of braising in the rich milk.

The guests are slowly coming out of their stupor induced by the rich and eagerly eaten pasta, the sauce is standing by in the blender ready to be seasoned, the beef is ready to be sliced for the platter and the potatoes are fully cooked and remain in the slowly simmering water on the range. The last bit is to finely chop chives for the garnish.

Earlier in the day Tyler had collected a handful of the robust green stems—none woody but none wispy either. Now he cuts them just before he will use them, ensuring their freshness and bright flavors. He trims the ends, scanning the handful for errant stalks of grass that mistakenly were harvested with the valued chives.

A few years back, one of the half-my-age cooks was working for me in the kitchen. As I was quite impatient with his progress on dinner, I decided to shoulder my way to the cutting board to chop the chives for the garnish. I began a very predictable chopping with one of my less-than-sharp knives. I thought that my tidy pile of green rings was serviceable. He did not. With the authority of a twenty-three-year-old, he explained to me the need to have a fine, sharp knife to slice the delicate rings of chive stalk, rather than to crush and chop them as I had chosen to do. I was both embarrassed—slightly—and also intrigued, curious if I had always missed this finer point of cooking. Certainly, god is in the details.

Tyler is far more obsessive than I and easily and swiftly creates a fine plate of thinly sliced—not crushed—chives. The chives are then set aside and he can return to finishing the rest of the dish. Although he made a similar ramekinful of chopped chives for the pizzas, he wants chives freshly cut for the potatoes.

The potatoes have remained in the hot water on the back of the range, holding their temperature and finishing the last bit of cooking needed. They are drained into a colander in the sink, the water steaming as it is poured out. He brings them to the counter and each one individually is pulled out, gently smashed with the palm of his hand and placed on a small baking sheet. When all have been transferred, the tray is run out to the still-warm wood-fired oven. Its temperature has certainly dropped from the high of seven hundred degrees at the early part of the dinner for the cooking of the pizzas, but it is still ample to finish this small tray of potatoes.

The fire has died down to coals in the back of the oven, giving the oven a warm golden glow. Tyler slides the tray in, giving the potatoes a chance to grab a bit of smoke from the fire and a bit of char on their top edges from the heat still radiating down from the hot bricks. Scattered among the potatoes are the bay leaves they were cooked with. They too are beautifully charred by the glowing embers.

All the parts ready, Tyler begins to serve the meat course. With a thin-bladed knife, he slices through the tender meat, using the flat plane of his knuckles as a guide. When the two roasts are fully divided into identical slices, he slips the long-bladed knife under the first roast, guides it with his other hand and picks the roast up and sets it down on the first waiting platter. The knife is removed and the slices are gently pushed over, revealing the interior of the moist, braised beef.

The two stainless steel gravy boats are filled with the rich sauce waiting in the blender, and a small amount is placed on the bright white platter on one side of the line of braised beef. On the other side are laid the bay-leaf potatoes, fresh from the wood oven. They now have a bit of a crust, slightly charred, yet they retain the moist, flaky interior of a boiled potato. When all is ready, I run the two full platters to the table a few feet away.

The guests make a gallant effort, eating a tender slice of the braised beef, enjoying the richly bay-scented potatoes as well. They pass the mahogany sauce down the long table and pour a bit onto their plates, coating the beef and the potatoes deliberately. They are without question sated, yet do not want to pass on this fine course.

In a few minutes I begin to clear the table of everything not needed for dessert and coffee: the platters of beef and potatoes, the gravy boats, all of the dinner plates and silver as well. The salt cellars and the pepper grinders and the butter dishes are also removed. All that remains are the coffee spoons, the dessert forks, the wine stems and the water glasses. The guests fill the now-empty space on the table in front of them with their arms, some nearly putting their heads in their arms in quiet repose.

I give them a couple of minutes to catch their breaths before Tyler and I begin to cut and serve the dessert. On the side racks the two tomato upside-down cakes have rested since I pulled them from their pans hours ago. The tomato jam that I added on top has seeped into the dense butter cake below, but the cake is still fresh and moist. The large slices of heirloom tomatoes glisten.

Tyler delicately cuts each cake into a dozen slices. The butter cake is dense and finely textured. Each cut is precise and the edges hold that sharp point beautifully. Twenty of the slices are placed on French porcelain dessert plates, the wide borders a deep forest-green color with a thin gold band on the edge.

I hand the cake out to the near-slumbering guests. The cake is tasty and welcomed, but to my great sadness, many of the diners have little room for more food and only have a few bites of the ample portion. Some, however, will continue to nibble on the rich slice of cake while drinking their coffee and miraculously will finish the serving.

The final course of dinner at the farm is always my favorite, not because it is complicated or uniquely tasty, but rather because it surprises everyone who sees it prepared here for the first time. The last course is coffee.

Most of us prepare coffee daily or stop by our local coffee shop for an espresso or even grab a cup of drip out of one of those old vending machines. Few, actually very few, ever roast the beans themselves. At the end of every dinner at the farm we roast the coffee beans and brew the coffee.

I am fortunate to have a small coffee roasterie a five-minute bike ride from the farm. One of the original Seattle-area coffee roasters relocated to Vashon Island in the 1970s and the building and the equipment remain. A new operator has taken over the space and has agreed to sell me green beans. As we are so very used to seeing only roasted beans, it is a shock the first time to see the coffee beans before they are roasted. They are green and lack much smell, so it is hard to believe that they could produce a steamy, rich cup of morning brew. They are neither shiny nor aromatic and bear little resemblance to the final roasted bean. They are also dramatically less expensive than the roasted bean. Every few weeks I ride over to the roasterie and buy a few pounds of Costa Rican beans. With luck I can accompany one of the clerks downstairs to the stockroom where the beans are stored in burlap sacks. All around the room are plump, bulbous sacks stitched closed on one end, stamped with the country of origin on the side and with the top open and rolled down a bit. I walk around the dimly lit basement room imagining where these bags were filled—Jamaica, Ethiopia, Brazil, Costa Rica—and how they could possibly have ended up on Vashon Island, a few blocks from my farm.

After the guests have finished the last bit of cake, Tyler pulls down the largest steel sauté pan from the pot rack above the prep tables. It is especially large and heavy and shows its age. I bought this pan and its matching ones when I started my first job in the late 1970s. I was working as a waiter in a French restaurant and became enamored of all things French. Year by year they have been over the heat at every stove in every apartment and house I have lived in. Now they are shiny black on the inside, a bit warped and coated in a crusty blackened exterior.

Tyler pours a pound of the green coffee beans into the large sauté pan and turns the gas on high. The pan is large enough that with a firm shake of the handle the beans spread out, covering the bottom in a single layer. Each bean has contact with the soon-to-be-hot steel. As the pan begins to heat up, the beans begin to pop and move about the bottom. If there is room enough, many of the beans will spin rapidly as they begin to roast. It reminds me of the Mexican jumping beans we would buy at the dime store as a kid. Actually it reminds me of what I had hoped those novelty beans would do, but which they rarely accomplished. These beans from the sunny Central American jungles spin and pop with enthusiasm. Tyler shakes the pan often to rotate the beans and roast each

face of them. At the first pops of the beans, the husks begin
to dislodge. In the pan with the beans are small paper-thin
remnants of the outer coverings. Over the next couple minutes
all of the husks will come off of the beans, their light weight
causing them to fly about the stove as Tyler shakes the pan to
keep the roasting even.

Like clockwork, the diners a dozen feet from the gas stove
begin to notice what Tyler is cooking. Through the entire meal
they have kept an eye on his activities but generally have
attended to their food and conversation. They have all seen a
cook chop vegetables or drain noodles or slice a beef roast. But
the room now has started to fill with both the smoke from the
nearly fully roasted beans and the intense aroma of coffee. The
formally sedate eaters, fully satiated by the previous courses,
now come alert and watch Tyler's every movement. He has
no shyness and picks up the heavy steel pan to dramatically
blow the last remaining husks from the smoking beans, in the
process showing off his heavily tattooed gym-toned arms. I
am never quite sure if those around the table are focusing on
the mocha-colored beans or the rampant sexuality of the cook.
No matter; their gaze is back at the hearth and the making of
their dinner.

The coffee beans will continue to pop and smoke and get
gradually darker as Tyler leaves them on the heat. If he has
kept them in motion for the majority of their cooking time,
their color will be consistent and even. If he has spent more
time posing and less attention to the beans in front of him, one
bean face will be light tan, the other face blackened.

I like the beans to be nearly black in color; a French roast,
if you will. If they are actually black, the burnt-ness will come
through in the final cup of coffee. When they are merely tan in
complexion, I find little depth in the cup. When they are just at
that great midpoint between the two worries, they will begin
to exude oil; a glossiness. Tyler pours the steaming beans into
a large mixing bowl and shakes them to get as much steam out

as possible. The general theory of coffeemaking is that coffee beans should not be ground for twenty-four hours after they have been roasted. We may sacrifice a bit of quality, but showing off the roasting is worth it.

After a few minutes, Tyler takes the still-warm beans, grinds them finely and pours the aromatic grounds into two large French-press pots. A robust teakettle on the back of the stove holds enough boiling water to fill the two glass carafes of the coffeepots.

Even if those around the long fir table had no interest in drinking coffee this evening, they will, if only to be a part of the long process of brewing this last course. Around the light fixtures of the high-ceilinged dining room hangs a cloud of smoke from the roasting. The aroma of freshly roasted coffee fills the space. All eyes were on the strong-armed cook flipping the beans in the heavy blackened pan. Drinking a cup of the dark, rich coffee cut with a dram of cream fresh from the cows all the diners met when they arrived a few hours ago completes the evening; completes the meal.

I have nearly forgotten the small butter cookies I baked this morning. Almost as an afterthought I place them on a couple of plates and put them in the center of the table, next to the creamers. A couple guests may try them, maybe a half dozen. I worry little, knowing that I will find some in the morning and enjoy them myself. Perhaps Daisy and Byron will nibble on them as well.

When the guests have finished sipping the rich coffee, they slowly begin to finish their conversations and prepare to get up from the table. Nearly all of the twenty live in Seattle and need to take a ferryboat back to the city. At this hour, few boats run the route from Vashon to Seattle. The ferry system is designed primarily as a commuter service and few if any inhabitants of Vashon are headed to work at this late hour on a Saturday evening.

The diners have been lulled into a bit of a gastronomic slumber. It is dark out by this point and they have little idea where they are or what time it is by looking out the many-paned windows in the Cookhouse. Their entire attention for these past four hours has been on this long fir table, lit from above by the illuminating halogen lights beaming down on the platters of food and their plates in front of them.

The conversations have been intense, especially as bottles of wine have been consumed. It is difficult, if not impossible, to keep an idle chatter up for this length of time, and all have delved into deeper topics than the usual dinner party fluff. I expect that they each believe that they will simply sit at their comfortable seats around the long planked table and in a few more minutes the sun will rise behind them and Tyler will begin to fry eggs and bacon; I will come to the table with large ceramic platters filled with breakfast and more coffee and perhaps some sweet pastries as well.

And then one single person is reminded of the ferry schedule, and of the time, and of their agreement with their child care, and of the work they want to accomplish on Sunday, and of all the other travails of their modern life. And this chatter will rapidly pass down one line of the table and up the other side and all will be checking their phones and schedules and looking to see if they have had emails or texts in the past four hours since they walked into Cookhouse and left their lives behind.

The spell is broken and in a matter of a few minutes all twenty of my friends will be standing at the end of the table, finding their coats on the rack by the door, exchanging email addresses with their table mates and heading to their cars. I can only stand back and watch it all unfold. Tyler too will quickly assemble his knives and tools into his black knife bag, grab his coat and head for the door to join them all on the late boat.

I hug and thank each in turn as they pass through the clumsy French doors, through the large bay leaf sentries and into the darkness that engulfs the farm on this fall evening. I can hear the chatter as they make their way down the sidewalk and find their respective cars, but I hold back, staying in the quiet of the brightly lit—but now empty—Cookhouse. In a couple of minutes all the cars will slowly wind down the long driveway, past the Cookhouse, around to the creamery, past the barn and out the long, rough gravel road to the paved county road a thousand feet beyond. I stand and savor the memory of the feast, the friends and all that has happened this evening, before I too head out of the Cookhouse for the Log House a few feet away.

This dinner was certainly special and unique. Few eat such lengthy meals or ones where the food was all grown on one farm. It is a luxury that rarely occurs. Most meals are eaten in a few minutes or perhaps two hours at most and are made up of ingredients grown all over the country or perhaps even all over the world. I prefer this dinner, made with my beef and vegetables and cheeses and fruits and so on, but I am loath to judge how others eat.

I do hope, however, that the twenty guests who traveled out to Vashon this afternoon get a sense that their dinner was begun months if not years before they walked into the Cookhouse. That this meal was made not just from the labor of Tyler and myself, but rather included the hands of Jorge and Ben, Dustin and Leda, Michiko and Bill and even Wayne. Many took part in the production of this food. Wayne has no idea that the cow that he bred nearly a year earlier would give him a role in this fine dinner tonight. Leda is aware that folks sit around the table and have dinner, but I doubt that she realized the small kale plants I traded with her for cheese would be the basis for our poached eggs tonight.

The table still has most of the last course left: the coffee-pots, the cups and saucers, the wine and water glasses, the cookie plates, napkins and spoons, the menu cards. I leave them till morning. I should finish up and put all of the dirty dishes through the dishwasher, returning the clean plates and glasses to the cupboard, but I don't. Partly because I am tired, but also because I want the meal to continue. Tomorrow I will go back to making cheese. Ben will arrive early and milk the cows. The regular routine will continue. The excitement of having Tyler here for the day and twenty friends for dinner has ended.

I open the French doors of the Cookhouse and exit the warm room. Byron awakes from his spot under the table. Daisy left an hour ago after the beef course was served. Her interest is only in the meat courses and once they are finished, she returns alone to the Log House for the night. Byron clumsily passes through the one open door of the double French doors and heads down the concrete sidewalk to the house. I follow him, closing the door behind me, the cremone bolt awkwardly locking the door. As I pass between the two mature bay leaf trees I look back, the lights still on in the Cookhouse, illuminating the table with the dirty dishes remaining. It is a beautiful scene and I savor it as I head to bed, confident that the guests enjoyed the best possible meal. My hope is that they enjoyed the evening, certainly, talking with friends, eating, drinking and savoring the food. But also I hope, as they ride home on the hulking state ferry crossing Puget Sound in the still darkness, that they reflect on this meal.

Tomorrow they will go to their local grocery store and pick up some vegetables and meat and put together a meal. My hope is that they look at that tomato a little differently, that quart of cream with a bit more curiosity. Before the dinner began, they parked next to the orchard, walked through the vegetable gardens and went out to see the new baby calf and the milking cows in the paddock by the barn. When I spoke at the beginning of dinner I gave them a bit of the history of the food and how it was grown. They didn't have a chance to meet Leda, to chat with Wayne about artificial insemination or to realize that Dustin tended to the vegetables through the summer. I believe, however, that they do now have a better understanding of where their food comes from, that there is a story to every part of their meal. And not just last night's farm dinner, but every meal: the meals that they will cook for themselves tomorrow and the days after that.

Recipes

Squash Soup

1 large (9–10-pound) winter squash—preferably Brodé Galeux d'Eysines or other firm heirloom squash
3 tablespoons butter
1 large yellow onion, peeled and roughly chopped

3 cloves garlic, peeled and halved
3 cups water
Approximately 1½ cups milk
Salt
Pepper

Prepare the squash: peel, halve and scrape out the seeds and pulp. Cut into large chunks (approximately one inch square). You will need eight pounds prepared squash.

Melt the butter over medium heat in a large, heavy-bottomed pot. Add the chopped onions and allow to sweat, stirring often. Add the squash cubes and continue cooking until the squash just begins to soften.

Add the garlic and water to the pot and bring to a boil. Reduce the heat and allow to simmer, stirring often. Slowly cook until the squash is soft, about sixty minutes. Reduce the heat to low and continue cooking for thirty minutes to allow the mixture to reduce.

Let cool, then puree in batches in a blender until completely smooth. Add milk as needed to thin the soup. Season to taste with salt and pepper.

Yield: 4–5 quarts

Quince Membrillo

4 pounds quinces   Sugar

Peel, quarter, core and stem the quince. Chop into rough chunks and put in a heavy-bottomed sauce pan.

Add water to the pan and put it on the heat. Allow the quince to cook slowly, stirring constantly to keep it from sticking, adding more water as necessary. When the quince is completely soft and fully cooked, remove the pan from the heat.

Puree the quince in a blender until smooth. Add an equal amount of sugar as the quince by volume or by weight.

Return the sweetened quince to the saucepan and continue to cook slowly, reducing the volume and allowing it to thicken.

Pour into a shallow cake pan lined with parchment paper.

Set the pan in a cool oven and allow the quince to thicken overnight.

Invert the pan onto parchment paper, cut the membrillo into individual shapes and wrap with plastic wrap.

Yield: 2 quarts

Pickled Pumpkin

One 4–5-pound firm pumpkin   1 tablespoon black peppercorns
2 cups white vinegar   1 tablespoon coriander seeds
1½ cups water   2 fresh bay leaves
½ white onion, peeled and   2 tablespoons kosher salt
   quartered   1 tablespoons sugar
8 garlic cloves, peeled and
   smashed

Halve and peel the pumpkin, and remove the pulp and seeds. Cut into one-by-two-inch blocks. Slice on a mandoline into one-eighth-inch slices. Transfer the pumpkin slices into a four-quart bowl or gallon jar. You should have two to three quarts of loosely packed slices.

Place the remaining ingredients in a nonreactive two-quart saucepan.

Bring the liquid to a boil and pour over the pumpkin slices, making sure to cover them. Place a plate on top to keep the pumpkin submerged. Refrigerate. The pickles will be ready in two days.

Yield: 2 quarts

Hard rolls

½ tablespoon sugar
1½ cups warm water (100–110 degrees)
½ tablespoon active dry yeast
4 cups bread flour, plus more as needed—I use King Arthur

1½ tablespoons whole wheat flour
1½ tablespoons Diamond Crystal kosher salt

Combine the sugar and warm water in the bowl of an electric mixer with a dough hook attachment. Sprinkle the yeast on the surface and allow it to begin foaming, about five minutes.

Sift together the bread flour and whole wheat flour. Add half the flour mixture to the yeast mixture while the mixer is running on low speed. Once incorporated, slowly add the remaining flour and the salt. Continue mixing until the dough is smooth and has completely pulled away from the sides, adding more bread flour as necessary. Take the dough out of the mixer and finish kneading briefly by hand on a floured board.

Place the ball of dough in a clean large bowl and cover. Let proof at room temperature until it begins to rise, two to three hours, then refrigerate overnight.

The following day, take the dough from the refrigerator and divide it into eight equal pieces. On a lightly floured board, form each piece of dough into a smooth ball. Place the rolls on a baking sheet at least four inches apart and cover loosely with a towel. Let the rolls rise at room temperature for five hours, until fully proofed.

Preheat the oven to 400 degrees.

Dust the tops of the rolls with a bit of the bread flour, then bake them on the top rack until golden brown. Let cool completely on the baking sheet.

(continued)

Just before serving, reheat the rolls again in a 400-degree oven to fully crisp them and to warm them through. This cooling and reheating step is crucial for proper texture and flavor development.

Yield: 8 rolls

Green Salsa

2 cups tomatillos, preferably milperos
1½ cup water
¼ cup roughly chopped medium onion
1 clove garlic—whole, peeled

1 loosely packed cup cilantro leaves, no stems
1 teaspoon salt
½ tablespoon freshly ground pepper

Combine the tomatillos, water, onions and garlic in a small saucepan and bring to a boil. When mixture comes to a boil, reduce heat to simmer until the tomatillos have burst, about one minute for small tomatillos and two to three minutes for larger ones.

Strain mixture, reserving liquid.

Transfer mixture to a blender together with the fresh cilantro. Puree, then add salt and pepper and one-quarter to one-half cup of the reserved liquid; puree fully.

Allow to cool and then taste for seasoning, adding more liquid as needed.

Yield: 1½–2 cups

Red Salsa

2 cups tomatillos, preferably milperos
2 cloves garlic, peeled
3 small to medium red chilies, such as serrano Anaheim or cayenne

¼ medium onion, chopped
1 teaspoon salt
½ teaspoon freshly ground pepper
¼ medium onion, finely diced

Heat a small dry sauté pan (preferably steel or cast-iron, not non-stick) over high heat.

Add the whole tomatillos to the hot pan in a single layer, moving them around as needed to sear all sides. Small tomatillos will need three to five minutes, larger ones will take several minutes more. Remove and reserve.

Add the garlic to the pan and sear; allow to blacken, turning as needed. Remove and reserve.

Split the chilies and remove the seeds, stems and inner membranes. Quickly sear the peppers in the hot pan, just long enough for them to begin blistering but not burn, about ten seconds. Remove and reserve.

Combine the tomatillos, garlic, chilies, chopped onion, salt and pepper and one-quarter cup water in a blender. Puree. Add another one-quarter cup water and continue blending until smooth. Taste for seasoning and add more water as needed.

Allow to cool fully, then stir in the finely diced onion.

Yield: 2–2½ cups

Noodles

4 cups all-purpose flour   Flour for kneading and rolling
6 whole large eggs, at room
 temperature

Sift the flour onto the countertop and form into a large doughnut shape. Crack the eggs into the center of the flour. With a fork, whisk the eggs until combined. Slowly combine the eggs and the flour with the fork, whisking until all of the flour is incorporated.

Knead the dough until it is a smooth ball—about ten minutes. Wrap the dough in plastic wrap and allow it to rest for at least two hours at room temperature.

Unwrap and divide the dough into eight portions.

Roll the dough out using a pasta sheeter and then cut into desired pasta shape.

Yield: 2 pounds pasta dough, enough for 7–8 servings

Black Pepper Crackers

2 cups all-purpose flour, plus
   more for dusting
1 tablespoon baking powder
2 teaspoons coarse salt, plus
   more for sprinkling

2 tablespoons butter or lard
12 tablespoons cold water or
   milk
Freshly ground black pepper for
   garnish

Sift the flour with the baking powder and salt into the bowl of a food processor.

Quickly pulse to mix the dry ingredients.

Add the butter or lard and pulse until the fat is well distributed.

While the processor is running, add the cold water or milk tablespoon by tablespoon until the dough just begins to come together—approximately twelve tablespoons.

Stop the processor, and collect the dough into a ball by hand.

Wrap the dough with plastic wrap and let rest for at least two hours at room temperature, or refrigerate overnight.

Preheat the oven to 350 degrees.

Unwrap and roll out with a pasta sheeter until the second to the last setting, using just enough flour to prevent sticking.

Cut the dough into desired shapes with a pizza cutter, prick with a fork and gently lay onto unlined baking sheets.

Sprinkle with salt and pepper as desired.

Bake at 350 degrees until golden.

Yield: up to 100 1-by-6-inch crackers, depending on thickness

Béarnaise Sauce

1 tablespoon finely diced
   shallots
1 tablespoon white wine vinegar
2 egg yolks
4 ounces very warm clarified
   butter

2 tablespoons finely chopped
   fresh tarragon
Salt

Combine the shallots, vinegar and two tablespoons water in a small saucepan; bring to a simmer. Allow to reduce by one-third, then cool.

In a small mixing bowl, combine the yolks and reduced shallot mixture; whisk to thoroughly blend. Set the bowl over a pot of gently simmering water, and continue whisking until the mixture is thick and has increased in volume. Immediately take the bowl off of the heat and continue whisking to prevent the yolks from overcooking.

Continue to whisk, and slowly add the warm clarified butter in a thin, steady stream. Stir in the tarragon and salt to taste. Adjust the consistency with one to two teaspoons warm water.

Serve immediately.

Yield: ¾ cup

Butter Cookies

1 pound unsalted butter—at room temperature
1 cup sugar

4½ cups all-purpose flour, plus more for dusting
½ cup rice flour

Preheat the oven to 350 degrees.

Sift together the flours and set aside.

Combine the butter and sugar in the bowl of an electric mixer and mix with the paddle attachment until well incorporated but not whipped—two minutes on medium-low.

Switch to low speed and slowly add the flour mixture to the butter mixture. Mix just long enough for the dough to come together.

Roll out the dough on a lightly dusted wooden counter until one-quarter inch thick. Cut with a cookie cutter into small rounds and gently move to cookie sheets lined with parchment paper.

Bake until the edges are just brown—twenty-two to twenty-eight minutes.

Yield: 6–8 dozen 2-inch rounds

Pizza Dough

1½ cups warm water (100–110   ½ teaspoon active dry yeast
   degrees)   4 cups bread flour, plus more for
½ tablespoon sugar   kneading
2 tablespoons lard or butter   1½ tablespoons kosher salt

Combine the water, sugar and lard or butter in an electric mixer bowl. Sprinkle the yeast on the surface. Allow the yeast to proof—five minutes.

Place the bowl in the mixer and attach the dough hook.

Combine the four cups flour and the salt. With the mixer on low, slowly add the flour mixture to the yeast mixture. Continue adding the flour mixture until the dough comes together and forms a ball.

Remove from the mixer and continue to knead the ball on a countertop dusted with flour. Knead the dough by hand until it is smooth and elastic, adding flour as needed.

Place the dough in a mixing bowl, cover and allow to proof at room temperature for an hour. After the dough has begun to rise, place in the refrigerator and allow to further proof overnight.

The next day, remove the dough from the refrigerator, divide into four equal pieces, cover loosely with a cloth and allow to rise at room temperature until ready to roll out and bake.

Yield: 4 nine-inch rounds

Tomato Jam

2 quarts Sun Gold tomatoes   1 cup white sugar
   (yellow cherries)   ½ cup water
1 cup packed brown sugar

Combine all of the ingredients in a large, heavy saucepan, preferably low and wide.

Place over medium heat and cook until the tomatoes begin to split and break down.

Lower the heat and cook slowly, stirring often until the jam thickens—one and a half to two hours.

To test the jam for the proper consistency, take a spoonful off the heat and let cool on a small plate—look for a golden, jam-like thickness that is still pourable.

Let cool, ladle into jars and refrigerate.

Yield: 2 pints

Tomato Upside-Down Cake

Inspired by Paul Bertolli/*Cooking by Hand*

4 tablespoons unsalted butter
½ cup packed brown sugar
A variety of flavorful ripe
    tomatoes—cherry tomatoes,
    heirlooms
1½ cup flour

1½ teaspoon baking powder
¾ cup unsalted butter
¾ cup white sugar
3 eggs, at room temperature
1½ cups tomato jam

Preheat the oven to 350 degrees.

Butter and line a nine-inch circular cake pan with parchment paper.

Melt four tablespoons butter and the brown sugar in a small saucepan and pour into the cake pan.

Slice the tomatoes into half-inch slices, arrange on the bottom of the pan in the brown sugar/butter mixture. Fill the pan as tightly as possible with large and small tomatoes. Use cherry tomatoes to fill in small spaces.

Sift the flour and baking powder to fully mix, set aside.

Whip three-quarters cup butter with the white sugar in an electric mixer on high until light and fluffy—five to ten minutes.

Reduce mixer speed to medium, and add the eggs one at a time, mixing thoroughly after adding each one.

Slowly add the flour mixture to the butter/egg mixture, scraping down the sides as needed. Mix until barely incorporated. Finish mixing the batter gently by hand.

The batter will be thick. Spoon it into the pan, gently and evenly covering the tomatoes without disturbing their placement.

(continued)

Bake at 350 degrees until a toothpick inserted in the center comes out clean—fifty to sixty minutes.

Remove from the oven and cool partially—five minutes. Invert onto an ample cake plate while still warm.

Spoon a thick layer of tomato jam over the warm cake and serve with additional jam.

Yield: 1 nine-inch-round cake

Acknowledgments

I wish to thank those who have made this book possible: my agent Elizabeth Wales, whose insight and patience have helped me through this process; and Maria Guarnaschelli, my editor at W. W. Norton, whose continued support and commitment have been instrumental. My team at Kurtwood Farms: Benjamin Scott-Killian, Jorge Garnica, Jennifer Sung, Julie Grunwald, Dustin Schulte, Tyler Palagi, Ben Ash and Kelsey Kozak. They keep the cows milked, the cheeses made and the farm running despite my times of absence while writing. Without them I would still be in the barn, slowly cajoling the cows into the milking parlor.

Index

abomasums, 24, 128
acidity, 22–23, 25, 175–76, 179
acorn squash, 99
affinage, affineurs, 55–56
aging, of cheese, 26, 39–49, 52–53,
    55–56, 195, 246, 247
Agriculture Department, U.S.,
    22
air lock, 42
Alaska, botulism in, 135
albumin, 175, 179–80
alfalfa hay, 15, 37, 126, 147
    expense of, 19, 57
Alice (cow):
    birth of, 9, 10–18, 23, 124, 148
    breeding of, 57–60, 147
    calving of, 147–50, 171
Amanda (cow), 148
Ambition shallots, 63–64, 211,
    234, 259
American larch, 73
amino acids, 30, 247
anaerobic bacteria, 134–35
Andi (cow), 17, 23, 124, 171
anthropomorphizing, 174
antipasti course, 5, 153, 161, 167,
    170
    six sensations of, 248–53
apple cider vinegar, 255
apples:
    trees, 166, 174, 188–89
    varieties of, 86–87
April, 96–97, 111, 113, 153
Arcadia, 53–55
Archimedes' screw, 131, 132
artificial insemination (AI), 57–60,
    147, 283
arugula, 60, 111–13
asparagus, 85, 88, 96, 135, 242
August, 115, 124

autumn, 12, 104
    early planting for, 49–56, 115
    harvest in, 61, 153

Baby (cow), 16–17
bacteria:
    in canning, 134–35
    in cheese making, 23
baking powder, 204, 206–7
balance scale, 168, 206
banneton baskets, 249–50
Bar-le-duc jelly, 107
barn, 40, 52, 56, 83, 95, 175, 194,
    243
    cleaning of, 89–90
barter, 77, 82, 92
baskets, 249–50
basmati rice, 95
batter, for cake, 204–8
bay laurel trees, 163, 221–22, 226,
    235, 281, 283
bay leaves, 163, 221–22, 272,
    275–76
beaches, 102–3, 141–42, 165
beans:
    green, 135
    for tacos, 210, 214–15
béarnaise sauce (*sauce Béarnaise*),
    174, 256–60
    recipe for, 290–91
beds, raised garden, 84–86, 88,
    90, 96, 105, 116, 119, 155, 160,
    225–26, 242–43
    plant starts in, 90–92
    tending of, 109–13
beef, 5, 120
    freezer storage of, 141–46,
    164–65
    processing of, 124–30, 137–41
beef cuts, 139–40

beefsteak tomatoes, 67
beef stock, 140
bees, beekeeping, 97, 117, 120–23
bell peppers, 103, 123, 210
Ben (farm worker), 33–37, 95, 110,
  114–15, 120, 125–30, 138–40,
  147–49, 185, 232, 282, 283
benches, for greenhouses, 61–62,
  77, 100, 103, 122
bench scraper, 200–201, 233
Bertolli, Paul, 203, 207, 293
Bilet, Maxime, 219
Bill (author's friend), 68–72, 282
  death and legacy of, 72–74, 102
Bill's Tomatoes, 67, 69–74, 100,
  101–2, 131, 211
birch boletes, 154
birch trees, 187
Black Beauty zucchini squash, 99
blackberries, 119, 133, 155
black currants, 107
black pepper crackers, 197–98,
  233, 249–50
blenders, 214, 217–20, 273–74, 276
"blood" temperature, 22
blueberries, 85, 88, 91, 111
Blue Hubbard squash, 160
boiling, 180, 262, 268–69
bok choy, 111–13
bolting, 112, 113, 257
boning knives, 138, 140
Boo (cow), 10, 14–17
bottom round (beef cut), 140, 146,
  268
  for braised beef, *see* braised beef
botulism, 134–35
boulders, 39, 46
boule (ball shape), 249
box graters, 270
Boy (bull calf):
  birth of, 23, 148
  slaughtering and butchering of,
    124–30, 190, 211
braised beef:
  preparation of, 189–92, 197,
    208, 220–21, 224, 271, 272
  sauce for, 272–76

serving of, 222, 253, 276
brassicas:
  plant starts for, 79, 81
  seeds of, 64, 225
bread crumbs, 199, 233, 269
bread dough, 176–79, 183, 185–86
  baking of, 187
breakfast, 35, 37
breeding:
  AI procedure in, 57–60
  of cows, 57–74, 147
Brideshead Revisited (Waugh), 51
Brillant, M. Frédéric, 219
brining, 37–38, 39
brisket, 127
broccoli, 81, 91, 96
Brodé Galeux d'Eysines winter
  squash, 99, 161
  for squash soup, 192–94, 285
broiler, 213
brown-butter-and-sage garnish,
  245
Brussels sprouts, 80–82, 90, 242
bucket milkers, 32–33
bulk milk tank, 16, 20, 35, 149,
  171, 173, 176, 191
bull calves, 15, 148
  as commercial loss, 13, 23–25,
    124, 149–50
  see also Boy
bullet hinges, 40–41
bulls:
  as breeding alternative to AI,
    57–58
  danger of, 58
Burton, Wash., 141–42, 145, 164–65
butchering, 138–41
butter, 5, 177, 185, 256, 291
  brown, 244–45
  making of, 9, 17, 173–75, 179
  for sauce, 258
  used in feast, 193, 199, 205,
    206, 208, 217, 243, 244–45,
    260, 266, 268
butter churn, 173–75
butter cookies, 208–9, 280
  recipe for, 291

butterfat, 56
buttermilk, 174, 179
Byron (dog), 3, 17, 18, 129, 183–
84, 186, 197, 235, 280, 283

cabbages, 5, 81–82, 90, 91, 96,
160, 225–26, 242
for slaw, 253–56
cake, tomato upside-down, 174,
203–10, 276–77, 293–94
cake pans, preparing, 204–5, 207
calcium, 10, 149
calving, 9, 10–18, 23–24, 57, 60
birth process in, 12–14, 147–49
separation after, 14–17
Cambros, 28–29, 38, 39
Camembert-style cheese, 20, 43
canning, 133–37, 176
carmelizing, 267, 273
carrots, 91
casein proteins, 25, 175, 179
castration, 8, 124, 149
cayenne peppers, 103, 123, 210
centrifuge:
for cream, 171–72
for honey, 121–22
chanterelle mushrooms, 155,
158–59
as earthy antipasto, 250–51
Charentais melon, 243
Charmant cabbage, 225
cheese cave:
ceiling of, 42–44, 46
cheese storage in, 50, 153,
194–96
choosing site for, 44
designing and building of,
43–47
doors to, 40–42, 47–48, 50, 52,
194–96
interior of, 42–44, 194
structural integrity of, 44–46,
50–52
cheesecloths, 27–31, 37, 181, 186
cheese festivals, 36
cheese making:
author's goal in, 7

checking on cheeses in, 50, 195
as commercial enterprise, 6–8,
19, 36, 43, 56, 82, 116, 119,
141, 149, 283
milk in, 14, 16, 21–24, 173
new model for, 55–56
pathogen contamination in, 183
process for, 21–32, 37–38, 141,
175
whey as by-product of, 175
cheese mites, 53
cheese molds, 27–32, 37, 53
cheese press, 31–32
cheeses, 5, 256
aging of, 26, 39–49, 52–53,
55–56, 195, 246, 247
attempted varieties of, 43
in barter, 77, 82, 92
Camembert-style, 20, 43
for feast, 195–96
grating of, 270
hard, 17, 19–20, 26, 247, 254, 270
serving of, 246–48
cheese vat, 21–23, 25–26, 28–30,
32, 38
Cherokee purple tomatoes, 100
cherry tomatoes, 67, 91, 100, 131,
155, 203, 205–6, 243, 292, 293
cherry trees, 188
chervil, 95
chestnut trees, 85–88, 188
chickens, 37, 82, 106, 119, 130,
150–52, 162, 173–74, 184, 210
slaughtering and processing of,
151–52
chicken stock, 152
chicken tractors, 150–51, 173–74
chili peppers, 103, 123, 178,
210–14, 234, 239, 288
Chinese wire strainer, 132
chives, 95, 225, 234, 274–75
chocolate persimmons, 87
cilantro, 112, 214, 216
cipollini onions, 63, 72, 267–68
coagulation, 24–26
coffee, 35, 76
at feast, 276–80

coffee beans, 5
  roasting and grinding of, 277–80
coffee roasteries, 277–78
coffee shop, author's, 176–77
colanders, 181, 183, 186–87, 275
collards, 82
colostrum, 14, 16, 149, 171
compost, 88–90, 94, 98, 112,
  128–29, 160
Constolato Genovese tomatoes, 67
Cookhouse, 21, 32, 35, 40, 50, 57,
  69, 70, 71, 83, 92, 94, 95, 99,
  116, 121–22, 125, 127–31,
  137–39, 145, 150, 163, 165,
  167, 175, 176, 219, 221, 223,
  226, 248, 254
  in feast preparation, 154, 155,
  185–86, 190, 193, 198–99, 210,
  234
  as venue for feast, 3, 72,
  235–36, 240, 242, 243, 281–83
Cookhouse dinners, as commercial
  venture, 6–8, 56, 119–20, 177,
  184, 218, 255
cookie dough, 208
cookies, 5, 208–9, 280, 291
Cooking by Hand (Bertolli), 203,
  293
Copra onions, 63, 192–94, 234
coriander, 163
Cornell University, agricultural
  program at, 33
Corno de Toro peppers, 210
Costa Rican coffee beans, 278
Costato Romanesco squash, 99
cows, Jersey, 5, 7, 58, 102, 119,
  123, 138, 184, 243
  author's affection for, 10–11, 23,
  33, 34, 45, 55, 56, 90, 126
  author's herd of, 13, 17, 20, 32,
  47, 54, 56, 124, 171, 189, 195
  digestive process of, 128
  grass vs. hay for, 19–20, 113,
  124, 147
  hierarchy in, 16–17, 32
  manure production of, 88–90
  wet nursing of, 14–17

  see also breeding; calving; milking
crackers:
  as crunchy antipasto, 249–50,
  253
  for feast, 197–98, 233
  recipe for, 290
Craigslist, 149
cream, 5, 9, 256, 280
  in butter making, 173–75
creamery, 83, 105, 182, 194
cream separator, 171–73
crows, 91–92, 243
crystals, in cheese, 247
cucumbers, 105, 111, 121, 162
  seeding of, 100, 101
Culinaria France, 107
cultures, in cheese making, 22–23,
  141, 175
curds, 24, 25, 179
  cooking of, 26–27
  cutting of, 26
  pressing of, 29–30
  separation of, 26, 28–29
currants, 84, 105–7, 141
  pickled, 107–9, 253
cutting, of pasta dough, 231–32
C. van 't Riet Company, 30

dahlias, 117
dairies, commercial, 24
Daisy (dog), 3, 18, 184, 197, 235,
  280, 283
Dawn (architect), 43–44
dead bolt locks, 41, 47
December, 98
deer, 243
deglazing, 192, 267–68
Dehillerin of Paris, 219
Delicata winter squash, 99
dessert course, 203–10, 271, 276–77
dibber, 93–94
Dinah (current cow), 10–14,
  16–17, 124, 171
Dinah (original cow), 14–15, 56
Dinah's Cheese, 20, 77, 82
dining table, 3–4, 18

dirty cooking, 267–69
Docton, Wash., 76, 82, 102
Docton Road, 83
dough:
  preparation of, 176–79, 183,
    185–86, 198–203, 208, 220–21,
    227–33, 244
  see also bread dough; pasta
    dough; pizza dough
dough hook, 177–78
Douglas fir:
  in cheese cave doors and shelv-
    ing, 40–42
  in dining table, 3–4, 18, 184, 280
  trees, 47, 102, 158, 187
draining:
  of butter, 175, 178
  in cheese making, 28–32, 176
  of pasta, 269
  of ricotta, 181, 183, 184,
    186–87, 251
draining table, 28, 37, 176
Dustin (farm worker), 112–13,
  130–36, 155–56, 159, 166, 196,
  210, 282, 283
Dutch cheese vat, 182–83
Dutch flathead cabbages, 225–26

Early Girl tomatoes, 67, 131
eggs:
  free range, 35, 119, 173–74,
    199, 210
  and kale, 256–65
  in making pasta, 199–201, 231,
    289
  nests of, 174
  poached, 174, 253, 256–65
  production of, 150–51
  used in feast, 174, 185, 199–
    200, 207
eggs Florentine, 256–57
egg yolks:
  for béarnaise sauce, 258, 290
  for pasta, 199–200
  separating of, 260
emulsified sauces, short- and long-
  term, 260–61

et in arcadio ego, 50–53
eye of round (beef cut), 140

farmers' markets, 60
farming:
  author's love of, 54
  in Eastern Europe, 173
  emotion vs. science in, 33–35
  environmental standards in,
    110–11
  large commercial, 11, 24, 59–60,
    148
  new generation in, 112–13
  romance vs. reality of, 54–55
  see also Kurtwood Farms
farm workers:
  cultural range of, 33–34, 79–
    82
  see also specific individuals
fats, 255–56
fava beans, 141
feast:
  aftermath of, 3–9, 281, 282–84
  afternoon of, 219–26
  author's contemplation of, 6,
    282–83
  author's role at, 235–36,
    243–44, 246–50, 253, 270, 272,
    276–77, 281–82
  beginning of, 227–65
  dairy products for, 171–84
  eighteen months before, 19–38,
    196
  end of, 280–82
  evolution of, 6–8
  four days before, 154–70
  guests at, *see* guests, at feast
  legacy of, 282–84
  long range preparation for, 9,
    17–18, 72, 196, 226, 282
  lunch on day of, 186, 210–16,
    217, 227
  menu for, 4–5
  morning of, 185–216
  nine months before, 57–74
  preliminary preparation for,
    124–46

feast (*continued*)
  recipes for, 285–94
  second half of, 266–84
  shared experience of, 272
  spring before, 75–104
  summer before, 105–22
  two weeks before, 147–52
  two years before, 10–18, 226
  Tyler's role at, 235–44, 248–57,
    259–61, 263–64
February, 61, 64, 100, 117
fennel, 121
ferryboats, 7, 75–76, 102, 280–81,
  283
fingerling potatoes, 98, 118
flank steak, 211, 213–16
flies, 124
flipping:
  in cheese making, 30–31, 38,
    52–53, 55, 195
  of compost piles, 80, 129
flocculation time, 25
Flora (cow), 171
flour, 5, 176–77, 197–203, 207,
  208, 236, 239
flowers:
  garden beds for, 85, 88, 116–17,
    119
  plant starts for, 79, 81
followers, in cheese making,
  27–28, 30–32, 37
food processors, 197–98, 218
4 x 4 (cow), 171
frames, honey, 121–22
France:
  artistic influence of, 40–41
  culinary traditions of, 55, 161,
    163–64, 167, 200, 218–19,
    233–35, 245, 249, 252, 258,
    278
Francesca's Cheese, 20, 26
  for feast, 196, 246, 270
Frédéric (carpenter), 40–42, 53
freezer storage:
  on farm, 141, 152, 183, 261
  in Sandy's meat locker, 143–46,
    164–65

French Charentais melon, 100
French-press coffee, 5–6, 280
French rolling pins, 208, 229–30
frogs, mating call of, 96–97
fruit production, 86, 119, 155
  overabundant, 105–6, 108
fruit trees, 85–88, 165, 243

gambrel, 127, 129, 138–39
garlic, 163, 234, 267, 285, 286,
  288
  harvesting of, 117–18
  planting of, 49–50, 63, 112
  in salsa, 211, 214
garnishes, 224–25, 245, 274–75
gate valve, 28–29
geese, 107–8
Georgia, 63
geraniums, 117, 225
German silver service, 245–46
germination:
  temperature for, 65–66
  of tomatoes, 72–73
gizzards, chicken, 151–52, 183,
  199, 266–68, 270
globulin, 175, 179–80
gluten, 202, 229, 233
goat cheese, ugly secret of, 24
goats, 24, 54, 56
golden chanterelles, 158–59
Gouda cheese, 43
grafting, 86
Grana-style cheese, 43
grapes, 155
grass, encroaching by, 84
grated cheese, 72, 270
Greece, 54
green beans, 135
greenhouses:
  author's, 60–62, 65–67, 71–73,
    79, 99–104, 122–23, 210, 242
  Bill's, 69
  Leda's, 76–82, 103
green salsa, 210–11, 214–15
  recipe for, 288
green slicing cucumbers, 100
green tomato chutney, 133

guests, at feast, 3, 6, 8, 72, 74,
  152, 153, 184, 216, 235,
  242–46, 252, 253, 264
  arrival of, 227, 235–36
  changed perspective of, 282–84
  departure of, 280–82
  satiation of, 271–74, 276–77,
    279–81
  shared experience of, 272, 281
gutting:
  of chickens, 151–52
  of steer, 128–29

Halley (cow), 148
hallmarks, silver, 245–46
Halloween, 61
hanger, 128
hard rolls, 176–78, 183
  for bread crumbs, 233
  making of, 186, 220–21, 224, 243
  recipe for, 287
  serving of, 244–45
hawthorn trees, 188
hay, *see* alfalfa hay
hearts:
  chicken, 151–52, 199
  pork, 254–55
heating mats, 65, 71, 100, 102
heat spells, 115–17
heifers, commericial value of,
  13–14, 24
heirloom:
  as pretentious term, 258–59
  squash, 160–61
  tomatoes, 67, 118–19, 131, 203,
    258, 277, 293
herbicide, ethical dilemma over,
  110–11
herbs, 84, 95, 178, 197, 234, 239,
  241, 251
  beds of, 224–25
hollandaise sauce, 258
hollyhocks, 81–82, 116
Holstein cows, 56
honey, 56, 97, 120–22, 133, 251,
  255–56
Hubbard squash, 64

hydration, of pasta dough, 202–3,
  231
hydrostatic pressures, 45

iceberg lettuce, 223
Idaho, botulism in, 135
identification:
  of beef cuts, 140
  of mushrooms, 153–54
  of onions, 64
  of plant starts, 91
  of squashes, 99
immune system, of cows, 14
interns, Japanese, 79–82
invasive weeds, 114
iPhones, 25, 27, 80, 136, 152, 204
irises, 119
irrigation, 122–23

jalapeño peppers, 103
jam, jelly, 107, 109, 133, 155–56,
  159, 177
  see also quince membrillo
Japan, agricultural colleges of,
  79–81
Jefferson, Thomas, 259
Jersey cows, *see* cows, Jersey
Joel (former cook), 202
Jonathan apple trees, 85–88,
  188–89
Jorge (farm worker):
  farm tasks of, 7, 16, 20–21, 23,
    33, 36, 49, 57, 62, 73, 89–90,
    98, 106, 109–11, 114–15, 120,
    122, 148–49, 159–60, 191, 210
  in feast preparation, 184, 185,
    282
  lunch prepared by, 210–16, 217
  Mexican heritage of, 215
  wife of, 183, 211
July, 111, 113
June, 61, 105, 111, 113
Justin (former cook), 254

kale, 80, 82, 96
  for feast, 222–24
  poached eggs and, 253, 256–65

kir, 106–7
kitchen garden, 66, 85, 205, 222
    tending of, 109–12
kneading, 177–78, 201–2, 229
kosher salt, 37–38, 179, 180
Krieger, Louis C. C., 153–54
Kurtwood Farms:
    author's history on, 6, 14–15,
        34, 36, 56, 80, 86–88, 130, 165
    author's love of, 51, 54, 243
    commercial aspects of, 6–8, 13,
        20, 36, 54, 56, 82, 112, 119,
        124, 149–50, 175, 182
    evolution of, 56, 119–20
    expenses of, 19, 56, 60, 83, 97,
        102, 124, 149–50, 175
    feast grown on, 5, 244, 282–84
    French influence on, 218–19
    guest's-eye view of, 242–43
    large farms compared to, 11, 148
    location of, 76, 83
    produce shared with workers
        at, 120, 121, 137
    see also various components

Lacinato kale (Dinosaur kale;
    Tuscan kale), 222–23, 256–65
lactation, 32
lactic acid, 175–76
lactose, 23, 175
lamination, of pasta, 228–30
lard, 95, 178, 191–92, 256, 261, 266
Laval, Gustav de, 173
lava rocks, 213
lawn mowing, 87–88
leavening, 197–98, 204, 206–7
Le Creuset casserole pan, 191,
    220, 272–73
Leda (grower), 63–64, 70, 90, 103,
    210, 282, 283
    farm of, 76–82, 91–92, 102–3,
        116
leg (beef cut), 139–40, 165, 170,
    185, 261, 268
    in feast, see braised beef
lemon balm, 225
lemon cucumbers, 100, 121

lettuce, 91, 111–13, 223
lilies, 88, 116–17, 119
lintel, 50–51
livers, chicken, 72, 151–52, 183,
    199, 267–68, 270
Log House, 18, 21, 32, 51–52, 69,
    83, 84, 96, 121, 126, 184, 186,
    219, 282, 283
loin (beef cut), 139
long-day onions, 62–63
Long Island Cheese squash, 99
    for pickling, 160–64, 250
lovage, 225
lunch, 95
    on feast day, 186, 210–16, 217,
        227
lung cancer, 72
lyres, 26

madrone trees, 47, 187
Magda Lebanese squash, 99
make room, 22–23, 28, 31–32,
    36–38, 39, 55, 59, 175, 182
mandolines, 162–63, 254
manger, 11, 23
manure, 11, 125, 150
    in compost, 88–90, 94
March, 79, 94–96, 100
Marmande tomatoes, 67, 205
Martha (cow), 171
mason jars, 133–37
Matt (farm worker), 60
Matt (Leda's husband), 77–79, 82
Maury Island, Wash., 75–76, 79,
    102
May, 101, 111, 113
    awakening of farm in, 19, 32
McGee, Harold, 261–62
meat locker storage, 143–46,
    164–65
melons, 5, 101
    seeding of, 100
menu cards, 4, 244, 282
Mexico, traditions of, 215
Michiko (author's friend), 153–59,
    250, 282
    dog owned by, 157–58

micro-planers, 270
"Mignonette" alpine strawberries,
   80, 82
milk:
   in cheese making, 16, 21–24, 146
   coagulation of, 24–26
   cooking with, 194–95, 273–74
   in feast preparation, 171–84,
      191–92, 198
   quality of, 14, 20, 25, 35, 56
   raw, 56
   skimmed, 173
milk fever, 10, 148–49
milking, 21, 32, 57, 120, 149, 171,
   175, 232–33, 242
   evening, 34, 114, 116, 191
   hierarchy in, 16–17, 32
   morning, 32–33, 34, 114, 138,
      159, 184, 283
   vacuum system for, 16–17,
      32–33, 62, 138, 149
milking parlor, milk room, 11, 17,
   22, 32–33, 34, 61–62, 147, 175,
   191
milk production, 7, 14, 20, 124
   annual breeding for, 24
mise en place, 233–35, 236, 239
mixers, 177–78, 206–8
Modernist Cuisine (Myhrvold,
   Young and Bilet), 219
molasses, 177
molds, in cheese making, 27–32,
   37, 175–76
Monsanto, 110
morels (*Morchella esculenta*),
   153–54
mowing, pleasures of, 113–15
mozzarella cheese, 47
mud, 125
muffins, 35, 37
muktuk (whale skin), 135
Mushroom Handbook, The
   (Krieger), 153–54
mushrooms:
   foraging for, 153–59, 250
   serving of, 250–51
Myhrvold, Nathan, 219

Netherlands, 30, 93
New York, N.Y., pizza of, 240
nicotiana, 80
noodles:
   recipe for, 289
   see also pasta
nut trees, 85–86

October:
   calving in, 10, 17–18
   planting in, 49–50
   timing of feast for, 3, 5, 17, 146,
      153, 194, 203
offal, 129
oils, 255–56
olfactory sense, in cooking and
   eating, 209, 220, 247, 279
omasum, 128
On Food and Cooking (McGee), 261
onions, 163, 250, 286, 288
   in cooking, 95–96, 192–94, 197,
      199, 219, 234, 267–68, 285
   harvesting of, 49, 159–60, 165
   planting of, 92–96, 119
   root cutting of, 93–94
   in salsa, 211, 214
   seeding of, 61–66, 92
   two growing periods of, 62–63
oregano, 224, 234
Oregon, botulism in, 135
organ meats, chicken, 151–52

Pacific tree frogs, mating of, 96–97
paddocks, 11, 16, 56, 60, 125
pappardelle, 232, 268
paring knives, 151
parsley, 224
pasta, 72, 232, 268
   alternative method for, 203
   cooking of, 166–69, 272
   dishes, 152, 174, 199, 234, 253
   plating and serving of, 269–71
   recipe for, 289
   sauce for, 266–71
pasta dough, 8, 198–203, 227–33
pasta roller, pasta sheeter,
   228–31, 233

paste, in cheeses, 247
paste tomatoes, 67, 69–70
pasteurization, 22
pastures, 47, 56, 102
    clearing trees for, 188–89
    expansion of, 19–20
    maintenance of, 113–15, 120
    rotational grazing on, 33, 35
    in spring, 32
pâte de fruits, 167
peaches, 87
pears:
    trees, 166, 174
    varieties of, 86, 87, 243
pectin, 169
peels, 239–40, 249
pepper, black, 5, 163, 233, 250
peppers, 120, 122–23, 210–11
    planting of, 61, 103–4
Persimmon tomatoes, 67, 100,
    131
pesticides, 106
pests, 105–7, 112, 113
phygelius, 80
Piano Row, 76
pickled pumpkin, 161–94, 244,
    253–54
    recipe for, 286–87
    as sour antipasto, 250, 253
pickling, 107–9
    defined, 162
pigs, 17, 39, 54, 184
    feed for, 16, 30, 43, 56, 132, 151,
        152, 162, 167, 172, 174, 175,
        192, 200, 210, 260
    slaughter of, 120, 125–26, 130,
        138, 141
Pineapple tomatoes, 67, 100, 131,
    205
pineapple upside down cake, 204
Pink Champagne currants, 105
Pink Lady apple, 87
pizza, 72, 74, 189
    for feast, 196–97, 205, 217, 224,
        236–43, 275
    serving and eating of, 241–42
    styles of, 240–41

pizza dough, 176, 178–79, 183,
    186, 197, 236–39
    recipe for, 292
plant starts, 77, 79–83, 100, 102
    buying vs. growing, 81, 91–92
    planting of, 90–92, 103–4,
        111–12, 115
plates, 248–49, 253, 264, 269, 271
plum trees, 174
poached eggs, 174
    and kale, 256–65
    methods for, 261–63
Pollan, Michael, 35
pommes gaufrettes, 162–63
poppies, 117
pork, 120, 141, 261
potatoes:
    for feast, 221–22, 272, 275–76
    harvesting of, 119–21, 159
    planting of, 97–98, 119
    varieties of, 98, 118
potting soil, 66
power take off (PTO), 114–15
precipitation, in ricotta making,
    180–81
pressing, in cheese making, 29–32,
    37
proofing, 177, 220, 236, 244, 249
proteins, 30, 35, 128, 175, 247, 261
    denaturing of, 179–80
pubescence, 166–67
pumpkin, 5, 49, 116, 160
    pickled, 161–64, 244
    seeds of, 64
puree, 217–18
purple potatoes, 98

quenelles, 252
quenelles de brochet (footballs of
    pike), 252
quince membrillo (quince paste;
    quince cheese), 167–68
    recipe for, 286
    as sweet antipasto, 248–50, 253
quinces (*Cydonia oblonga*), 5,
    165–69, 248, 286
    cooking as imperative for, 166–67

raccoons, 150
racemes, 108
radiccio, 82, 90–91
raspberries, 84
raw milk, 56
red bell peppers, 103
red cabbage, 82
red currants, 105
red salsa, 210–11, 214–15
  recipe for, 288–89
refrigeration, cheese cave vs.,
  43–44
rennet, 24–26
reticulum, 128
Rhode Island Reds, 150
riboflavin, 30, 176, 181
rice flour, 208
ricotta:
  failed commercial venture with,
    182–83
  making of, 175–76, 178–84,
    186–87
  as rich, creamy antipasto,
    251–53
rifle, 126
rising, of dough, 178, 249
ristras, 210, 234
roast beef, 95
Robot Coupe food processor,
  197–98
rolling:
  of pasta dough, 228–31, 237,
    252
  of pizza dough, 237–38
rolls, *see* hard rolls
rondeau, 131–32, 136, 155,
  168–69, 193, 266
rose geraniums, 225
roses, 119
Rouge Vif d'Etampe squash, 99,
  160
Roundup, 110–12
rubbing, of cheeses, 30–31, 38,
  52–53, 55
Rubine Brussels sprouts, 80
rumen, 128
ruminants, 128

russet potatoes, 98, 118
Russian kale, 222

saddle (beef cut), 139
sage, 224, 243, 244
salad:
  greens for, 111–12, 119
  see also slaw
Salatin, Joel, 35
salsas, 210–11, 214–15
  recipe for, 288
salt, 5, 163, 175, 176, 179, 191,
  197–98, 207, 221, 233, 266,
  268
  in cheese making, 37–38, 39
  in ricotta, 179–80, 251
Sandy (store owner), 142–43, 164
Sandy's store, 141–45, 164–65
sang de boeuf (beef blood), 126
Sara (author's friend), 72
sautéing, 267
  of kale, 261
  pan for, 278
Savoy cabbage, 225–26
scale (size and volume), in cooking, 254–55
scales, balance, 206
  vs. digital, 168
scaling, of dough, 186
"Science of Nature and Environmental Systems and Agroecosystem Science," 34
scimitar knives, 126, 138, 254
seasonal pond, 96–97
Seattle, Wash., 8, 54, 76, 78, 102,
  176, 189, 245, 257, 277, 280
Seckel pears, 87
seed catalogs, 60, 67
seeds, 64–65, 259
  saved vs. purchased, 69–70, 211
semolina flour, 236, 239, 242
September, 61, 124, 133, 150
  calving in, 60
shallots, 63–64, 211, 234, 258–61,
  264, 290
sheep, 54, 56
sheeter, 228–31

shelving, 42
  flipping of, 53–56
short-day onions, 62–63
shoulder (beef cut), 139
shrubs, currant, 105–8
Shun knife, 249
Sidney's Pizza Café, 238
sieve, 181, 183, 186–87, 218, 220
silver service, German, 245–46, 264, 271
silver skin, 140, 190, 213
skirt steaks, 141, 146, 165, 211
slaughtering:
  of bull calves, 24, 120, 124–27, 130, 190, 211
  of chickens, 151–52
  of male goats, 24
slaw, 253–56
  dressing for, 255–56
smoker, 97, 121–22
Sneeboer Company, 93
soil blocks, soil blocker, 66–67, 98, 100–101
sorrels, 225
soup course, 161, 192–94, 245–46, 253
soup stock:
  beef, 140, 197
  chicken, 152
Spanish pine, 73
Spanish white sugar melon, 100
spices, 163
spinach, 256–57
spring, 19, 72, 75–104, 111, 133, 150
  as season of optimism and hope, 91, 95–96
  seeding in, 60–72
spruce, in shelving, 42, 53
squash blossoms, 99
squashes, 105, 111, 112, 115, 120, 121
  seeding of, 61, 98–101
  seeds of, 64
  varieties of, 99, 160–61, 165
  see also pumpkin

squash soup, 161, 189–90, 192–94, 197, 217–20, 224, 243–46
  recipe for, 285
squirrels, 255
stagiaire, 200
stalls, 10–12, 23, 147
stand mixers, 177–78, 206–8
Steiner, Rudolph, 35
Stella (cow), 148
sterilizing, 134–35
sterling, as term, 245–46
Stewart, Martha, 177
stirring, in cheese making, 22–23, 26–27, 29
stirring wand, 26, 29
stockpot, oversize, 136–37, 176, 179–81, 266
straw:
  as bedding, 11
  manure layered with, 89, 94
strawberries, 80, 82, 85, 88, 111, 120, 155
Stuart (contractor), 45–46, 50–51, 85, 88
sugar, 5, 163, 205, 207, 208, 274
  in dough, 176, 177
  in jam making, 156
  in onions, 63
  in quince membrillo, 168–69
sulfer, in onions, 63
summer, 5, 6, 49, 54, 91, 104, 105–22, 150, 153, 222
  before the feast, 105–22
  financial advantage of, 19
  height of, 114–15
Sun Gold tomatoes, 67, 131, 155, 205–6, 211, 292
supermarket products:
  author's limited use of, 5, 213, 244
  eschewed by author, 94–95, 133, 135, 181, 206, 211, 221–22, 283
supersalination, 37–38
swallows, 115
Sweet 100 tomatoes, 67, 205
sweet peas, 117, 119
syringe, 59

tacos, 141, 210–16
tajarin, 199
tall-pot poaching method, 262
tamis, 198, 207
tarragon, 258, 264
Taxi tomatoes, 67, 131, 205
temperature:
    in canning, 134–35
    in cheese cave, 41–42, 43–44,
        46–47, 50, 195, 246
    in cheese making, 22, 25, 27,
        29, 182–83
    of compost, 89
    in Cookhouse, 98–99
    and egg production, 150–51
    freezing, 104
    in greenhouse, 65–66, 71,
        122–23
    for poaching, 261–63
    for ricotta, 176, 178–80, 182
    in slaughtering and butchering,
        125, 129
    in wood-fired oven, 236–37,
        240
Thanksgiving, 104
thermophilic bacteria, 89–90
thermophilic cultures, 22
throwing, of pizzas, 238
thyme, 224, 234
Timmermeister, Kurt:
    culinary goal of, 219, 223–24
    environmental ethical dilemma
        of, 110–11
    evolution to management of,
        112, 114
    farming experience of, 6, 14–15,
        34, 36, 56, 80, 86–88, 130, 165,
        204, 243
    legacy of, 88
    personal characteristics of,
        7, 12, 21, 27, 33, 34–37, 43,
        54–56, 60–61, 83, 91–92, 94,
        99, 102, 107–8, 116, 126, 133,
        138, 204
    public vs. private personality of,
        236
    restaurant and cooking experi-

ence of, 3, 162–63, 176–77,
    193, 200, 204, 218–19, 227,
    236, 252, 257–58, 265, 278
    role at feast of, 235–36, 243–44,
    246–50, 253, 270, 272, 276–77,
    281–82
tobacco, seeds of, 64–65
tomatillos milperos, 141, 211–12,
    214, 288
tomatoes, 49, 79, 122
    for cake, 205–7, 209, 277
    harvesting of, 130
    planting of, 100–102, 104, 112,
        119
    seeding of, 61, 66–72, 98, 100,
        101
    varieties of, 67, 100, 118–19,
        203
tomato jam, 155–56, 159, 203,
    210, 277
    recipe for, 292–93
tomato sauce, 72, 74, 109, 120
    making of, 130–37, 153, 205
    for pizza, 178, 196–97, 205, 236,
        238–40, 242
tomato upside-down cake, 174,
    203–10, 276–77
    recipe for, 293–94
Tomme cheese, 43
tongs, 268–69
top round (beef cut), 140
tortillas, 213–15
tractors, 36, 78, 84, 89, 114–15,
    125, 127–30
Tramp Harbor, 102
trees:
    cutting of, 85–86, 88, 188–89
    dwarf vs. standard, 86
    maturity of, 86–88
    propogation of, 69, 73
    water-loving, 96, 116
    as wood for oven, 188–89
    see also specific varieties
trends:
    in fruit varieties, 86–87
    in vegetables, 223, 259
Tromboncino summer squash, 99

Tyler (cook), 8, 120, 121, 140, 152
  in feast preparation, 184,
  186–87, 189–94, 196–203,
  205, 208–10, 214, 216, 217–26,
  227–34
  role at feast of, 235–44, 248–57,
  259–61, 263–64, 266–83
tyrosine, 247

udders, 13, 14, 36, 147–49, 171

vacuum pump, 16–17, 62, 138, 149
Vashon Island, Wash., 8, 54,
  75–76, 82–83, 102–3, 141–42,
  164–65, 277–78, 280, 282
  history and character of, 68, 75
Vashon-Maury Island Heritage
  Museum, 76
veal, 24
vegetable gardens, 7, 219
  raised beds of, 84–86, 88,
  90–92, 96, 105, 116, 119, 155,
  160, 225–26, 242–43
  tending of, 109–13
vegetables, 56, 211, 218
  farm grown vs. industrially
  produced, 119
  fashionable trends in, 223, 259
  heirloom, 67, 118–19, 131,
  160–61, 258–59
  moving from spring to fall
  planting of, 111–12, 115
  seeding of, 60–72, 79
veterinarians, 10
Victorio strainer, 130–33
Vidalia onions, 63
Villandry, France, 219
vinaigrette, 251, 253, 255–56, 258,
  260, 265
vinegar:
  for pickling, 108–9, 162–64, 250
  in poaching, 262
  for vinaigrette, 251, 253,
  255–56, 258, 260, 265

Walla Walla onions, 63
walnut oil, 255–56

walnut trees, 255
Washington, botulism in, 135
Waugh, Evelyn, 51
Wayne (AI tech), 57–60, 147, 282,
  283
weeds, weeding, 109–15
wetlands, 96–97
whey, 24, 38
  ricotta made from, 175–76,
  178–84, 186–87
  separation of, 26, 28–32, 175–76
whipped butter, 206–8
whisking, 260
white cannellini beans, 210
white chanterelles (*Cantharellus
  subalbidus*), 158–59
white pine blister rust, 107
whole wheat flour, 177
William's Pride apples, 174
willows, 116
wilting, of kale, 261
wine, 5, 48, 107, 142, 218
  at feast, 236, 242, 243
winter, 6, 12, 19, 32, 33, 50, 54, 57,
  71, 77, 79, 83, 90, 133, 151, 153
  as best time for slaughtering,
  125
  vegetable storage in, 94, 160
Winterbor kale, 222
winter squash, 99, 160–61,
  192–94, 285
wood-fired brick oven, 8, 178–79,
  187–89, 205, 224, 236–37,
  239–40, 275
  structure and use of, 187–89
World War II, 172–73, 218
worms:
  in composting, 129
  as pests, 105–6

yeast, 176–77, 220
Young, Chris, 219
Yukon Gold potatoes, 98, 118,
  221–22

Zamorana, La, 186
zucchini, 111

About the Author

Kurt Timmermeister grew up in Seattle. At the age of twenty-four he opened Café Septieme, a café reminiscent of the Paris neighborhood where he had lived and worked while studying abroad. Two decades and three restaurants later, he left Seattle and the restaurant business and bought a four-acre plot of land on Vashon Island. Starting with just a single Jersey cow, Kurtwood Farms is now a thirteen-acre dairy farm with a vegetable garden, creamery, and cheese cave, and home to a dozen Jersey cows that provide the milk used in the award-winning Dinah's Cheese, as well as LogHouse and Flora's Cheeses. In his first book, *Growing a Farmer: How I Learned to Live Off the Land*, Timmermeister recounted the joys and struggles of small-scale farming.